LAW ENFORCEMENT

&

CRIMINAL JUSTICE

An Introduction

LAW ENFORCEMENT
&
CRIMINAL JUSTICE:

An Introduction

Paul B. Weston
Sacramento State College

Kenneth M. Wells

Goodyear Publishing Company, Inc.
Pacific Palisades, California

Contents

Chapter IV

Chapter V

Chapter VI

Chapter VII

Chapter VIII

Chapter XIV

Chapter XV

Chapter XVI

Illustrations

Preface

It is common in community life in America for all citizens to expect certain fundamental freedoms and rights: the services of police officers who are paid to maintain order, detect crime and arrest offenders; the due process of law from state and federal law enforcement agents; and judicial review to protect all citizens from injustice. Additionally, the control of crime now extends from its prevention to the rehabilitation of convicted criminals. But all this is very new. The American police were no more than constables in villages and towns and a watch in the cities 150 years ago. Only a little over a century ago, the Bill of Rights had to be augmented by the Fourteenth Amendment's ban against the deprivation of any citizen's life, liberty, or property without due process of law, and only contemporary judicial review has protected citizen's rights against abridgment by state and federal agents. Lastly, the strategy for preventing crime and changing law breakers' behavior has only recently changed from the long prevailing and ineffective storage of criminals.

The origin and aim of the criminal law and legal process is the place of beginning in this text. Then, role, theories, and practices of the agents and agencies of criminal justice are reviewed in alignment with the book's theme of criminal justice as a system to maintain domestic tranquility and control crime. Lastly, this is an open–end text. The past and the present are viewed as frames of reference for new horizons in law enforcement and criminal justice.

This is an introduction to the people and the procedures comprising America's methodology for protecting the citizen and community against crime, and to change the behavior of lawbreakers. It is a detailing of the components of a single system made up of legislators, the judiciary, and agents of the executive branch of government—and of the criminal offender and his victim or victims.

After the introductory chapter on law and legal process, there are two chapters detailing the history of police in America and their mission and role. This is followed by three chapters on the offenders and the victims of crime, typologies of criminals, and the causative factors in criminal behavior.

Chapters seven to twelve contain material about fair trial and the due process of law. *En bloc*, these six chapters concern the constitutional rights of the individual, and how they have been both threatened and safeguarded. Chapter seven deals with the conflict between individual rights and the power of government; chapter eight and nine relate to the conduct of judicial proceedings and its goal of a fair trial before an impartial jury for all persons accused of crime; and the last of these chapters discuss the reality of plea negotiations (conviction without trial), prejudicial publicity, and justice for juveniles—all of which threaten the concepts of fair trial and due process.

Chapter thirteen is concerned with the activities of organized crime, its corruption of public officials, the threat to government inherent in its vast profits, and the secrecy of its operations.

The next two chapters are concerned with crime and punishment, and corrections and rehabilitation. Chapter fourteen covers the ethics of punishment, the alternatives to sentencing, the individualization of corrections through probation and parole supervision, and the treatment programs for imprisoned offenders. Central to the theme of this chapter is a segment about the need of, and dimensions of, a data base about offenders to guide the decision makers, from sentencing judge to parole authorities. Chapter fifteen contains four case studies of offenders, and a view of corrections and rehabilitation in action. Two of the cases also develop drug abuse and its relationship to criminal behavior and the rehabilitation of offenders.

The final chapter is an overview of law and of the criminal justice process, its agents, and its clients as a system. There is a review of functional roles in this fragmented system, basic conflicts, and new horizons in education for careers in law enforcement and criminal justice.

Each chapter of this text has been footnoted to guide and encourage further study, and a list of selected references at the end of each chapter provides guidelines not only to further study, but also to the development of a personal library in law enforcement and criminal justice.

LAW ENFORCEMENT

&

CRIMINAL JUSTICE

An Introduction

Chapter I

Law and The Legal System

Systems of law and systems for the determination of guilt do not spring forth full grown. Our present system of justice is the product of centuries, and perhaps millenia, of trial and error. In addition to the experience of history, the complexity of civilization must determine the methods by which men determine codes of conduct and execute sanctions for disobedience of those codes.

Making the Law

There is a trend to reliance on the criminal law to control human behavior that threatens the security of persons and property. However, legal controls require respect as well as obedience for true viability. Where did the criminal law come from? What means or authority causes obedience to the law?

We can speculate that when man began living in family units there was a need for interpersonal problem solving. The particular code of conduct was determined on the basis of day–to–day disputes and the arbitrary and changing decisions of the one in authority. The natural choice for the role of lawmaker was the family authority figure: usually the father, or the oldest member of the family. Because of his longer experience, the oldest member may have been considered the wisest. Respect, awe, fear, or a combination of the three, resulted in obedience to his decisions.

We may also reason that as families grew into communities of families, one or more of the experienced or strongest members became the leaders; and the leader or leaders settled disputes and determined the codes of conduct for the community.

As populations grew and were joined together to form nations, the codes of conduct were established by the authority of physical force, the gods, or both. The sanctions for disobedience were either penalty in this world, or damnation in the next. The authority or leader had to be sufficiently powerful to physically force obedience or speak and act as a god's representative, or even as a god himself.

One of the many illustrations of the early codes of conduct and the basis for obedience is found in the story of Moses.[1] After Moses led his people out of Egypt they began to disobey him. It was then that God told Moses he would come in a cloud and speak to the people in Moses' behalf. Having done so, He called Moses to the top of Mount Sinai where He gave him the commandments and ordinances with this admonition:

> For I, the Lord, your God am a jealous God, visiting the iniquity of the fathers upon the children to the third and the fourth generations of those who hate Me, and showing steadfast love to the thousandth generation of them that love Me and keep My commandments.[2]

These commandments and ordinances covered most of the major present–day crimes. For instance:

Murder: You shall not kill.[3] Whoever strikes a man so that he die shall be put to death. But if he did not lie in wait for him, but God let him fall into his hand, then I will appoint a place for you to which he may flee. But if a man wilfully attacks another to kill him treacherously, you shall take him from my altar, that he may die.[4]

Adultery: You shall not commit adultery.[5]

Theft: You shall not steal.[6]

Protection of Property: If a thief is found breaking in and is struck so he dies there shall be no blood guilt for him.[7]

Perjury: You shall not bear false witness against your neighbor.[8]

Kidnapping: Whoever steals a man, whether he sells him or is found in possession of him, shall be put to death.[9]

1. Exodus.
2. Exod. 20:4.
3. Exod. 20:13.
4. Exod. 21:12.
5. Exod. 20:14.
6. Exod. 20:15.
7. Exod. 22:2.
8. Exod. 20:16.
9. Exod. 21:16.

Arson: When a fire breaks out and catches in thorns so that the stacked grain or the standing grain or the field is consumed, he that kindled it shall make full restitution.[10]

Embezzlement: For every breach of trust, whether it is for ox, for ass, for sheep, for clothing, or for any kind of lost thing, of which one says, "This is it," the case of both parties shall come before God; he who God shall condemn shall pay double to his neighbor.[11]

Rape: If a man seduces a virgin who is not betrothed, and lies with her, he shall give the marriage present for her, and make her his wife. If her father utterly refuses to give her to him, he shall pay money equivalent to the marriage present for virgins.[12]

Sodomy: Whoever lies with a beast shall be put to death.[13]

These and similar regulations formed the code of conduct for the people of Israel by the direct authority of God through Moses. Because of the subsequent spread of the Judeo–Christian ethic, it is the foundation upon which our present system of criminal justice is based.

Violating the peace of an individual often led to blood feuds and *wergeld,* but in later years vengeance was subordinated to *composition.** Violating the king's peace was an offense punishable by *outlawry.* The outlaw was considered an enemy of the community—no one could harbor or aid him—and killing the offender was lawful. In extending the concept of king's peace and in making decisions about outlawry, the community began to codify the antisocial and unfair deeds and the measure of their punishments. In Anglo–Saxon England this marked the transition from private law to public law.

In the English, or common law** system, which we have to a large degree inherited, the tribunal hearing the original factual circumstances in the disputes or accusations made the decision whether the acts were violations of the basic code of conduct, or acts which should additionally be deemed criminal. These decisions adding crimes to existing law were written down and records were kept, so that when a similar factual circumstance occurred the deciding tribunal could apply to the precedent of the former case for guidance. In this

10. Exod. 22:6.
11. Exod. 22:9.
12. Exod. 22:16.
13. Exod. 22:19.

* *Composition* and *wergeld* are similar; *composition* was the sum of money paid by an aggressor to the victim or his family as satisfaction for a wrong or personal injury, usually by mutual agreement; *wergeld* was the "price" of a homicide or other violent crime. It was paid by the aggressor, but the payment was apportioned between the victim (or the family), the community, and the king.

**"Judge–made" law: within the English legal system, the principles and rules of action derived solely from ancient usages and customs, or from judgments and decrees of courts enforcing such usages and customs. Collaterally, the doctrine of *stare decises* is the policy of courts to stand by precedents.

way, each new case and decision added to the basic code of conduct. This mountain of law created by court decision followed the early colonists from England and remained the primary method of determining what was a crime.

Following the American Revolution and the experiences of federal and state legislative governments, more and more states compiled the body of law into codes, criminal and civil, which now have become the only source of the substantive law* and subject to interpretation only by courts of competent jurisdiction.

Statutory law is not essentially different from common law. The common law (or adjudicative law) results from decisions in real–life criminal proceedings; statutory law is the enactment of legislation prior to any actual trial for its violation, but postdates some expressed need for such legislative action. On the one hand, the court waits for the situation to develop in controversy; on the other hand, the legislative action is a response to a developing situation. In the common law, the judicial decision arrayed the rule of the law together with the reason for the decision. Statutes and their provisions of law normally contain nothing more than the essential elements of law. They are assertive, rather than explanatory.[14]

The major problem of statutory law is the proper application of statutory language to individual events alleged to be crimes. The author of a legislative act may not intend the meaning expressed in the legislation. A statute defining a crime is subject to reasonable interpretation on the basis that statutory law is not what the lawmakers intended to say, but rather what they succeeded in saying.[15] What the law *is* may vary because of the meaning of the words used in the law and inferences drawn from its structure and general content.

Courts do not have unlimited power to assess meaning to the words of a law in a *criminal code* or *penal law* (the codification of statutory law), but one of the roles of the courts in the American legal system is the appropriate application of statutory laws to cases before the courts. Judicial interpretations and applications of statutory laws are crucial to the development of justice under statutory law. When such judicial action is founded on principles and policies related to the ultimate purpose of establishing sound foundations for a tolerable and durable social order, then statutory law develops coherence and intelligibility. The quality of rational interpretation then becomes a quality which is characteristic of the body of *unwritten* laws (the common law).[16]

*That part of the body of law creating, defining, and regulating rights.

14. Lon L. Fuller, *The Anatomy of the Law* (New York: Frederick A. Praeger, 1968), pp. 84-91.

15. Ibid., pp. 13-18.

16. Henry M. Hart, Jr., "The Aims of the Criminal Law," *Law and Contemporary Problems* 23, no. 3 (Summer 1958): 401-42.

Law and its making, by court decision or legislative action, has been characterized as an order directed to the citizens of a community by its government, and the words *command* and *duty* are particularly useful in understanding the making of laws, the sanctions for their enforcement, and the nature of voluntary compliance. In 1832, John Austin discussed these two terms as follows:

> *Command:* A command is distinguished from other significations of desire, not by the style in which the desire is signified, but by the power and the purpose of the party commanding to inflict an evil or pain in case the desire be disregarded. If you cannot or will not harm me in case I comply not with your wish, the expression of your wish is not a command.

> *Duty:* Being liable to evil from you if I comply not with a wish you signify, I am *bound* or *obliged* by your command, or I lie under a duty to obey it. If, in spite of that evil in prospect, I comply not with the wish which you signify, I am said to disobey your command, or to violate the duty it imposes.

> *Command* and *Duty:* Wherever a command has been signified, a duty is imposed.[17]

The Law of Crimes

The concept of criminal law as a command and a duty carries over to the purpose of law—to prevent or reduce the incidence of behavior that is viewed as antisocial. This is a utilitarian objective. The retributive view of law has long been rejected for the view of law as a device for deterrence—to modity the future behavior of offenders and others who might be tempted to commit criminal acts.

A crime is an act committed or omitted in violation of a law forbidding or commanding it, and for which a punishment is assigned on conviction. The penalties for crime may be death, imprisonment, fine, removal from public office, or disqualification to hold public office. A *capital crime* is one for which the punishment may be death; a *felony* is a serious crime for which the offender may be sentenced to state prison for more than one year; and a *misdemeanor* is a lesser offense for which the punishment should not exceed one year. Some jurisdictions add a *minor offense* or *infraction*, which is less than a misdemeanor and usually associated with vehicle and traffic violations. The seriousness of a criminal offense has always been related to the penalty assigned for its violation, and the punishment is contained in the judgment and sentence of the trial judge after a verdict of guilty. In most areas, the sentence imposed determines whether the crime is a felony or misdemeanor.

17. John Austin, *The Province of Jurisprudence Determined* (New York: Noonday Press, 1863; originally published in 1832), p. 14.

Clearly written statutory criminal law with its sanctions (penalties) assigned according to the seriousness of the offense is a fair warning against criminal behavior, and a means of securing voluntary compliance. The criminal law tends to group or categorize crimes and criminals in relation to the nature of the offense and the punishment established by law. Distinctions as to the act done that was criminal led to the legal typology of misdemeanors and felonies. This division based on the gravity of the offense was also linked to punishment.

Severe punishment, death and lengthy sentences of imprisonment, lead to a category of *serious offenses.* These are the traditional crimes of violence, of death, and of injury to the victim. The FBI in its role of recorder and reporter of offenses known to police, has placed five serious crimes in its Index of Crimes. These are: murder, non-negligent manslaughter, forcible rape, robbery, and aggravated assault.

Crimes based upon the moral code change as the times change; victimless crimes (based on moral concepts rather than the concept of injury) are being modified or done away with completely. Homosexual acts have been accepted, prohibited, or ignored depending upon the historical period of time. Presently a homosexual act is a crime. However, it is either being ignored by enforcement officers or repealed by the legislatures. The whole subject of obscenity as a crime is being reevaluated in the light of the right of an adult to choose what he reads, sees, and hears as long as there is no injury to another. Until recently abortion was a crime in most western countries, but many jurisdictions are now drastically revising their abortion laws, or eliminating abortion as a crime.

Until now legislation concerning drunkenness, sexual variations, gambling, and blue laws have established as crimes those acts which are popular with many citizens of any community. This overreach of the criminal law has contributed to our criminal population and made any typology of offenders more difficult. An array of various types of criminals and a study of their characteristics would be much simpler if the criminal law retrogressed to its primitive origins and attempted, as its function, no more than the protection of "the king's peace," and of persons and property. When a particular form of behavior (gambling, prostitution, etc.) is forbidden by law, participants are led into contacts with the criminal subculture and other criminal activities. The popularity of forbidden goods and services has led to the development of career criminals and profit–motivated criminogenic organizations, and to the growth of criminality. Many customer–victims resort to a variety of crimes in order to secure funds for the high–priced forbidden goods and services.[18]

Special interest groups also influence state legislatures in creating

18. Norval Morris and Gordon Hawkins, *The Honest Politician's Guide to Crime Control* (Chicago and London: University of Chicago Press, 1969), pp. 2-24.

new crime areas, and increasing or decreasing the punishment for existing ones. The crime of theft illustrates the power of special interests to try to protect their particular product against criminals. *Grand theft*, a felony in California,[19] is the unlawful taking of money, real property, labor, or personal property exceeding a value of $200. *Petty theft*, a misdemeanor in California, is any unlawful taking of property valued at $200 or less. However, if the property is domestic fowls, avocados, olives, citrus or deciduous fruits, nuts or artichokes, then grand theft is the unlawful taking of such property exceeding a value of $50. If the property is an automobile, firearm, horse, mare, gelding, any bovine animal, any caprine animal, mule, jack, jenny, sheep, lamb, hog, sow, boar, gilt, barrow or pig, it is a grand theft regardless of the value. A separate section of the law on thievery makes dog stealing a grand theft if the value of the animal is in excess of $200.[20] An additional section makes dog stealing for the purpose of sale, medical research or other commercial uses, a grand theft without regard to the value of the dog.[21]

Acts previously lawful are frequently made criminal by legislative edicts which are the result of the ever–increasing complexity of our civilization. We often add to our basic moral–criminal offenses and special interest offenses. These are the offenses which have to do with health, safety, government, and welfare of the individual. These new laws regulate the manufacture, sale, and use of products: drugs, explosives, fireworks, swimming pools, atomic energy development, paints, cosmetics, foods (human and pet consumption), bakeries, canneries, housing, and many others. They also regulate the actions of persons or business organizations to license lawyers, doctors, hospitals, bars, restaurants, and the like. In addition they protect or combat disease: communicable disease control, sanitation, garbage disposal, sewer control, cemeteries and undertakers.[22] In California alone, laws fill over 50 volumes of codes which cover every conceivable relationship of man to man, man to machine, man to activity, and man to animal.

Criminal law is also affected by the political reality of lawmakers responding to the public mood. Certain crimes have a scare value by which the vocal and visible activity of legislators gains votes, and actiol s to increase penalties are considered good politics. Narcotic and dangerous drug abuse offenses are an excellent example of political reasons for a particular punishment at a particular time.

Marihuana, in the 1960s and 1970s, is and will be the subject of

19. *California Penal Code*, Section 484 to 486.
20. Ibid., Section 487.
21. Ibid., Section 487.
22. *California Health and Safety Code*.

moral, social, and political concern. This concern is quite visible in the history of the law prohibiting its possession, use, and sale. The possession of marihuana was not a public offense in the state of California until 1929, at which time the legislature enacted a statute making the possession of marihuana a crime punishable as a misdemeanor (a maximum of six months in the county jail). By 1945, the punishment for possession of marihuana was imprisonment in the county jail for six months to one year, or in the state prison for not more than six years. The punishment for possession of marihuana was then the same as for the possession of hard drugs (opium, heroin and cocaine).[23]

In 1959, the maximum penalty for possession of marihuana had increased to ten years in a state prison. In 1961, after a great deal of public agitation about the use of marihuana, there was a basic change in the offense and its punishment. The Penal Code was amended to punish possession by *deleting* that portion of the section on the illegal possession of marihuana which authorized the judge to sentence a first offender to imprisonment in the county jail for not more than one year (a misdemeanor). In its place the following mandatory punishment was specified: ". . . shall be punished by imprisonment in the state prison for not less than one year nor more than ten years, and shall not be eligible for release upon completion of sentence, or on parole, or on any other basis until he has served not less than one year in prison."[24]

In addition, the above section of law provided that persons who had been previously convicted of a narcotic-type felony shall be punished by imprisonment in state prison for not less than two years and no more than twenty years; and must serve, in prison, at least two years. Furthermore, that if the person had been twice previously convicted of a narcotic-type felony, the punishment for possession of marihuana was imprisonment for five years to life with a minimum of five years spent in prison.

For the next seven years a conflict raged between those who claimed marihuana was a dangerous drug and those who argued it was no worse than alcohol. During those years, the great majority of persons convicted of marihuana offenses were young people in college or high school—persons who had no connection with crime other than their experiments with marihuana. In 1968, the law was again amended by the legislature to reinsert the option of the judiciary to sentence first offenders to the county jail (a misdemeanor). The punishment for the second and third offense remained the same.

The use of drug or narcotic laws as a political tool is also evident in the evolution of punishment for the unlawful possession of danger-

23. Ibid., Section 11713.
24. Ibid., Section 11530.

ous drugs.[25] In 1945, the offense was codified with the punishment of a fine of $50 to $500, or imprisonment in the county jail not to exceed six months (a misdemeanor). In 1949, the minimum fine was raised to $100.[26]

In 1965, after the rise of the hippie culture which made the abuse of dangerous drugs a visible and growing problem among college–age men and women as well as children in the high schools and junior high schools, the law was amended and recodified to provide for: ". . . a fine of not more than $1,000 or by imprisonment in the county jail not exceeding one year . . . ."[27] Additionally, the penalty section of this law specified that if the person had been convicted of a similar drug or narcotic offense he should be punished by imprisonment "in the state prison for not less than one year or more than five years (a felony) or . . . in the county jail for not more than one year."

In 1968, as the abuse of dangerous drugs grew, and as the public reacted adversely to the hippies' activities associated with drug use, it became good vote getting strategy for lawmakers to get tougher on drug users. The law was amended to drop the alternate punishment of a fine and add, for the first conviction, the alternate imprisonment of from one year to ten years in state prison. In addition, for the person who had been previously convicted of a similar offense, the alternative county jail sentence (a misdemeanor) was deleted and the sole punishment was imprisonment in state prison from two years to twenty years, and it was also specified that a minimum of two years had to be served *in* the prison.

As a contrast to the above punishments, examine the following review of the punishments specified in California law for the commission of the basic crimes:

1. Murder second degree, five years to life

2. Manslaughter, not exceeding fifteen years

3. Robbery, five years to life (first degree), one year to life (second degree)

4. Burglary, five years to life (first degree), one year to fifteen years (a felony), or county jail (a misdemeanor, second degree)

5. Theft, one year to ten years (a felony), or county jail (a misdemeanor—petty theft, $200 or less).

Narcotic or dangerous drug abuse, in California and many other

---

25. Hypnotic drugs, barbituric acid derivatives, amphetamines, lysergic acids (LSD) and others.
26. *California Health and Safety Code*, Section 29026.
27. Ibid., Section 11910.

states, has become an offense punishable by equal or greater penalties than those offenses which leave injured or dead victims at crime scenes. Therefore, any review of criminal law must recognize not only the relationship of the specified penalty for crimes in determining the grade of crime, but must also be aware of political realities as lawmakers respond to many influences in their enactment of new criminal laws, or in amending the laws relating to crimes.

The Determination of Guilt

Guilt is the opposite of innocence. It is the basis of a person's confession to a crime: *I am guilty.* It is the jury verdict when a defendant is convicted of one or more charges in the accusatory pleading (*indictment* or *information**): *guilty.* In the American legal system, guilt in a criminal proceeding is personal. Crimes always are committed by persons—and in a limited sense by corporations—but not by states. There is a doctrine of legal responsibility of corporations and states which imposes a collective liability, but a criminal act is difficult or impossible to justify on some legalism which transfers responsibility from the perpetrator to some collective organization.

Very early in man's development he chose one or more of his tribe to be the judge in disputes or accusations, and to determine where the truth lay. Those chosen as judges were the oldest (most experienced), the wisest, or the individuals who were deemed the agents or representatives of God or the gods.

The ancient books of the Bible illustrate the indirect intervention of God to settle disputes.[28] The well–known incident of the judgment of King Solomon in determining who was the mother of a child illustrates, as decisionmaker, the supportive nature of divine intervention:

> And all Israel heard of the judgment which the King had rendered and they stood in awe of the King because they perceived that the wisdom of God was in him, to render Justice.[29]

Divine intervention was sought as a resource for determining guilt or innocence in criminal proceedings by tribal leaders in Africa, and the medieval governing groups in England during the eighth through the twelfth centuries. In England, they used the *ordeal* to determine whether an accusation was true or false. The ordeal involved either a hot iron, boiling water, fire, or cold water. The process sought the

---

*In many states a prosecutor may use either method to bring a case to trial. The indictment originates with a grand jury hearing; the information with a preliminary hearing in court.

28. Num. 27:1–11; 36:1–13; Joshua 17:1–6.
29. I Kings 3:28.

direct intervention of God for a minor miracle to show guilt or innocence. Later, in the wager of battle, there was some trust in the belief that the innocent antagonist was to receive divine assistance.

The ordeal of the hot iron required that a fire be kindled within the church. The accused was seated in front of the fire and all those interested and the clergy surrounded him. The iron bar was laid on the fire and heated. After a prayer for God's assistance, the accused lifted the iron bar and carried it nine yards from the fire. When he laid down the iron he was taken to the vestry by the priest. His hands were wrapped in linen cloths. After three days, the cloths were removed. If an infected stripe was found in the mark of the iron he was considered guilty. If the wound was clean he was deemed innocent.

In India the ordeal of fire was quite similar; the accused was required to walk barefoot on the fire. Of course, innocent persons would be uninjured by the ordeal.[30]

The ordeal of boiling water was involved in an incident in Africa. There was a theft in the camp and the Barotse tribesmen asked permission to try a boiling water test to identify the thief. Some 60 natives, men, women, and children, lined up and the test and its purpose were explained to them. No one disagreed to the test. A fire was built and a large pot of water placed on it. When the water came to a boil, a smaller pot of cold water was placed next to it. Then each of the 60 "suspects" walked up to the pots. The ritual was to immerse the right arm into the cold water, then place it in the boiling water. When each of the natives had taken the test, he was told to return at the same time the next day. In theory, the individual who had lost some skin or showed blisters would be guilty. When the natives returned the next day, each passed by and showed his arm. Only one of the 60 showed any sign of a burn, and he confessed.[31]

The ordeal of cold water (*judicium acquae frigidae*) required, after suitable prayer, that the accused be lowered into pure water. If he sank, that is, the water accepted him, he was innocent. If he floated, that is, the water rejected him, he was guilty. It was believed that the pure element would not receive into its bosom anyone stained by a crime.[32]

As late as 1594, Jacob Rickius, a learned jurist, who as judge in the court of Bonn had ample opportunity to consider the value of the ordeal of cold water, vividly described the usefulness of the ordeal when a judge was confronted by a serious crime and worthless evidence. His elaborate discussion of all the arguments in favor of the ordeal may be condensed into this observation: (1) use the ordeal

30. Henry Charles Lea, *Superstition and Force*, 4th ed. (Philadelphia: Lea Bros. & Co., 1892), p. 303.

31. Margaret Carson Hubbard, *African Gamble* (New York: G. P. Putnam & Son, 1937), p. 129.

32. Lea, *Superstition and Force*, p. 318.

when the offense is so difficult to prove that there is no other certain evidence than the ordeal; (2) without it, courts would be destitute of absolute proof—which would be an admission of the superiority of the Devil over God—an unacceptable conclusion. Judge Rickius concluded that he never administered the ordeal when the evidence was sufficient for conviction, nor when there was insufficient proof to justify the use of torture.[33]

Trial by battle was performed either by the parties involved or their champions. It was thought that God would not allow the wrongdoer to triumph over the party in the right. Therefore, the winner of the fight was the victor in the lawsuit. Vestiges of this concept existed in England until 1819, when the English Parliament acted to abolish this last form of nonlegal trial. A system of *waging the law* and *trial by jury* began the nonviolent legal process to determine the guilt or innocence of persons accused of crime.

To *wage the law* was to produce in the court the number of witnesses demanded by the judge to declare the accused guiltless. When the accused produced a sufficient number of friends to testify in his behalf, he was acquitted. Friends of an accused who testified in support of his oath were called *compurgators* and, in effect, they would swear to the credibility of the accused. These "oath helpers" did not testify to any personal knowledge of the crime as an event, but only to their belief in the accused's story given under oath. Exoneration of criminal charges by compurgation was a valued right of English citizens, and it was not wholly abolished until 1833.[34]

Waging the law is no doubt the origin of one of our present rules of evidence: that the accused may produce character witnesses to testify to various qualities of the defendant which may bear on his guilt or innocence. For instance, in California this rule is stated as follows:

> Evidence of the defendant's character as to those traits which ordinarily would be involved in the commission of a crime such as that charged in this case is relevant to the question of the defendant's guilt or innocence because it may be reasoned that a person of good character as to such traits would not be likely to commit the crime of which the defendant is charged. Evidence of good character may be sufficient to raise a reasonable doubt whether the defendant is guilty, which doubt otherwise would not exist.[35]

While there is no Presumption that the defendant is of good character, when evidence is introduced of good reputation regarding the traits involved in the crime charged, a California judge must instruct

33. John H. Wigmore, *A Kaleidoscope of Justice* (Washington, D.C.: Washington Law Book Co., 1941), p. 16.
34. Marcus Gleisser, *Juries and Justice* (New York: A. S. Barnes and Co., 1968), pp. 31–33.
35. *California Evidence Code*, Sections 1100–1102.

a jury that character evidence (waging the law) of itself may be sufficient to raise a reasonable doubt as to whether or not a defendant is guilty.[36]

Originally the trial jury was a jury of witnesses. The jury was made up of the witnesses in the case, and their verdict was the summary of their knowledge of the crime and its surrounding circumstances. Trial by jury probably originated with early Spanish kings as a form of inquest or inquiry; it was introduced into England by the Norman invaders.

Apparently, at one time there was a belief among the agents of criminal justice that the jurors should be chosen for their knowledge of the defendant and his crime. This is one step removed from a jury of witnesses. The following tale illustrates this belief: William of the Palace was accused of stealing from the king's treasury. When arraigned in court, he demanded a trial by jury. The sheriff was asked by the court if he had a jury. The sheriff replied:

> I am proud to say it will be an excellent jury for the Crown. I myself have picked and chosen every man on the panel. I have spoken to them all, and there is not one whom I have not examined carefully, not only as to his knowledge of the offense wherewith the prisoner stands charged; but of all the circumstances from which guilt can be collected, suspected, or inferred. All the jurors are acquainted with him, eight out of the twelve have often been known to declare, upon their troth, that they were sure one day he would come to the gallows, and the remainder are fully of the opinion that he deserves the halter. My Lord, I should ill have performed my duty, if I had allowed my bailiff to summon the jury at hap–hazard, and without previously ascertaining the extent of their testimony. Some, perhaps, know more and some less, but the least informed of them have taken great pains to go up and down in every hole and corner of Westminster, they and their wives; and to learn all they could hear, concerning the prisoner's past and present life. Never had any culprit a better chance of having a fair trial.[37]

The present form of the trial jury dates back to the time of the Tudors. The modern jury now provides a court with 12 persons who have no discernible bias against the defendant or the prosecutor, or preconceived beliefs as to the outcome of the particular case at hand. The functions of a modern jury include: (1) the determination of the credibility of witnesses, (2) the weighing of the evidence, and (3) the drawing of justifiable inferences from proven facts.

---

36. *California Jury Instructions—Criminal*, rev. ed. (St. Paul, Minn.: West Publishing Co., 1958), pp. 60–61.
37. John H. Wigmore, *A Kaleidoscope of Justice*, pp. 24–25.

The Admissibility of Evidence

As we have already discussed, the ordeals did not require any formal evidence other than the accusation in order to put the accused to the test. In practice, however, the accused was put to the ordeal only after he had been accused under the prosecutor's oath and the oaths of others, or a public reputation of guilt, or after capture while in fresh pursuit with *hue and cry*.*

In waging the law, the evidence admitted at trial was relevant only to the good or bad reputation of the accused and he was judged on that alone. Of course, the ancient right of compurgation was based on the concept that a guilty person's friends would know whether the accused was guilty, and if he could find a meaningful number of them to uniformly testify to his plea of innocence and his credibility as a witness he was likely to be innocent.

During the time when jurors were chosen because of their knowledge of the crime or the accused, there were no rules concerning what could be told to and discussed by the jurors in order to decide the issue of guilt or innocence. The only rule of evidence at this time prevented the accused from testifying in his own defense.

It was not until persons without knowledge as to the facts of the crime and the activities of the accused were selected as jurors, that rules developed for presenting evidence to the jury. The rules were few to begin with and became more complex as a concept of fairness became more and more important to the ideal of justice. The system now practiced in the United States is deeply concerned with fairness to the accused and with the eventual ascertainment of the truth. Justice in our present system is equated with fairness; and truth is the desired result of the equity of the system. Thus rules of evidence have developed to maintain and insure that the government acts justly toward each of its individual citizens who may be suspected, accused of, or tried for the commission of a crime.

In fact, ongoing rules for the admissibility of evidence stress the doctrine of fair trial, and enhance it by the concept of *due process* for the purpose of avoiding the conviction of the innocent and preserving the basic sense of security of citizens in a democratic society. Fairness and legality of the methods by which law is enforced are of increasing concern to the American judiciary and is a major theme of twentieth-century judicial policy.

The essence of this theme in modern judicial policy was stated in the dissenting opinion of Mr. Justice Louis D. Brandeis in the 1928 case of *Olmstead* v. *United States:* [38]

*In old English law: a loud outcry with which felons were pursued (all who heard were bound to join the pursuit).

38. 277 U.S. 438 (1928), pp. 471–85.

The protection guaranteed by the Amendments is much broader in scope. The makers of our Constitution undertook to secure conditions favorable to the pursuit of happiness. They recognized the significance of man's spiritual nature, of his feelings and of his intellect. They knew that only a part of the pain, pleasure and satisfactions of life are to be found in material things. They sought to protect Americans in their beliefs, their thoughts, their emotions and their sensations. They conferred, as against the Government, the right to be let alone—the most comprehensive of rights and the right most valued by civilized men. To protect that right, every unjustifiable intrusion by the Government upon the privacy of the individual, whatever the means employed, must be deemed a violation of the Fourth Amendment. And the use, as evidence in a criminal proceeding, of facts ascertained by such intrusion must be deemed a violation of the Fifth.

Experience should teach us to be most on our guard to protect liberty when the Government's purposes are beneficent. Men born to freedom are naturally alert to repel invasion of their liberty by evil–minded rulers. The greatest dangers to liberty lurk in insidious encroachment by men of zeal, well–meaning but without understanding.

And if this Court should permit the Government, by means of its officers' crimes, to effect its purpose of punishing the defendants, there would seem to be present all the elements of a ratification. If so, the Government itself would become a lawbreaker.

Will this Court by sustaining the judgment below sanction such conduct on the part of the Executive? The governing principle has long been settled. It is that a court will not redress a wrong when he who invokes its aid has unclean hands. The maxim of unclean hands comes from courts of equity. But the principle prevails also in courts of law. Its common application is in civil actions between private parties. Where the Government is the actor, the reasons for applying it are even more persuasive. Where the remedies invoked are those of the criminal law, the reasons are compelling.

The court's aid is denied only when he who seeks it has violated the law in connection with the very transaction as to which he seeks legal redress. Then aid is denied despite the defendant's wrong. It is denied in order to maintain respect for law; in order to promote confidence in the administration of justice; in order to preserve the judicial process from contamination. The rule is one, not of action, but of inaction. It is sometimes spoken of as a rule of substantive law. But it extends to matters of procedure as well.

But the objection that the plaintiff comes with unclean hands will be taken by the court itself. It will be taken despite the wish to the contrary of all the parties to the litigation. The court protects itself.

Decency, security and liberty alike demand that government officials shall be subjected to the same rules of conduct that are commands to the citizen. In a government of laws, existence of the government will be imperilled if it fails to observe the law scrupulously. Our Government is the potent, the omnipresent teacher. For good or for ill, it teaches the whole people by its example. Crime is contagious. If the Government becomes a lawbreaker, it breeds contempt for law; it invites anarchy. To declare that in the administration of the criminal law the end justifies the means—to declare that the Government may commit crimes in order to secure the conviction of a private criminal—would bring terrible retribution. Against that pernicious doctrine this Court should resolutely set its face.

Courts are attempting to insure fair trials for persons accused of crimes. Judicial control over the admissibility of evidence has been a significant factor in the development of the law almost from the year of Mr. Justice Brandeis' opinion cited above. The prosecutor and police have had many practices declared unconstitutional and evidence secured in such circumstances excluded upon timely application by the defense for legal relief from the use of unlawfully secured evidence. Initially, the concern of the judiciary was the Fourth Amendment right to privacy and then it was extended to the Fifth Amendment privilege against self-incrimination. Recently it has been concerned with the right to counsel, not only at trial, but also during any critical stage of the pretrial period (such as police lineups or interrogation sessions).

Selected References

Books

Fuller, Lon L. *Anatomy of the Law.* New York: Frederick A. Praeger, 1968.
Gleiser, Marcus. *Juries and Justice.* New York: A. S. Baines & Co.; London: Thomas Yoseloff, 1968.
Wigmore, John H. *A Kaleidoscope of Justice.* Washington, D.C.: Washington Law Book Co., 1941.

Periodicals

Hart, Henry M., Jr. "The Aims of the Criminal Law," *Law and Contemporary Problems* 23, no. 3 (Summer 1958): 401–42.

Cases

Olmstead v. United States, 227 U.S. 438 (1928).

Chapter II

The American Police—From Colonial Times to 1900

The patterns of law enforcement in American have been closely aligned with municipal and county governments, rather than state and federal governments. For over two centuries, police services have provided for the control of criminal acts and the enforcement of local laws whenever a community and its local government believed police protection was necessary. In the settlements of colonial America, police services were viewed as necessary because "public watchmen" were essential to the protection of life and property. In rural areas and frontier communities, the employment of a sheriff, marshal or constable was viewed as essential because a willing and capable person was needed to confront armed criminals and bring them to justice.

The history of law enforcement in the United States reveals a steady growth in the number of police units but no trend toward consolidation into statewide police systems or one with national jurisdiction. Police units, because of their functional role in municipal and county governments, have similarities in the scope of their authority, prevailing practices, organization, and management, but there is no such thing as an American police system.[1]

The American police "system" has its roots in the Norman and Anglo–Saxon concept that groups of people have a basic responsibility to guard against unlawful conduct in their community. In sixteenth-century England, the watch was a nighttime patrol which safeguarded the lives and property of the people of a community. Several of the

---

1. Bruce Smith, *Police Systems in the United States* (New York: Harper & Row Publishers, 1940), pp. 21–28.

residents of a town or village performed this duty each night. Assignments were rotated among the local citizens and service was compulsory—a civic responsibility. The *parish constable* system in England was also compulsory and without pay. The parish was a small community, and each resident parishioner was liable to one year's service as a constable. In addition, the parishioner performed his regular occupation. As communities increased in size, parishioners who did not wish to serve as constables were allowed to hire substitutes. In time, this led to the development of the role of constable as a paid agent of the parish.[2] The London Metropolitan Police, organized in 1829 by Robert Peel, was a natural evolution of the watch and the constable systems into an agency which served to protect the local citizens and their property.

The office of constable predates the monarchy of England and its origin can be traced to the time of the Saxons. When the Statute of Winchester was enacted in 1285, during the time of Edward I, one of its provisions was that two constables should be chosen from each *Hundred*. A Hundred contained ten *tithings*.* This unit had a corporate or community responsibility for the crimes of individual members of the Hundred. It was a control device initiated under the Saxon organization of England, but its roots go back to ancient German groups.

At that time, the law required that a constable should be *idoneus homo***;* to have honesty to execute the office without malice, affection, or partiality; knowledge to understand what he ought to do; and ability as well as substance or estate, to enable him to conduct himself with utility to the public.[3] Early court decisions in both English and Scottish courts establish the fact that the constable was not an employee of a town or village, or a servant of the crown. He exercised his function and duties as an independent holder of a public office. He was a "professional citizen," paid to discharge the responsibilities of all citizens, but with an obligation only to the community as a whole. He was personally liable for false arrest, and he could not claim any of the immunities granted to servants of the crown. Additionally, a constable could not seek the refuge of the military services—the claim of acting upon orders of a superior.[4]

---

2. Patrick Pringle, *Hue and Cry—The Story of Henry and John Fielding and Their Bow Street Runners* (Great Britain: William Morrow and Co., 1964), pp. 12–16.
*Made up of ten *freeholders* (persons with title to realty), or *frank-pledges* (men who gave pledges, put up surety, or acknowledged the corporate responsibility) and their families.
**A responsible person; a good and lawful man.
3. Patrick Colquhoun, *A Treatise on the Police of the Metropolis* (Montclaire, N. J.: Patterson Smith, 1968, originally published in 1806, London), pp. 386–87.
4. Michael Banton, *The Policeman in the Community* (New York: Basic Books, 1964), pp. 5–6.

Unlike the British police system, the European police were nation-wide forces under the control of national governments. However, these systems had overtones of political control; of providing central governments with apparatuses for the control of citizens. Rather than being organized as watches to protect life and property in a community, these huge national police forces were organized primarily as political security police. In place of constables, these forces used military personnel.[5]

Fear of change may have been the major factor in developing what we now term the English model of policing. An attempt by Oliver Cromwell to establish central government control of localities may have contributed to this basic reluctance to change. In 1655, Cromwell divided England and Wales into 12 police districts, each under an army general and a force of from 100 to 1,500 armed men. Cromwell abandoned this project as a failure after 18 months because the people of England and Wales bitterly resented the system. Cromwell ordered the return to the constable system.[6]

Since the early settlers of our country had their roots in both the British Isles and Europe, there was a possibility that the natural growth of police services in the new land might have been patterned after the French or German models, instead of the British. The European police model, however, was in conflict with the new nation's rejection of tyranny. After the American Revolution, the new constitution provided for the preservation of order but not at any loss to individual liberty or fundamental freedoms. It is not surprising that the authors of a document stressing the citizen's right to personal freedom rejected a police model inherently oppressive because of central government control and potential unresponsiveness to the will of the people.

The framers of the United States Constitution adopted a federal system of government in which the powers are divided between the central government and the state governments. The Tenth Amendment reserves to the states respectively or to the people "all of the powers not delegated to the United States by the Constitution, nor prohibited by it to the states."[7]

The enumerated powers of the United States government are few, and a lesser number relate to the enforcement of laws related to crime and criminals. The federal government has the power to punish for counterfeiting; to define and punish crime on the high seas and against the law of nations; to declare the punishment for treason; to arrange

5. Raymond B. Fosdick, *American Police Systems* (New York: Century Co., 1921), pp. 76–81.
6. Pringle, *Hue and Cry*, pp. 12–16.
7. Tenth Amendment, U. S. Constitution: "The powers not delegated to the United States by the Constitution, nor prohibited by it to the States, are reserved to the States respectively, or to the people."

the extradition of fugitives; and to try criminal actions in federal courts. However, general law enforcement is reserved for the states. Within the states, the enforcement of law is generally delegated to the political subdivisions: cities, counties, towns, and villages.[8]

Local Government and the Police

When the United States Constitution established a federal system of government it also established two power centers: (1) the national government, and (2) the state governments. Centralization is common in federal government. Decentralization is the pattern of operations within states, with the state being divided into counties for this purpose.

The county as a unit of local government is an Anglo–Saxon heritage. The basic territorial jurisdiction for local government in that period was the *shire.** After the time of William the Conqueror, the shire became a county. In the colonies, in 1634, the populated area of Virginia was divided into eight shires or counties. In Massachusetts, colonists adapted a smaller unit of English local government to their needs; they formed towns, geographical areas roughly centered on one or more villages. In the Middle Atlantic colonies, both towns and counties were established. By the time of the Civil War, the county was established in its present and traditional form as the basic geographical subdivision of the state.

The county is the main political base for party organization. The political leader of the county is usually a key figure in local politics. Elective and appointive positions in the county government are a source of patronage for the political party in power.[9] Since the county is also the basic subdivision of the state court system, every county has a courthouse. This structure has traditionally served as the center for county government in its performance of the two types of functions characteristic of this unit of government: (1) duties required by the state, (2) activities not required by the state but permitted.[10]

The concept of home rule for city governments became firmly established in America as urban centers struggled with the problems of growth and the concept of self–government. In the middle of the

8. Arthur C. Millspaugh, *Crime Control by the National Government* (Washington D.C.: Brookings Institute, 1937), pp. 43–48.
*One of the earliest territorial subdivisions of government in England.
9. Herbert Sydney Duncombe, *County Government in America* (Washington, D.C.: National Association of Counties Research Foundation, 1966), pp. 3–33.
10. Paul B. Wager, ed., *County Government Across the Nation* (Chapel Hill, N.C.: University of North Carolina Press, 1950), pp. 10–20.

twelfth century the term *civitas** began to have a precise meaning: a compact settlement having a special law with rights of self–government for its free men. It was normally walled, had a market, and some commerce and industry. The factor which encouraged the growth of a city was its focus as headquarters for trade and institutions which provided goods and services for the residents of the surrounding area. In ancient Greece and Rome *civitas* embodied the concept of a city–state: a small unit with a central focus for its life and activities.[11]

While the specifics vary from state to state, the general idea is that when a community has reached the population levels normally earning classification as a city, control of local affairs is within the scope of a municipal government. Once incorporated as a local government unit, a municipality is self–governing within certain limits, and is not inter-fered with by the state government and its legislature. In California, the state's constitution was amended in 1879 to curtail the power of the state legislature in municipal affairs and to allow cities to run their own affairs.[12]

The primary business of local self–government is to provide public services. The cost of these services to the taxpayer depends upon the expertise and integrity of local public officials and employees. Howev-er, local government is often linked to local politics.

The "courthouse gang" refers to a group influential in decision making in county government and politics. The composition of this elite group in the local political scene varies from county to county, but there is little doubt that this group of local residents is the most powerful force in county politics.[13] Americans, from the time of the original settlements along the eastern seaboard, have believed that positions in a municipal government belong by right to the residents of the community, and that well–paying jobs in a municipality's government are a means of taking care of "worthy elements" among the city's residents—and voters.[14]

Before the turn of the century, urban police forces were tainted by the corruption in government. Political interference with day-to-day police operations was common. The residents of large cities identified police with corrupt city politics and the equally corrupt local govern-ment. Appointments to high police positions were made in accordance

---

*The equivalent term in French was *ville;* in German, *stadt;* in Greek, *polis;* and *town* in English.

11. Robert E. Dickinson, *City and Region* (London: Routledge and Kegan Paul, 1964), pp. 20, 49, 60.

12. Eugene P. Dvorin and Arthur J. Misner, *Introduction to California Government* (Reading, Mass.: Addison–Wesley Publishing Co., 1966), pp. 97–99.

13. John C. Bollens, in association with John R. Bayes and Kathryn L. Utter, *American County Government* (Beverly Hills, Cal.: Sage Publications, 1969), pp. 24–25.

14. Thomas R. Adam, *Elements of Government—An Introduction to Political Science* (New York: Random House, 1960), pp. 265–67.

with the interests of the dominant political party. Municipal leaders were quick to respond to changes in public sentiment, and they used the device of short tenure to make certain that the police leader was equally responsive. It was a time of political partisanship and corruption.[15]

Municipal Police

The community of New Haven in the colony of Connecticut used special constables in place of a night watch as early as 1668. The law enforcement problem was centered at the iron works (the only industry in New Haven), and was primarily concerned with disorderly persons. In 1673, New Haven's selectmen (elected at a town meeting) appointed two constables for one–year terms to supplement the citizens who served as special constables. Apparently, this combination satisfied the town's residents, because the night watch was not reestablished until the hostilities of King Phillip's War in 1675–77 threatened the safety of the community and its residents.[16]

In July 1772, the city fathers of Williamsburg, Virginia, roused to action by the activities of thieves (including the burglary of the local post office), created a town watch of four "sober and discreet people," whose duties were described as: "To patrol the streets of this city from ten o'clock every night until daylight the next morning, to cry the hours, and use their best endeavours to preserve peace and good order, by apprehending and bringing to justice all disorderly people."[17]

In 1801, the people of the community of Boston approved the establishment of a continuous night watch. Prior to this time, the people of Boston and its surrounding towns and villages would only be required to perform watch duty as required by local conditions. This continuous duty as public watchmen was incompatible with the earlier concept of watch service as a civic responsibility (refusal to serve required production of a substitute), and funds were voted to pay members of the watch. The watch patrolled the city of Boston from 10:00 P.M. or 10:30 P.M. to sunrise. The men on patrol were asked to cover their assigned section (or beat) once each hour and to prevent or suppress all disorders and disturbances. Members of the watch were

15. Smith, *Police Systems in the United States*, pp. 4–10, 206–7.
16. Rollin G. Osterweis, *Three Centuries of New Haven, 1638–1938.* (New Haven: Yale University Press, 1953), pp. 70–73.
17. Arthur P. Scott, *Criminal Law in Colonial Virginia* (Chicago: University of Chicago Press, 1930), pp. 218–19.

authorized to stop and examine all persons reasonably suspected of unlawful designs and to question them as to their business and the purpose of being about the streets at night.[18]

New York City, at the beginning of the nineteenth century, had a history of both a citizen's watch and military patrols, and the city was protected by a high constable, constables, marshals* and a night watch. In 1801, a local law made the high constable responsible for the peace of the city and the enforcement of all state laws and ordinances of the municipal corporation. This public officer was appointed by the mayor and supervised 16 constables. Constables were elected annually in each of the *wards*, political subdivisions of the municipality. City marshals were appointed by the mayor. In 1811, the state legislature limited the number of marshals in New York to no more than 60. Both constables and marshals served the various courts of the city and were essentially a day police force. The night watch served from sunset to sunrise. There were only 72 watchmen in 1800, but by 1826 the night watch consisted of 400 men. These men were divided among three watch districts in the city, each with a watch house. The entire watch was supervised by the Watch Committee of the city's Common Council. This council appointed all watchmen, captains, and assistant captains of the watch.[19]

In 1832, the state legislature—reacting to the pleas of the mayor— raised the allowable number of city marshals in the city of New York to 100. In 1845, the number of watchmen on nocturnal patrol in the growing city totaled 1,096. However, it was not until 1845 that New York City reformed their police structure along the lines of London's police.[20]

The civic responsibility of policing the city was established as the objective of a reorganized police force.** This objective was stated simply and became part of the city charter:

> The Police Department and Police Force thereof has the power and it is their duty, at all times of the day and night to:

18. Roger Lane, *Policing the City: Boston 1822–1885* (Cambridge, Mass.: Harvard University Press, 1967), pp. 7–10.

*Termed "little sheriffs" because their work was also concerned with local courts as well as law enforcement. The provost marshal is a military officer responsible for military police and the administration of justice. Marshal is derived from an old German word *marah* (horse) and *scalh* (servant), a person who cared for horses.

19. James F. Richardson, *The New York Police—Colonial Times to 1900* (New York: Oxford University Press, 1970), pp. 7–21, 32–33.

20. Richardson, *The New York Police*, pp. 29–49.

** The word *police* did not become common until late in the nineteenth century. F.W. Maitland in *Justice and Police* (London: Macmillan and Co., 1885) suggests a definition: "Such part of social organization as is concerned immediately with the maintenance of good order, or the prevention or detection of offences."

a. Protect life and property

b. Prevent crime

c. Detect and arrest offenders

d. Preserve the public peace

e. Enforce all laws, ordinances and provisions of the Administrative Code over which the Police Department has jurisdiction.[21]

In 1843, the legislators of the state of New York established a three–man Board of Police Commissioners for New York City and took the first step in the history of the country to eliminate the political control of urban police forces which had dominated this branch of government since colonial days. Prior to this time, arrangements for the control of police had been in the hands of common councils or mayors, public officials with broad executive power. The New York Board of Police Commissioners consisted of the mayor, the recorder, and the city judge. It was an administrative body that had full control of the good order and discipline of the police force. It was a model promptly adopted by other urban areas in the United States: New Orleans (1853); Cincinnati, San Francisco (1859); Detroit, St. Louis, Kansas City (1861); Buffalo, Cleveland (1866). From 1870 to 1880 most of the population centers of the country placed control of their police forces under a two- to twelve-man police board or commission.[22]

However, police boards in urban centers soon became political tools when state legislators enacted laws placing the appointing power in the hands of the governor. State control of such boards represented maneuvering by political parties at state levels to gain control over the police in a city usually dominated by the opposition party. When New York City's Board of Police Commissioners was placed under state control in 1857, the membership was increased to five, and the governor promptly appointed four members of his own political party and one man from the opposition. Maryland imposed a state controlled plan in Baltimore in 1860: four commissioners of police to be chosen by the state legislature. Missouri, Illinois, Massachusetts, Michigan, Ohio, Louisiana, Indiana and California, also imposed state control over local municipal police in the years from 1857 to 1888.[23]

State political control of these police boards soon clashed with the home rule concept of municipal self–government. In 1870, New York City's local control of police was restored under a new city charter; in 1891, Michigan lawmakers eliminated state control in the city of Detroit as a contribution to effective local self–government; and, in 1902

21. *Rules and Regulations* (New York: New York City Police Department, 1956), p. 10.
22. Fosdick, *American Police Systems*, pp. 76–81.
23. Ibid., pp. 80–96.

the Ohio legislature rescinded any authority of the central government in cities. Under this law, the municipal authorities of Ohio cities have full control of police and their management.[24]

Critics said that bipartisan police boards or commissions never worked well and never would. These boards simply provided a means for the two leading political organizations to run the police force in a partnership under a gentleman's agreement. Municipal government requires a mayor with courage and conviction to place law enforcement and the administration of justice above political ambition or advantage by appointing a competent person as the police executive and then supporting this public official as long as he is honest and faithful to his duties and responsibilities.[25]

The abandonment of the police board as an effective management technique led to a restoration of single-handed leadership in police forces in urban areas. The one-man system of executive control was substituted for the multiheaded control of police boards in city after city: New York and Detroit in 1901; Boston in 1906; Cleveland in 1908; Omaha in 1912; and Buffalo in 1916.

Detectives

Francis Tukey, a young attorney, was appointed as city marshal for Boston, Massachusetts, in 1846. His instructions from a reform mayor were to reorganize the night and day watch into a police force. Within a year, he installed a detective force. He transferred the most capable policemen to this new unit, several of whom were men who had served as constables before Tukey's appointment, and he specified that a detective's duties were to ferret out serious crimes and detect those who had committed them. Tukey was the first American police official to recognize the existence of certain police functions which a uniformed policeman cannot perform, because his uniform and badge publicly identify him as a police officer.[26]

It has long been recognized that criminal offenders who are not arrested at the crime scene or in flight from it, are likely to be professional criminals who have learned how to evade the uniformed police on patrol. While every crime scene can tell its story to modern evidence technicians and skilled investigators, the detectives in the early years of policing had to outwit the professional criminal by being knowledgeable about criminals and their *line.* They tended to special-

24. Ibid., pp. 106–8.
25. William McAdoo, "Why the Police Are Not More Effective," in *The American City,* ed. Anselm L. Strauss (Chicago: Aldine Publishing Co., 1968), pp. 270–77.
26. Lane, *Policing the City,* pp. 44–66.

ize in the detection of pickpockets, hotel and boardinghouse thieves, confidence men, and bank burglars.[27]

At this time a precept of detectives was: "Criminals usually stick to their line." This belief led to the later development of *modus operandi* as a technique of criminal investigation—identifying a criminal from his method of operation recorded in reports of prior crimes.

George S. McWatters was the first American detective to write a nonfiction book on American detectives.[28] He was a New York detective who believed that without him and his fellow detectives the civilization of New York could not be maintained, and anarchy of a sort would prevail throughout the country. "Vigilance committees," McWatters wrote, "would be needed in all our cities, and be made up of inexperienced citizens, who—not knowing what to do—would make confusion more confounded, and run riot themselves."

McWatters was of the opinion that detectives were not fully understood by the majority of the people, who never knew how much of their peace and security depended upon the quiet, silent, effective operations of *master detectives*. This author describes the work of master detectives as follows:

> His field of labor is usually more thorny, and his work at times not only very perplexing, on account of the subtle characters he has to deal with, but very laborious in view of the much traveling, nights and days, which many jobs occasion. The tracking of bank robbers, searching for the hiding–places of their stolen treasures, and various like things, will suggest the great amount of real, hard, physical labor the detective sometimes has to perform. Only he can do it. He cannot delegate his powers to any great extent. If he employs others, it is only as aids, not as substitutes. He is expected to know everything in the ways of business, regular and irregular. If he would succeed as a detective of bank robbers, especially, he must not only know all the rogues in that class, but he must understand what class of "workmen" they are; for these industrious hard-working bank robbers all have different ways of doing their work; possess different degrees of skill; and when the robbery of a bank is reported to a detective, his first inquiry is directed to the manner in which the work was done. So the detective's calling is one which demands not only much cunning, but much general and accurate knowledge of human character, and not a little acquaintance with all sorts of business.[29]

Thomas Byrnes of the New York City police was considered the country's leading detective in post–Civil War years. Byrnes became chief of detectives in the New York City Police Department and he

---

27. Duncan Matheson, "The Technique of the American Detective," *Annals* 116 (November 1929): 214–18.

28. George S. McWatters, *Knots Untied: or Ways and By-Ways in the Hidden Life of American Detectives* (Hartford, Conn.: J. B. Burr & Hyde, 1871), pp. 659–61.

29. McWatters, *Knots Untied*, pp. 652–53.

made his record in this position in a variety of ways. He trained his detectives in criminal techniques. When a theft occurred, his men were generally able to name the thief, making identification from their knowledge of the style of work of professional thieves: the signature aspect of a crime. Byrnes and his subordinates also built a network of informers in whose interest it was to report on other criminals. When these techniques proved inadequate for the solution of particular cases, Inspector Byrnes had no hesitation about resorting to the third degree—or approving its use by his detectives. He personally solved the Manhattan Savings Institution robbery by patient inquiry in the underworld until he accumulated enough scraps of information to move in on the suspects and extract their confessions.[30]

Rural and Frontier Policing

While the first urban police forces in America had their origin in the watch and constabulary, the origin of policing in rural areas is the ancient English office of sheriff as representative of the crown.* The central government's control over the office of sheriff did not survive long in America. Control stabilized at county levels of government and the office became an elective one, with the county's electorate choosing a sheriff at two–, three–, or four–year intervals.

The sheriff of a rural area during the time of colonial and post-colonial government was probably a merchant or landowner of considerable wealth. But as the frontier moved southward and westward, the average incumbent sheriff was no more than a householder of the community. Additionally, the western sheriff never had much opportunity to perform the tasks of assisting local magistrates and tax collecting, which were characteristic of their early English counterparts. For the first time in the history of this office, the sheriff became personally active in the enforcement of law. This heroic figure of frontier history was no longer the "king's steward," but was an armed protector of life and property known for the frequency of his shoot–outs with gun–carrying cattle rustlers, horse thieves, and stagecoach and train robbers.[31]

The function and duties of the office of sheriff have been described as follows: "The sheriff is the conservator of peace in his county, and while serving in this capacity is the sovereign power of the state. He has a duty to commit all persons who break the peace, or attempt to do so, to jail, and to pursue and capture all felons and 'other misdoers'

---

30. Thomas Byrnes, *1886—Professional Criminals in America* (New York: Chelsea House Publishers, 1969; originally published in 1886), pp. xii–xxvi.
*The *reeve* was a public official of a shire who had some law enforcement duties. He was called the shire–reeve, believed to be the origin of the word sheriff.
31. Smith, *Police Systems in the United States*, pp. 75–89.

and he may command a *posse comitatus*—by a summons every person over 15 must obey."[32] The posse comitatus was the *levee en masse* of the adult male population of a county, which a sheriff might summon to his aid in preserving the peace, pursuing felons, etc.

Towns and villages within a county often hired constables or town marshals as their agents of law enforcement. Their territorial jurisdiction was limited to the boundaries of the village or township.

While the jurisdictional boundaries of sheriff, constable, and town marshal were usually respected in rural areas, the incumbents in these positions along the western frontier generally ignored them. The sheriff usually deputized his fellow lawmen and thus authorized countywide law enforcement jurisdiction, and sheriffs of adjoining counties were usually happy to have professional assistance in apprehending criminal offenders.[33]

At the request of a sheriff or other local public official, a governor of a state can summon the state militia (National Guard) for law enforcement duty. This system supports the office of sheriff as it allows the larger unit of government to step in and help when necessary. However, the reverse is not always true. Sheriffs may be unwilling to respond to the direction of a governor. After all, sheriffs are elected officials of a local government unit and are not in the employ of the state.[34]

State Police

In order to protect the lives and property of 30,000 American colonists during the Texas Revolution in 1835, a police force commonly known as the Texas Rangers was organized. Three companies of 56 men each were authorized; the men were enlisted for one year and placed under the command of a major and three captains. The rangers were neither state militia nor a unit of the federal armed forces. They were armed men in a military–civilian organization. They were allowed $1.25 a day for "pay, food, clothing and horse service." On its frontier to the west, the residents of Texas justly feared the menace of roving bands of Indians intent on arson and murder. On the southern frontier of Texas, Mexican soldiers and citizens disputed the right of the Anglo –American residents to seize land they considered part of Mexico. The Republic of Texas was the governing unit of this territory from 1836

32. August Vollmer and Alfred Parker, *Crime and the State Police* (Berkeley, Cal.: University of California Press, 1935), pp. 15–16.
33. Carl W. Breihan, *Great Lawmen of the West* (New York: Crown Publishers, Bonanza Books, 1963), pp. 10–12.
34. Bruce Smith, *The State Police—Organization and Administration* (Montclair, N. J.: Patterson Smith, 1969; originally published in 1925 by the National Institute of Public Administration, New York, N.Y.), pp. 15–36.

to 1845. In 1836 legislation provided for additional companies of mounted volunteers for the ranging service to protect three border counties. In 1844 and 1845, additional companies were formed for other counties along the western and southern frontiers of Texas. When Texas entered the Union in 1845 as a state, the rangers served as scouts for the U. S. Army in its fight with the Mexican army to preserve the border of Texas as United States territory.[35]

The Arizona Rangers were organized in 1901 and the New Mexico Mounted Police in 1905. The assigned duty of both units was patrol, similar to the ranging of the Texas Rangers. In 1905, the Commonwealth of Pennsylvania established a state constabulary. In earlier years, Massachusetts and Connecticut appointed a few constables with authority to function within a statewide jurisdiction, but neither group was a police force managed by a commanding officer. Pennsylvania, in fact, was the first state to initiate a force similar to the Texas Rangers, but with general law enforcement authority rather than specific border or frontier service.[36]

The concept of a state police did not spread rapidly. It was road-blocked by organized labor's resentment of the gathering of great numbers of state policemen in one place for strike duty. The Pennsylvania State Police were used for duty at many strikes as were other state police forces. The presence of a concentration of professional police attempting to preserve the peace and protect life and property may have frustrated some of the legitimate demands of organized labor. Legislators responsive to the voting power of an industrial area hesitated to be supportive of the state police concept. However, the rejection of the concept of a state police may not have originated in the use of such police in labor disputes, but rather from a local community's rejection of any armed force entering that community and taking over the privileges of the familiar local police.[37]

State police are an excellent solution for the problem of policing rural areas, substituting full–time, salaried, and trained police for part–time, and often untrained sheriffs and constables. In New York, the state police have *troops* of police distributed at various zone headquarters and substations throughout the state, and they have the responsibility—along with the county sheriffs—for law enforcement outside of cities. The state police have the power to go into cities and make arrests whenever necessary. This police organization has proven itself for the past half-century to be a professional police force in the finest sense of the term. The troopers are known and respected by citizens throughout the state of New York.

35. Walter Prescott Webb, *The Texas Rangers* (Boston: Houghton Mifflin Co., 1935), pp. 21–34, 91–95.
36. Smith, *State Police*, pp. 36–42.
37. Ibid., pp. 53–65.

Other states have units with similar powers, but many states have restricted the jurisdiction of their statewide police to traffic law enforcement. The California Highway Patrol is a nationally recognized professional police unit, but its jurisdiction is the highways of the state and its personnel, by legislative action, are termed state traffic officers, rather than state policemen. However, this specialization has been very effective as it concentrates a statewide police in a crisis area, the control of traffic, and at the same time provides local police and sheriff's deputies with a back–up force of highly trained police officers.

Federal Law Enforcement

The Judiciary Act of September 14, 1789, not only established a system of federal courts, but also established the Office of Attorney General and the position of federal marshal. U. S. marshals were appointed in each of 13 federal districts for four-year terms. Assigned duties were to serve the federal courts and execute all lawful precepts directed to them under the authority of the United States. The U. S. marshal was empowered to appoint deputies and to command all necessary assistance in the performance of his assigned duties. In 1792, Congress granted U. S. marshals the same common–law powers in executing the laws of the United States as sheriffs possessed in their respective counties in the states.[38]

The U. S. marshal was the first agent of law enforcement in the federal government. He had the same powers under federal jurisdiction that sheriffs possessed at local levels, and his authority to command assistance equaled the ancient rights of sheriffs to call out the able–bodied men of a county in a posse comitatus.

In 1861, the attorney general was given control and responsibility for United States district attorneys and United States marshals. In 1870, Congress authorized a Department of Justice in the federal executive system and made the attorney general its chief executive.

In 1889, a U. S. marshal shot and killed a California citizen named Terry in the line of duty. The marshal acted in defense of the life of a judge he was protecting on orders from the U. S. attorney general. The U. S. marshal was jailed by California authorities. His defense was that he had acted pursuant to the law of the United States, and he sought review and release in an application for a writ of *habeas corpus.** The case terminated in the U. S. Supreme Court.[39] In its opinion the court commented that there was a "peace of the United States," and

38. Rita W. Cooley, "The Office of U. S. Marshal," *Western Political Quarterly* 12, no. 1, part 1 (March 1959): 123–40.

*Literally: produce the body; a legal remedy for persons unjustly imprisoned.

39. In re Nagle, 135 U.S. 1 (1890).

that the U. S. marshal in this case was as much entitled to protect this peace as a California sheriff would have been in protecting the local peace under the same circumstances.[40]

The Secret Service had commenced operations against counterfeiters of the national currency in 1865 under legislation enacted by Congress to restore public confidence in the country's money. Inherent in this legislation, which provided funds to detect and arrest persons violating the counterfeiting laws, was the authority to act against persons violating these laws and other federal laws regarding the U. S. treasury. This new unit became a branch of the Treasury Department. The Secret Service was a small force in comparison to the awesome responsibilities of this new agency of law enforcement. Washington became the headquarters of the Secret Service, and its 30 investigators were distributed across the country in 11 field offices. In the announcement of the initiation of this group of federal agents and its single area of interest, U. S. marshals in each federal district were asked to cooperate.

The Secret Service operated under yearly grants of authority by Congress in annual appropriations acts providing various amounts of money for operating expenses. It was at the turn of the century that the protection of the president was assigned to the Secret Service (informally in 1901 after President William McKinley's assassination; formally in 1903 when Congress included this duty in its annual appropriations act funding the Secret Service).[41]

The Division of Inspectors of the Post Office Department existed as early as 1878. The U. S. Post Office Inspection Service is responsible for internal security (administrative inspection of post offices and postal accounts) and the detection of crime. In 1886 the office of chief inspector of this service was approved by a congressional appropriation of funds for this purpose. It quickly became a nationwide operation with postal inspection districts and a force of postal inspectors. Cases assigned to these men have included the rifling of mail, embezzlement, the transmission of forbidden matter, post office burglaries, and the robbery of postal employees and trains and other conveyances transporting mail.[42]

As late as 1906, Congress was authorizing the temporary assignment of Secret Service personnel to the Department of Justice; and it was not until 1909 that Congress appropriated sufficient funds for the attorney general to create and maintain a small detective force. These men were assigned to a new subdivision of the Department of Justice,

40. In re Nagle, p. 69.
41. Walter S. Bowen and Harry Edward Neal, *The United States Secret Service* (Philadelphia: Chilton Co., 1960), pp. 14–16, 126, 190–92.
42. Albert Langeluttig, "Federal Police," *Annals* 146 (November 1929): 41–54.

the Bureau of Investigation—renamed the Federal Bureau of Investigation (FBI) in 1935.[43]

The Congress of the United States was apparently reluctant to take any action likely to contribute to the establishing of a national police. The intent of Congress was made clear by limiting the U. S. marshal's duties to crimes defined by federal statutes and to legal processes concerned with U. S. courts; by carefully delineating the restricted enforcement areas assigned to the Secret Service and the Postal Inspection Service; and by its delay until 1909 in providing investigations for the U. S. Department of Justice.

The post–Civil War years may have contributed to Congress' reluctance to install any federal police with general criminal jurisdiction. The states participating in the Civil War as part of the Confederacy were placed under the control of the United States Army. This was the only federal agency available to administer the national government's reconstruction policy. This policing under central government control was authorized by martial law. Military personnel serving as provost marshals were in charge of one or more districts. Military commissions and provost courts* functioned under federal control in place of the civil courts of many areas of the South.[44]

President Andrew Johnson's Proclamation of Peace on April 2, 1866, began the long process of changing over from military to civilian control in the South. The preamble of this proclamation is illustrative of the federal control over the region during this period.

> Whereas standing armies, military occupation, martial law, military tribunals, and the suspension of the privilege of the writ of *habeas corpus* are in time of peace dangerous to public liberty, incompatible with the individual rights of the citizen, contrary to the genius and spirit of our free institutions, and exhaustive of the national resources, and ought not, therefore, to be sanctioned or allowed except in cases of actual necessity for repelling invasion or suppressing insurrection or rebellion. . . .[45]

Police Status at the End of the Nineteenth Century

The history of the law enforcement officers who served their communities as constables, sheriffs, deputy sheriffs, or members of a city's

---

43. Harry Overstreet, and Bonaro Overstreet, *The FBI in Our Open Society* (New York: W. W. Norton & Co., 1969), pp. 11–28.
*Derived from the use of provost marshal to designate the law enforcement official in the army.
44. John Richard Bennett, *The South As It Is: 1865–1866* (New York: Viking Press, 1965), pp. 220–23.
45. James E. Sefton, *The United States Army and Reconstruction: 1865–1877* (Baton Rouge, La.: Louisana State University Press, 1967), pp. 5–33, 78.

police force from colonial times to 1900 has structured many of the stereotypes about police now held by the public. One that has apparently earned its right to a natural death and an R.I.P. burial is the stereotype of the "dumb cop." It is true that long ago, police applicants satisfying the rudimentary physical requirements of height and strength, were tested only as to their friendship with the political party in power at the time.[46]

A second stereotype slowly fading from the public mind is the image of the brutal policeman. Unfortunately, this was fostered in earlier years by press reports of police brutality when accused persons were interrogated. The *third degree* became the catchword for the employment of methods which inflict suffering, physical or mental, upon a person in order to obtain information about a crime.[47] Decisions of the U. S. Supreme Court in confession cases set new standards for police interrogations and police acceptance of these decisions erased this stereotype, or—at least—partially erased it from the public mind.[48]

However, there is a strong suspicion that another element in the public attitude about police brutality is an Anglo–American fear of a strong police force, first manifested in England in 1829, when Robert Peel proposed a municipal police. This fear is part of our national psychology, and is probably the major reason for our fragmented American police system.[49] Fear and distrust of government authority by a citizenry intent on preserving their fundamental freedoms, provided a receptive audience for every tale of police third degree methods.

The basic distrust of an armed, uniformed, and disciplined body of police is reflected in the failure to provide tenure for city police chiefs and the continuing popular election of sheriffs. Lack of tenure for an adequate number of years and popular elections are both devices used by communities for control of local police, and they are both aligned with the citizens' distrust of an armed, uniformed, and disciplined police.

Lastly, and probably another carry-over from the watchman's role of colonial days, is the American public's attitude that police are solely responsible for controlling crime.[50] This may also be a side effect of the American image of the western frontier and its lawman, sheriff, or

---

46. Charles B. Saunders, Jr., *Upgrading the American Police—Education and Training for Better Law Enforcement* (Washington, D.C.: Brookings Institute, 1970), pp. 13–15.

47. Zachariah Chafee, Jr., Walter H. Pollack, and Carl S. Stern, *Mass Violence in America: The Third Degree* (New York: Arno Press and the *New York Times*, 1969), p. 19.

48. The series of cases commonly known as the "confession cases" begin with Brown v. Mississippi, 297 U.S. 278 (1936), and climax in Miranda v. Arizona, 384 U.S. 436 (1966).

49. Saunders, *Upgrading the American Police*, pp. 13–15.

50. Ibid., p. 13.

marshal who took direct and personal action against criminals.

The outstanding features of the American police at the end of the nineteenth century were its local characteristics and its communal control.

The nature and growth of a great nation shaped the law enforcement area of government during these years, and fast–growing communities set the stage for the development of modern police organizations. Police in America, in their growth to professional organizations of full–time, salaried personnel, did provide the citizens of a growing nation with the protection necessary to "insure domestic tranquility," and they contributed in no small measure to establishing justice, and providing for the general welfare.

Selected References

Books

Adam, Thomas R. *Elements of Government—An Introduction to Political Science* New York: Random House, 1960.

Bollens, John C., in association with Bayes, John R. and Utter, Kathryn L. *American County Government.* Beverly Hills, Cal.: Sage Publications, 1969.

Bowen, Walter S., and Neal, Harry. *The United States Secret Service.* Philadelphia: Chilton Co., 1960.

Browne, Douglas G. *The Rise of Scotland Yard.* London: George G. Harrap & Co., 1956.

Byrnes, Thomas. *1886—Professional Criminals in America.* New York: Chelsea House Publishers, 1969: originally published in 1886.

Duncombe, Herbert S. *County Government in America.* Washington, D. C.; National Association of Counties Research Foundation, 1966.

Fosdick, Raymond B. *American Police Systems.* New York: Century Co., 1921.

Lane, Roger. *Policing the City: Boston 1822–1885.* Cambridge, Mass.: Harvard University Pres, 1967.

Millspaugh, Arthur C. *Crime Control by the National Government.* Washington, D.C.: Brookings Institute, 1937.

McWatters, George S. *Knots Untied: or Ways and By–Ways in the Hidden Life of American Detectives.* Hartford: J. B. Burr & Hyde, 1871.

Overstreet, Harry, and Overstreet, Bonaro. *The FBI in Our Open Society.* New York: W. W. Norton & Co., 1969.

Pringle, Patrick. *Hue and Cry—The Story of Henry and John Fielding and Their Bow Street Runners.* Great Britain: William Morrow and Co., 1964.

Richardson, James F. *The New York Police—Colonial Times to 1901.* New York: Oxford University Press, 1970.

Sefton, James E. *The United States Army and Reconstruction: 1865–1877.* Baton Rouge: Louisana State University Press, 1967.

Smith, Bruce. *Police Systems in the United States.* New York: Harper & Brothers Publishers, 1940.

Webb, Walter P. *The Texas Rangers.* Boston: Houghton Mifflin Co., 1935.

Periodicals

Cooley, Rita W. "The Office of U.S. Marshal." *Western Political Quarterly* 12, no. 1, part 1 (March 1959): 123–140.

Matheson, Duncan. "The Technique of the American Detective," *Annals* 116 (November 1929): 214–18.

Cases

In re Nagle, 135 U.S. 1 (1890).

Chapter III

The Police Mission and Role in a Democratic Society

The peace officer role in the history of Anglo–American government predates the police role as law enforcer. The "king's peace" at one time signified the absence of any disorder. Loyalty to the monarch entitled the king's subjects to a certain measure of peace and security. As the chief magistrate, the king appointed his stewards to extend the royal protection to loyal subjects. Later, the monarch delegated some of his magisterial authority to persons in his service and assigned them responsibility for a specified territorial area, a shire. These men had vice–regal powers in the beginning, convening their own courts in the king's name. They were also empowered to call upon any of the king's subjects to assist them in keeping the peace. One of the roles of the posse comitatus was to handle serious disturbances. Later, great landowners—the lords of the manors—became responsible for the peace and security of their dependents.[1]

The modern police officer responds to the needs of twentieth-century communities by assuming the role of an employee hired to keep the public order and to provide various related general services. It is a dual role inasmuch as police must always be on the alert for violations of law, and many times, when peace–keeping efforts fail, police must switch roles and invoke the formal arrest process.

The prototype of twentieth–century police organizations, London's Metropolitan Police, was organized to serve this dual function. It was an arm of the administration of justice, bringing persons accused of crime into court for trial, but it was also an agency for keeping the

1. Douglas G. Browne, *The Rise of Scotland Yard* (London: George G. Harrap & Co., 1956), pp. 13–14.

peace by official action less than the formal legal procedure of arrest and arraignment.[2] In October 1829, the membership of the Metropolitan Police were warned about rudeness "on the part of the police toward persons asking civil questions"; and a month later, in November, they were cautioned "to preserve peace and good order" by all possible means. One hundred and thirty–five years later, in 1964, an article in an authoritative police science and criminology journal concluded with these words:

> The real significance of the Metropolitan Police lay in its example to the nation as a model for subsequent national police reform legislation and organization. It proved that an efficient police could greatly decrease the use of troops against civilians; that it could protect life and property; and that it could be compatible with the English constitutional concepts of liberty.[3]

The Police Mission

The evolution of American policing over a century and a half has developed the mission of police as one element of the criminal justice system. It is supportive of the entire process of the administration of justice, and as the most visible of its agents and agencies its role in law enforcement and apprehension is critical.

The goals to be achieved by police are generally summed up as the prevention of crime and disorder; the preservation of the peace; the apprehension of offenders; the recovery of lost and stolen property; and the protection of life, property, and personal liberties.

The primary police techniques for achieving these measures are the crime-prevention-and-deterrence method, the apprehension process, the regulation of noncriminal conduct, the provision of public services, and the protection of personal liberties by appropriate control of police behavior and interaction with other units in the criminal justice system.[4]

Most police officers see their function and the police department's mission as primarily that of law enforcement. However, urban living in high–density population centers, the continuing industrial revolution, and the increasing use of the automobile has realigned the police

2. Egon Bittner, "The Police on Skid Row: A Study of Peace Keeping." *American Sociological Review*, 32, no. 5 (October 1967): 699–715.

3. J. L. Lyman, "The Metropolitan Police Act of 1829," *The Journal of Criminal Law, Criminology and Police Science* 55, no. 1 (March 1964): 141–54.

4. *Municipal Police Administration*, edited by George D. Eastman (Washington, D.C.: International City Management Association, 1969), pp. 3, 209, 322.

mission with the basic responsibility of keeping order. The twentieth century introduced a whole new set of interrelationships, and equally new areas and avenues of conflict in these interactions. These order–keeping functions are more frequently aligned with the police officer as philosopher, guide, friend, or peace officer rather than the pursuer of criminals in the apprehension process.

The police mission in a democratic society is concerned with control, keeping the law from being violated, and apprehending law violaters, but it is also concerned with the maintenance of order. Thousands of police officers in all sections of the country, day after day, function as keepers of the peace to preserve domestic tranquility.

A functional continuum has been suggested as illustrative of the basic police mission. This continuum would have the helping function at one end, and the punitive function at the other end;[5] or the supportive functions at one end and the control functions at the other end of the continuum.[6]

That policemen are practicing social scientists is a reality long rejected by the academic world of social science and the professional arena of social work, but the facts of day–to–day performance of police as peace officers in many jurisdictions throughout the nation has established the police as de facto social scientists. The mission of police has not changed, but a basic part of that mission has developed as a function demanding new skills and more police manpower than the law enforcement segment of the police mission.

In a survey of the literature and commentaries on police management the following specific functions were outlined as goals for police:

1. Prevention and repression of crime

2. Maintenance of the peace (domestic tranquility)

3. Protection of persons and property (security)

4. Enforcement of laws

5. Detection of crime

6. Recovery of lost and stolen property

7. Apprehension of offenders

8. Regulation of noncriminal conduct

9. Protection of individual rights

5. Joseph D. Lohman and Gordon Misner, *The Police and the Community—The Dynamics of Their Relationship in a Changing Society* (Washington, D.C.: Superintendent of Documents, Government Printing Office, 1966: a report prepared for the President's Commission on Law Enforcement and Administration of Justice, 1966), p. 38.
6. Elmer H. Johnson, "Police: An Analysis of Role Conflict," *Police,* January-February 1970, pp. 47–52.

   10. Control of traffic

   11. Miscellaneous public services

   12. Preparation of cases for presentation in court.[7]

The dominance of the order–keeping function has led to its classification as the *first* objective of a police department and the classification of the law enforcement function as the *second* objective.[8] A study of 652 calls to an upstate New York police department spanning an 82–hour period is illustrative of the merit of this reorientation of the police mission. Researchers found significant evidence of police acting out a peace–keeping role. A patrol car was dispatched in 75 percent of the 652 calls. In reports by these responding police, over 50 percent of the citizens wanted help or some form of support for personal or interpersonal problems. This research team found that responding police attempted to solve the problem, or guided the citizen to someone who might solve his problem. In on–the–scene problem–solving, police were found to provide support, either by offering friendly sympathy to the caller, by giving authoritative information to the citizen, or by helping two or more disputants agree on some plan for resolving the problem.[9]

Police as Law Enforcers: The Apprehension Process

The apprehension process is within the core area of the traditional role of police as law enforcers. In response to an event, the police invoke the formal process of arrest and arraignment in court.

The apprehension process was first formalized by the hue and cry, an arrest procedure in which an alarm was raised upon the commission of any felony. The practice dates back to Edward I (1285), when persons fleeing the scene of a crime were easily identified and pursued. When a hue and cry was raised, every person—on a constable's order —had to aid in the pursuit of the felon, or be liable to fine and imprisonment. During the time of George II (1735), a regulation was promulgated which provided for a forfeit of five pounds for any constable who "neglects making hue–and–cry."[10]

The apprehension process is a sequence of actions taken as a re-

7. Lohman and Misner, *The Police and the Community*, p. 37.

8. James Q. Wilson, "Dilemmas of Police Administration," *Public Administration Review*, 28, no. 5 (September–October 1968): 407–17.

9. Elaine Cumming; I. Cumming; and Laura Edell, "Policeman as Philosopher, Guide and Friend," *Social Problems* 12, no. 3 (Winter 1965): 276–86.

10. Patrick Colquhoun, *A Treatise on the Police of the Metropolis* (Montclair, N.J.: Paterson Smith, 1969; originally published in 1795, London), pp. 388–89.

sponse to the event of a crime. The sequential action begins when a crime is detected by police, a victim or another citizen, or by an alarm device. The next step is a headquarters-to-patrol-unit broadcast over local police radio. Police on patrol respond and proceed to the crime scene. A search for the perpetrator of a crime has three phases: (1) *hot*, (2) *warm*, and (3) *cold*. The hot and warm searches are conducted at the crime scene and in the general area of the crime, respectively, and generally have a time limit associated with the time of the crime and the duration of the perpetrator's flight from the scene. The cold search may range far and wide, and its time span is limited only by the opportunities for getting results.[11]

Uniformed police, within the police function of patrol, usually conduct the hot and warm searches. Being on patrol nearby the scene of a crime, being available for instant receipt of the alarm broadcast, and having the mobility necessary to get to the crime scene without delay are the triology of factors which assign this portion of the apprehension process to police on patrol.

When the perpetrator is known to the victim, known to an eyewitness to the crime, or if there is an identification of a vehicle involved in the crime, the cold search is often initiated by the police radio dispatcher, and the patrol force often makes arrests on the basis of broadcasted data about the suspect, his vehicle, or both. When an arrest is not made in the first eight hours of the postcrime period, the case usually requires investigation.

When the victim can give no clue to the perpetrator's identity and there are no eyewitnesses (or such witnesses cannot provide any identification data), the search is investigative from its origin. The success of the apprehension process depends upon the ability of investigative personnel to identify the perpetrator from a study of the crime's circumstances and collected evidence: linkups to past crimes through comparison of modi operandi; the use of informants; or some combination of intuition and innovative handling of promising leads.[12]

Delegation of the continuing investigation—the cold search of the apprehension process—to the personnel of the investigative unit is necessary because the continuing investigation embraces all the work necessary for identifying the offender, apprehending him, and preparing the case for prosecution. The ready alert status of patrol officers and their assignment to the limited area of a post or sector interferes with this type of investigation. The cold search is more than surprising a perpetrator at a crime scene or skill in pursuing a criminal in flight from the scene. It is a search in which a patrol officer is likely to be

11. President's Commission on Law Enforcement and Administration of Justice, *Task Force Report: The Police* (Washington, D.C.: U.S. Government Printing Office) 1967 p. 58.
12. Paul B. Weston and Kenneth M. Wells, *Criminal Investigation* (Englewood Cliffs, N.J.; Prentice-Hall, 1970), pp. 89–106.

handicapped by his uniform, frustrated by his patrol duties, and limited by his assignment to a limited territorial area (post or sector).

The Peace Officer Role of Police

In keeping the peace, police are confronted with three main types of public disorder: structural, collective, and individual. Structural disorder results from noncriminal actions creating a collective disorder: the carelessly discarded match or cigarette can lead to huge conflagrations, and panic in a crowded restaurant or theater can result from an ill–chosen word such as "fire." The collective disorder results from the acts of several persons acting in concert. Riots, parades, demonstrations, meetings that become riotous, and mass picketing that gets out of hand are collective disorders. The common drunk or the "man down" are the classic illustrations of individual disorders— one is apparently an intoxicated person, the other is one lying in the street who may be drunk, sick, or injured.[13]

Peace keeping involves skills in the application of procedures to situations that do not involve the formal legal routine of arrest. Typical situations which are likely to result in action less than an arrest are:

1. *Supervision of licensed premises*—the inspectional role of police, from the scrutiny of licenses to the influencing of the licensee to cooperate with the police and other agencies of government —particularly in protecting the morals of young people.

2. *The regulation of traffic*—the control of noncriminal conduct.

3. *Minor criminal offenses*—the classic "low visibility" of American police when the law or the circumstances of the case are ambiguous and the police officer may act alternatively rather than make an arrest.

4. *Crisis–intervention*—intervention in family and neighborhood matters that have no criminal aspects (and often no legal aspects) in order to aid people in trouble; to arbitrate family disputes; to care for the sick, injured or intoxicated person; and to pacify the rowdy and unruly.

5. *Monitoring crowds and assemblies*—the police control role in an early stage of preventing disorder: monitoring is an informal control of groups in the incipient stages of disorder.

6. *People with special problems*—police concern with the less–than–

---

13. Arthur L. Stinchcombe, "Institutions of Privacy in the Determination of Police Administrative Practice," *The American Journal of Sociology* 69, no. 2, (September 1963); 150–60.

fully–competent persons: (a) children, (b) aged persons, and (c) the mentally ill; for people who are different—bohemians and vagabonds;[14] and the resident known criminal

Keeping the peace requires officers on patrol to know a great deal about their posts or sectors. Officers assigned to a neighborhood should not be transferred without reason and certainly not until several years have been spent in the same neighborhood. The concept of police residing in their work areas would promote a firsthand knowledge of local conditions. The old–time foot patrolman had a rare knowledge of his post, and he usually did not live at any great distance from it.

Peace keeping has been described as a "craft," and skill at keeping the peace is developed as a result of an apprenticeship rather than any formal training or learning by the study of a written body of special knowledge. From the long–term acceptance of police intervention in disputes, differences, and difficulties of family and neighborhood, there is a recognition that when police inspect, direct, inform, warn, and take other action less than an arrest, they do this in some accord with the circumstances of the event threatening domestic tranquility.

This on–the–job training in the skills of peace keeping involves some trial and error actions and some ground rule coaching in what *not* to do. The grading process in these skills is job–related: winning or failing to win the approval of associates in the police patrol unit. Gains in the performance of police in their peace–keeping role are not likely to result from the formalization of procedures, nor in extensive training programs. The most significant action to improve police skills in peace keeping is to reorient the police administrators to emphasize and adequately reward the patrol officer and to develop assignment patterns which will increase the patrol officer's knowledge of a neighborhood and the problems of its people.[15]

The Police Mission—Organizing and Managing

Organizations are: (1) goal–oriented, (2) psycho–social systems, (3) technological systems, and (4) an integration of structured activities.[16] They are made up of people with a purpose, who work in groups, who use knowledge and method in their work, and who attempt to work together in interdependent relationships, but with some structuring and integrating of individual activities.

The total task of achieving an organization's objectives is differen-

14. Bittner, "The Police on Skid Row," pp. 701–15.
15. Wilson, "Dilemmas of Police Administration," pp. 413–15.
16. Fremont E. Kast and James E. Rosenzweig, *Organization and Management—A Systems Approach* (New York: McGraw–Hill Book Co., 1970), pp. 5–6.

tiated so that particular persons or groups are responsible for the performance of specialized activities. Differentiation is segmenting an organizational system into subsystems, each of which tends to develop particular attributes in relation to the work that has to be done to achieve the objectives of an organization. In differentiation, there is a vertical dispersion of the work to be done and the responsibility for its completion among operating personnel.

The executive is responsible for organizing and controlling all activity in achieving the ultimate objectives of an organization. However, in a vertical differentiation he may establish program objectives for supervisors in charge of segments of the organization and delegate related duties to them. In turn, these officers in charge may set objectives for subordinates and delegate related duties. This is a pyramidal management structure. The various levels of management between the executive at the top and the operations personnel who turn out the product is primarily dependent upon the size of the organization. There must be sufficient levels in the vertical differentiation of an organization to provide adequate communication and control.

The three primary bases of horizontal differentiation are: (1) location, (2) function, and (3) product.[17] Universally, police forces in America use location as a primary organizational base. The municipal, town or village police department, the sheriff's office, and the state police are all responsible for certain geographical areas. This territorial jurisdiction is broken down into posts and sectors to secure a basic unit for the assignment of personnel. Concurrently, because police must provide services on a 24–hour and 7–day basis, there is also a universal division of work and responsibility by time. Not all posts and sectors are manned by police officers every hour of the day, but within the total territorial jurisdictional area of a police force there are one or more police officers on duty or available when required.

In theory, a police organization is segmented* into its major parts by function. In practice, however, it is a historical division of labor. In 1829, the first organized police force patrolled London to achieve objectives similar to the total responsibilities of police in community after community across America. It was a uniformed patrol force of full–time, salaried, professional police officers. In 1842, the first detective force was organized to supplement the work of London's uniformed patrol officers. In America, the same format was repeated time and again. First, there was the uniformed patrol force. Then, in a spin–off from this group, a detective division or criminal investigation bureau was authorized and organized. Therefore, the

---

17. Kast and Rosenzweig, *Organization and Management*, pp. 178–81.

*Segmented is used instead of the "departmentalized" of Kast and Rosenzweig because the word has a graphic dimension and does not conflict with the term "department" as used in the police service to indicate the entire police organization of a municipality.

first specialization in American policing was that of detective.

Later, when automobiles replaced the horse and carriage, a traffic division was organized in many police departments. The New York City police had equipped many of its officers with bicycles and this mobility permitted these men to stop runaway horses, reckless horse-and-carriage or horsecar drivers, and bicycle "scorchers" as well. However, these men were usually stationed in a "tough part of the city where there was a tendency to crimes of violence," rather than assigned primarily to traffic duty.[18] It was the advent of the motor vehicle into American life in the first quarter of the century that dates the police specialization in traffic control.

When youth delinquency became a community problem, youth or juvenile divisions were initiated and assigned to police for control at operational levels. The government intervened in the lives of young people whose health, morals, and safety were threatened by involvement in an immoral life or criminal acts. Post–World War I dates the advent of police specialization in the control of youth crime and juvenile delinquency.

Urban areas always recognized the relation of *vice* or *morals* to crime and the police mission, but it was not until post–World War I years that it was identified as major police problem. It was defined at this time as "including prostitution, gambling, and the illegal production, sale, and/or use of liquor and of narcotics."[19] Because of its known relationship to major crimes, a vice division became another major specialization within the police services for work related to its suppression and control.

If the product of police work can be described as things done to achieve planned results, then there is some segmenting by product in the police organization, but it is aligned with functional segmenting of the organization. In the patrol division, the product attempts to be crime prevention or deterrence. When this fails, then the desired product is the apprehension of the offender. The patrol division also attempts to produce peace, stability, and order. When this fails, the sought–after product is the control of disorder. In the detective division, the product is the solution of crime, the recovery of stolen property, and the apprehension of offenders; in traffic, it is voluntary compliance with reasonable regulations. In the control of youth crime and juvenile delinquency the product is first the prevention of such conduct, and second the rehabilitation of the offender. In vice control, it is the suppression and control of the crimes related to vice and morals.

The average organization of an American police department or

18. Theodore Roosevelt, *An Autobiography* (New York: Macmillan Co., 1919), pp. 202–4.
19. August Vollmer, *The Police and Modern Society* (Berkeley, Calif.: University of California Press, 1936), p. 81.

sheriff's office is segmented by function along the lines established by the emergence of major areas of specialization in the evolution of policing. This is functionally divided as follows:

1. The patrol division
2. The detective or criminal investigative division
3. The traffic division
4. The juvenile or youth division
5. The vice division.

The organizational structure of the police force of a major police department or sheriff's office depends a great deal upon its size. The division of work in a small police department may plan for one man to perform almost all of the police functions, or allow for some part-time specialization in the division of work. When a police force has a considerable number of men, the available personnel allows for more specialization.

Police Patrol

The post* or sector** is the area of individual responsibility in police patrol. The jurisdictional territory of a police department is divided into these smaller units on the basis of likely demand for police services. The major criteria determining post or sector boundaries are: (1) prior history of crime, (2) population, (3) land use and occupancies, and (4) traffic flow.

Police management analysts have long expressed the theory that the patrol officer is the central figure in achieving the police mission. The uniformed force of a police department is mainly concerned with general crime prevention work. This general protective service constitutes the foundation of all police services.[20] Uniform patrol is fundamental to police work, and not only does it discourage criminal acts, but it also creates a situation for securing information about crime and criminals. Police patrol is a technique for the service of protection and a means of collecting intelligence items likely to contribute to successful investigations.[21]

The patrol force is the backbone and action arm of a police department. Its uniform personnel are distributed throughout the communi-

---

*In some American cities and in Britain, the term used is beat.

**A term originating with police use of motor vehicles; in some police jurisdictions, a sector may include several foot patrol posts in its territory.

20. Elmer D. Graper, *American Police Administration* (Montclair, N.J.: Patterson Smith, 1963; originally published in 1921 by the Institute of Public Administration), p. 123.

21. Bruce Smith, et al, *Chicago Police Problems* (Montclair, N.J.: Patterson Smith 1969; originally published in 1931 by the University of Chicago), pp. 87–88.

ty and are in continual contact with citizens. It is the patrol officer who responds to the cry for help and arrives first at the crime scene. The patrol function, compared with the other major functions of a police department, is more complex and important, and the patrol officer needs knowledge and intelligence to perform adequately.

Patrol by uniformed police is a police activity designed to reduce the opportunities for the commission of crime and to create a belief in the mind of a potential offender that no opportunity exists to commit crime. Many crimes have been prevented or deterred by fear of police on patrol. An unknown number of criminals are dissuaded from a planned criminal act because of a basic fear that the criminal activity will be observed and police action will be swift and certain.[22] Crimes of emotion and passion, however, are not generally prevented by an awareness that police are about and on the alert for suspicious persons.

When policemen patrolled their posts on foot they developed a fabric of information about their assigned area that was invaluable to them in their work performance. The foot patrolman knew every person who managed or worked in the shops, stores, hotels, saloons, and restaurants on his post; and he had a vast, stored knowledge of people and past events in the neighborhood.

However, the foot patrolman in the early years of the twentieth century was generally out of contact with his headquarters, and lacked mobility. A recall signal system of lights and bells, installed on streetlight posts and in other prominent positions, attempted to alert foot officers to call their headquarters, but the response was poor. Bicycle patrol was the first attempt to improve the mobility of the foot–patrol officer. Theodore Roosevelt organized the first police–on–wheels unit when he established the "Bicycle Squad" in the New York City Police Department in 1895.[23] This new mobility allowed police to cover a greater area while on their patrol, or the same area more frequently. It also allowed them to reach crime scenes with some speed and to pursue criminals with more dispatch than pursuit on foot.

Motor patrol in the police service was aligned with the use of motor vehicles by criminals. High–speed pursuits of lawbreakers justified the purchase of high–speed motor vehicles for police use. The possession of such vehicles and their assignment to patrol officers extended their area of patrol, and greatly improved their response time in reaching crime scenes.

One–way radio installed in the early police automobiles improved the availability factor. The recall signal and the message were merged in the one transmission from the radio dispatcher at police headquar-

22. George W. O'Connor and Charles G. Vanderbosch, *The Patrol Operation* (Washington, D.C.: International Association of Chiefs of Police, 1965), pp. 23–30.
23. Roosevelt, *An Autobiography,* pp. 202–4.

ters. Two–way radio added a new capacity for acknowledging the receipt of the message, for checking its content when transmission difficulties or other problems warranted, for a patrolman–to–headquarters report of action taken, or to call for assistance. Three–way radio now offers vehicle–to–vehicle communication to supplement the headquarters–to–patrolman and patrolman–to–headquarters traffic.

Working in an automobile with direct radio contact to police headquarters through the radio dispatcher enables the officer on patrol duty to respond promptly to messages. This availability and mobility allows the patrol officer to reach the crime scene without delay, enhancing opportunities to take appropriate police action. It has also led to a greater involvement of the patrol force in the criminal investigation function of police.

The concept of a detective service in the police force fostered the practice of assigning unsolved cases to a detective for investigation. Unless the patrol officer apprehended the offender at the crime scene, or nearby in flight from the scene, a detective responded and conducted the investigation. The police duty of the foot patrol officer was that of the first officer at the scene. This ranged from first aid and calling for medical assistance when the victim was injured, to arresting the offender—if present—and "freezing the scene" until the arrival of one or more detectives.

Up to the midpoint of the twentieth century, the use of the patrol force was not equal to its functional assignment as the major enforcement arm of a police force. The detective concept monopolized the work of criminal investigation, and restricted the work of patrol officers.

The greatest advance in the second half of the twentieth century has been the increased use of uniformed patrol officers to conduct preliminary investigations of crimes. It was recognized that the patrol officer was capable of more than just giving aid to the injured or arresting the perpetrator of a crime. This increased use of patrol officers began with the smaller departments and state police units. The conservation of manpower and the low incidence of crime ruled out the full–time assignment of an officer to detective duty in a small police department or sheriff's office. The rural crime incidence and distance factor militated against this specialization in state police forces.

In time, large municipal police forces recognized the fact that officers on patrol could conduct the preliminary investigation when a case was not closed out by arrest at the time of the first police contact. The patrolman could interview witnesses and complainants and do the many other duties necessary to the foundation of further investigation.[24] The assumption of this portion of the classic role of a

24. O'Connor and Vanderbosch, *The Patrol Operation*, pp. 115–22.

detective has raised the function of a patrol officer beyond the established horizons of observing, protecting, and reporting.

The conduct of a preliminary investigation requires decision making as to whether a crime has been committed; determining the type of crime by category, and possibly by classification; searching for and collecting physical evidence; locating and interviewing the victim and witnesses; recording stories and taking statements; and building a theory of how the crime was committed.[25]

Along with the transfer of the preliminary investigation to the patrol force, there has been a trend to combine the patrol and criminal investigation functions under a common supervisor. The traditional separation of these two functions has handicapped staff planning, both in the improvement of the apprehension process and in the solution of crimes which occur in a series pattern.[26] This trend may develop, but to date it has failed to overcome the traditional division of a police department into two main areas: the uniformed force and the detective bureau or division. In fact, suggestions of consolidation in many police departments have backlashed and exacerbated the traditional rivalry between these two major police divisions.

Unit beat policing is an innovative British concept that recommends consolidation of these two functions into a new neighborhood police unit. Unit beat policing begins with a double assumption: (1) beat patrol is the basis of the British police service, and (2) police organizations have lost the struggle to provide adequate police patrol by conventional means. The concept of unit beat patrol is simple: a team of police will provide police service to a selected area. Each beat would be patrolled by a radio–equipped car manned by one or two officers and supplemented by two area constables and a detective constable.

The essence of unit beat policing is teamwork. The detective constable is responsible for the incidence of crime on the beat, and for help and guidance to patrol officers and area constables in the solution of minor crimes. The area constables and the patrol officers are responsible for learning the crime patterns in their assigned area and getting to know the people in it, and helping the detective constable. The basic unit consists of: (1) the car and assigned personnel patrolling the beat 24 hours a day, (2) two area constables patrolling in a manner and time most beneficial to achieving the unit's objectives, and (3) the detective constable.[27]

25. Weston and Wells, *Criminal Investigation*, pp. 25–30.
26. *Task Force Report: The Police*, p. 53.
27. Eric Gregory and Peter Turner, "Unit Beat Policing in England," *The Police Chief*, July 1968, pp. 42–47.

Evaluation and Control of Role Performance

Since the concept of crime and legal sanctions for violating laws belong to the legal system, police role performance as law enforcers is subject to review by the judiciary rather than by the managers of the police unit. Arrest, the first step in the formal legal prosecution of persons accused of crime, is rightfully subject to judicial review: (1) on the issue of probable cause justifying the police action; (2) on the lawfulness of the gathering of evidence; and (3) on the ultimate issue of guilt or innocence.

However, role performance in this law enforcer role is measurable by management. First, the offenses known to police tabulate the discernible universe of criminal operations. Second, the case clearance data reveals the cases cleared by arrest or other authorized administrative techniques for closing cases (unfounded; offender in prison; no further results possible; etc.). Lastly, the ratio of convictions to arrests indicates the successful prosecution of police cases.

The peace–keeping role of police is highlighted by police action less than an arrest. Therefore, there is no judicial review of police action. There is no criteria of probable cause, lawfulness of evidence gathering, or measure of guilt or innocence. There is no ratio of offenses known to the police and case clearances. Peace officers pretty much act without constraint or external direction. Control is exercised mainly through on–the–job consultation between supervisors and subordinates.[28]

There is a need to measure the peace–keeping role; to evaluate the ability of patrol officers to keep the peace on their post or in their sector. Supervisors and managers in the police organization will have to learn how to evaluate patrol officers on how they function as crisis interventionists in family fights, teenage rumbles, street corner altercations, and during civil unrest and other disturbances.[29]

Since a significant percentage of the called–for services of any police unit involves family crisis situations, there is a potential for evaluation of role performance in this area. Homicides and serious assaults are more likely to occur in family quarrels than in disputes with strangers, and death and injury to patrol officers responding to family quarrels occur with disturbing frequency. Evaluation of a patrol officer's effectiveness when intervening in family disputes may be based on the total number of family disturbances on his post or in his sector (in some comparison with a control area); the recidivism rate; the recurrence of complaints by the same families; a reduction in the number of homicides and assaults involving family members; and an improved survival

28. Bittner, "Police on Skid Row," p. 704.
29. Wilson, "Dilemmas of Police Administration," pp. 412–13.

rate among police responding to complaints of family trouble.[30]

Evaluating the role performance of police officers may also be achieved by a costs–to–benefits analysis. The decision to arrest, or to intervene in any other fashion, is a decision which can be analyzed on the net loss or gain to the suspect, the neighborhood, and the officer himself. The dimensions of this analysis are twofold. Is the situation within the law enforcer or peace officer role? Is the response police-invoked or citizen–invoked?

In police–invoked law enforcement, the officer's action is measurable in the area of initiative and job interest as well as by justification of the action taken. In citizen–invoked law enforcement the officer's conduct is measurable primarily as a report taker.

In police–invoked order maintenance, the police officer's intervention is measurable by the justification for his action and the outcome of the event: was intervention justified, and was order maintained or disorder controlled? In citizen–invoked order maintenance, an assessment can be made of the officer's handling of the complaint and the outcome of his action.[31]

A new and interesting concept in evaluating role performance by police is that each police department has a style of policing that can be determined by examining the policies and prevailing practices of a police force. The style of a police organization affords a convenient grouping of police organizations on the basis of the common characteristics of the role performance in these departments.

When police act as if keeping the peace rather than enforcing laws was their particular function, the department has a *watchman's* style. The law is used mainly as a means of maintaining order.

When police react to situations as law enforcers rather than peace officers, comparing observed behavior with the essential elements of a crime and making an arrest if all the essential elements are present, the police style of the organization is *legalistic*. A legalistic police style is usually the result of strenuous efforts by the management of a police organization to get the patrol officers to take the law enforcer's role and to measure community conduct against legal standards.

When the police of a community intervene frequently but nor formally, and seriously review all called–for service requests, the police style is *service*. In these communities, the police protect a local definition of law and order against threats by unruly local residents or outsiders.[32]

30. Morton Bard and Bernard Berkowitz, "Training Police as Specialists in Family Crisis Intervention: A Community Psychology Action Program," *Community Mental Health Journal* 3, no. 4 (Winter 1967): 315–17.

31. James Q. Wilson, *Varieties of Police Behavior—The Management of Law and Order in Eight Communities* (Cambridge, Mass.: Harvard University Press, 1968), pp. 83–89.

32. Wilson, *Varieties of Police Behavior,* pp. 140–226.

Role conflict is a factor in police behavior that is not uncommon. Therefore, in examining role performance, there is a need to review the conduct of an officer in order to determine whether one or more of the common means of handling role conflict are operating to handicap any effective work performance. These techniques range from compartmentalization, through delegation and extension, to raising barriers against intrusions on the officer's time. An officer can "compartmentalize" his work and hew to his selected role as law enforcer or peace keeper, disregarding the circumstances of an event. In "delegation," a patrol officer rejects and refers to another agency any part of a situation not in harmony with his selected role as law enforcer or Peace officer. In "extension," a patrol officer keeps himself busy in one role, law enforcer or peace keeper, and pleads lack of time to fulfill any other role. In discouraging people on his post or sector from inducing citizen–invoked police action, an officer erects "barriers against intrusion." Requests for some services, therefore, are rejected because the request relates to a nonpolice matter.[33]

In the control of police role performance the role of lawenforcer lends itself to controls inherent in the legal system and judicial review of police action. In the control of police behavior in the peace officer's role, there is a pressing need for new management measures which will allow evaluation of role performance: is the police intervention warranted and in alignment with the police mission to preserve the public order and insure domestic tranquility?

Selected References

Books

Banton, Michael. *The Policeman in the Community*. New York: Basic Books, 1964.

Kast, Fremont E., and Rosenzweig, James E. *Organization and Management—A Systems Approach*. New York: McGraw-Hill Book Co., 1970.

Lohman, Joseph D., and Misner, Gordon *The Police and the Community—The Dynamics of Their Relationship in a Changing Society*. Washington, D.C.: Superintendent of Documents, Government Printing Office, 1966; A report prepared for the President's Commission on Law Enforcement and Administration of Justice, 1966.

O'Connor, George W., and Vanderbosch, Charles G. *The Patrol Operation*. Washington, D.C.: International Association of Chiefs of Police, 1965.

President's Commission on Law Enforcement and Administration of Justice, *Task Force Report: The Police*. Washington, D.C.: Government Printing Office, 1967.

Weston, Paul B., and Wells, Kenneth M. *Criminal Investigation: Basic Perspectives*. Englewood Cliffs, N.J.: Prentice-Hall, 1970.

33. Johnson, "Police: An Analysis of Role Conflict," pp. 51–52.

Wilson, James Q. *Varieties of Police Behavior—The Management of Law and Order in Eight Communities.* Cambridge, Mass.: Harvard University Press, 1968.
– – –, *Municipal Police Administration.* Washington, D.C., International City Management Association, 1969, edited by George D. Eastman.

Periodicals

Bard, Morton, and Berkowitz, Bernard. "Training Police as Specialists in Family Crisis Intervention: A Community Psychology Action Program." *Community Mental Health Journal* 3, no. 4 (Winter 1967): 315–17.

Bittner, Egon. "The Police on Skid Row: A Study of Peace Keeping." *American Sociological Review* 32, no. 5 (October 1967): 699–715.

Cumming, Elaine; Cumming, I.; and Edell, Laura. "Policeman as Philosopher, Guide and Friend." *Social Problems* 12, no. 3 (Winter 1965): 276–86.

Gregory, Eric, and Turner, Peter. "Unit Beat Policing in England." *Police Chief,* July 1968, pp. 42–47.

Johnson, Elmer H. "Police: An Analysis of Role Conflict." *Police,* January–February 1970, pp. 47–52.

Lyman, J. L. "The Metropolitan Police Act of 1829." *Journal of Criminal Law, Criminology and Police Science* 55 (1964).

Wilson, James Q. "Dilemmas of Police Administration." *Public Administration Review* no. 5, (September–October 1968): 407–17.

BANK OF AMERICA'S FIVE MOST WANTED MEN

FOR BANK ROBBERY
$1,000 REWARD

AT LARGE — For robbery of the Silverlake-Glendale Branch, on July 8, 1968. Total taken at branch was $5,149. Suspect at left was unshaven at time of holdup, is Caucasian male, early 40s, 6'2", weighs about 190 to 200 pounds, dark complexion, dark hair, medium built. Suspect at right is Caucasian male, late 40s, 6'1", about 205 pounds, ruddy complexion, dark hair, heavy built. Both suspects wore sunglasses during holdup, made getaway in stolen car.

AT LARGE — For robbery of Bayview Branch, San Francisco, November 13, 1968. Simulated weapon. Gave verbal demand: "Lady, don't say a word. Lady, don't say anything." Total amount taken at this branch was $846. Suspect is Negro male, about 25 years of age, is 6'3", weighs 170 pounds. Had a Dilbert beard at time of holdup.

AT LARGE — For robbery of West-pro Santa Monica Branch, August 21, 1968. Simulated gun. Handed teller brown paper bag with instructions: "Put the money in the bag, put the money in the bag." Total taken was $1,470. Suspect is Negro male, about 29, 5'10", weighs 170 pounds. Had thin moustache at time of holdup and sunglasses.

AT LARGE — For robbery of Wilshire-La Brea Branch, July 11, 1968. Suspect is Mexican male in female clothing, in late 20s, is about 5'6", weighs 170 pounds. Simulated weapon. Had note reading: "Give me all of your money, put it in the envelope. Don't scream or say anything, I have a gun." Suspect got away with $2,051 and drove away in old, black Volkswagen. Was wearing black wig below shoulder length, lady's gold blouse with white buttons, dark colored jeans, sunglasses.

Here are five bank robbers who have not yet been apprehended. Law enforcement agencies are making every effort to apprehend them all. Bank of America will pay $1,000 for information leading to the arrest and conviction of each of the bank robbers shown. Please contact your local police or FBI office immediately, if you have any information about these individuals.

SOME INTERESTING FACTS

We read a lot about bank robberies, but very little about the bank robbers who have been caught, tried and convicted and who are serving sentences. Here are some facts:

Law enforcement agencies and the FBI have been successful in apprehending 80% of all bank robbers in a relatively short period of time after such robberies occur — that is four out of five bank robbers. These law enforcement agencies are also successful in recovering a substantial portion of the stolen funds.

The five bank robbers shown on this page were photographed while holding up B of A branches. The odds are that sooner or later all five will be apprehended, thanks to existing means of identification.

The type of photos shown above have provided police with a fairly accurate description of the criminal's physical makeup and other features which will assist in his apprehension.

There is more, however, which the pictures don't show. Bank robbers caught through camera identification are often wanted for other crimes as well — super market holdups, assault, muggings, purse snatchings, breaking and entering, forgery, theft, and so on.

The penalty for these crimes varies, the sentence for holding up a bank averages 15 years in a federal penitentiary.

Spread out over 15 years, the average take of $1,900 amounts to just over $125 a year, and most robbers obtain much less than this.

Do bank robberies pay? We'd let you be the judge.

Chapter IV

Crime: The Offender–Victim Relationship

The amount of crime in the United States is unknown. While there is some uniformity to police reports of known crimes, it is a tiresome detailing of figures against a broad population base. There are statistics without adequate data on the numbers of crimes that occur and remain undiscovered by or unreported to the police. While definite data on all crimes will never be known (murder and other secret crimes do not always out), there is a projection potential in field surveys of victims as to their knowledge of crimes. There appears to be a possibility of estimating the total incidence of any crime within a community for a given period of time by developing the "loss" between data developed in these field surveys of crime victims and the number of offenses known to police. For instance, one extensive survey of crime victims indicates that less than half of the thefts under $50 (petty thefts) are reported; and only slightly over half of the burglaries are known to police (37 percent of 473 cases; and 58 percent of 313 cases).[1] Surely, such data afford reasonable projection figures.

The availability of victims for crimes (individuals, business and other organizations), is the major socio-environmental factor contributing to the total amount of crime in America. The person intent on committing a crime must find an available victim. Except for insurance frauds and other crimes with fictitious victims, crime is a strange partnership between victim and offender, with the victim providing the opportuni-

1. Phillip H. Ennis, *Criminal Victimization in the United States* (Chicago, Ill.: National Opinion Research Center, University of Chicago, 1967; A report to the President's Commission on Law Enforcement and Administration of Justice), pp. 41–42.

59

ty for the crime and the offender capitalizing on the circumstances. Victim distribution ranges from victim–precipitated crimes to pure chance in victim selection.

In crimes against the person, the availability of victims is a result of residence, employment, and daily living patterns. Among the common major crimes, only rape limits its victims by sex; and crimes against children limit the victims by age. Otherwise, male adult victims predominate. There is a greater percentage of men working at night— a favorite time period for many crimes—and in high–crime areas. Additionally, many more men than women visit entertainment areas and roam about unescorted.

In major crimes against property, the availability of victims involves the type of structure or establishment (residence, store, and other commercial occupancies). Victims in these crimes are the householder, the retail store owner–operator, or the person or firm with property in commercial buildings. In auto thefts and theft from motor vehicles, the victim may be the owner of the vehicle or the person or firm owning the material stolen.[2]

The classification of victims places emphasis upon: the weak, the dull normals, and the mental defectives; and those who precipitate crime by their travels in high–crime areas, through dissolute living or by their own aggressiveness. The major categories in this classification are:

1. Children

2. Females

3. The aged

4. Dull normals and mental defectives

5. Acquisitive persons (the larceny-in-their-soul victims of frauds)

6. Wanton women

7. Tormentors [3]

2. Albert J. Reis, Jr., "Measurement of the Nature and Amount of Crime," in *Studies in Crime and Law Enforcement in Major Metropolitan Areas,* vol. 1 (Washington, D.C.: The President's Commission on Law Enforcement and Administration of Justice, 1967), pp. 43, 65–77.

3. Hans von Hentig, *The Criminal and His Victim: Studies in the Sociology of Crime* (Hamden, Conn.: Archon Books, 1967; originally published in 1948 by the Yale University Press), pp. 404–50.

Victim Distribution: The Place of Occurrence

Whenever a crime happens there is a *place of occurrence*. Penal codes and police records systems use the place at which a crime occurs to determine the seriousness of the offense. Bank robberies are often a federal offense, while liquor store robberies are violations of state law; the burning or burglarizing of a residence is a more serious degree of crime than setting fire to a factory or breaking and entering a store. Police record keeping uses the place of occurrence for subdividing the records of many crimes such as taxicab robberies, street robberies, residential burglaries, and commercial burglaries.

The place of occurrence is a key factor in the availability of a victim of crime. If no one is present in a street or public place, or in a home, store, or other occupancy, the murderer, rapist, or robber is without a victim. If there is nothing of value in a premises entered by thieves, there can be no stealing; if there is no unlawful taking away of another's property, there is no victim. Therefore, the place where the crime takes place supplies the victim of a crime.

The locations at which victims of crime are available to offenders is indicated from the following index headings used by many police departments in their records systems and in their analysis of crime patterns:

Street	Residence (except public housing)
Park	Railroad property or bus station
Taxicab	Bar and tavern
Automobile	Drug store
Truck	Supermarket
School property	Gas station
Public housing	Bank

Other businesses.

A study of criminal victimization in the United States for the U.S. Department of Justice reveals the place of occurrence of crimes in relation to the victim's residence, and whether they happened in a public place or building, or a private building or place. Citizens were queried in this study until persons were located who had been victims of crime in the year prior to these interviews. Facts about five crimes were probed; these were the crimes likely to have individual victims (as opposed to businesses or organizations as victims) and usually coming to the attention of police: (1) robbery, (2) aggravated assault, (3) rape (force), (4) grand larceny, and (5) auto theft. In a grand total of slightly over 2,000 such crimes discussed with their victims by interviewers, 29 percent occurred near* the victim's home, 23 percent were inside the residence of the victim, and 10 percent in other private buildings or

*Contiguous yard, sidewalk, driveway.

places; 24 percent occurred in public buildings or places; and 14 percent took place in taxicabs and places not specified. Since over half of these reported crimes occurred in or near the victim's home, it is apparent that residence is an important factor in determining who is to be a victim of crime.[4]

A Washington, D.C. survey of crime victims also provided data that victimization is related to the home: (1) close to 75 percent of all crimes reported by victims to survey interviewers happened in the home neighborhood of the victim; (2) approximately 60 percent happened on the residence block of the victim; and (3) fully 50 percent of the victims term the place of occurrence as home. The only other location reported with any frequency was the victim's place of employment.[5]

In armed robbery the reward factor is of secondary concern because the safety of the robber or robbers is the primary determinant in the selection of the victim. Banks, loan companies, and supermarkets offer the greatest reward in the amount of money likely to be on the premises at the time of the robbery, but these places are usually crowded. The normal robber, or robbery group of from two to four persons, cannot control more than two to four persons effectively during a robbery. The basic safety factor in robbery lies in the offender's control of victims, and it is this factor which accounts for the popularity of liquor stores as targets for robbery. A robber or robbery group often cruise the streets of a neighborhood, examining liquor stores and how many people are in them, and walk right in and rob the selected victim when the odds are no more than the clerk or owner and one or two customers. The rewards in any one of these liquor store robberies are not large, but one robber or robbery group often invade and rob two or three places a night.[6]

The Agent–Victim

Most criminals with rational motivation for crime (as opposed to the traditional motivation of kleptomaniacs* or pyromaniacs)** seek a perfect set–up. This requires a cooperating, if not consenting, victim.

4. Ennis, *Criminal Victimization in the United States,* pp. 37–40.

5. Albert J. Biderman; Louise A. Johnson; Jennie McIntyre; and Adriane Weir, *Report on a Pilot Study in the District of Columbia on Victimization and Attitudes Toward Law Enforcement, Field Survey 1,* President's Commission on Law Enforcement and Administration of Justice; Bureau of Social Science Research, Washington, D.C. (Washington, D.C.: Government Printing Office, 1967), p. 62.

6. Werner J. Einstadter, "The Social Organization of Armed Robbery," *Social Problems* 17, no. 1 (Summer 1969): 64–83.

*Thieves who steal because of a so–called compulsion, and not for gain.

**Fire setters, other than those who set fraud or revenge fires, or blazes to conceal another crime.

The term agent–victim originated in studies of the styles of robbery. It was found that robbers recognize a basic security in victims who cooperate. For this reason, targets are selected for attack and looting that are owned by corporations or large organizations, or in which the owner–operator is covered by insurance. The employee who becomes the victim in these robberies is viewed as an agent–victim: a person with no personal loss as a result of the robbery. The concept of the agent–victim includes the rationale that no employee is going to fight or resist when the money demanded by the robbers does not belong to him. This is also true, to an undetermined lesser extent, when the money may belong to the victim but the victim is covered by insurance (a lesser extent because a series of losses usually results in the cancellation of such insurance).[7]

This concept of the agent–victim contributing to the perfect set-up in robberies is in direct opposition to victim–precipitated crimes. The agent–victim's expected cooperation by–passes any possible provocation or contribution to the crime as an event. While resistance to robbery attempts cannot be construed as victim–precipitated crime, robbers do justify the use of force against their victims by claiming self–defense when the victim resists the armed robbery.[8]

Victim Distribution: The Opportunity Factor

The distribution of victims of crime among various social groups is not a factor of race, creed, or national origin, but of opportunity for the offender to commit a crime. Where people live and work, and the nature of occupancies in a neighborhood are the most valid criteria for determining who or what place will be the victim of crime. While thousands of words have been written on the white to nonwhite ratio of victims, it is meaningless unless some proof is developed that either group is more likely to be a victim of crime than the other—over and beyond the factor of residence, place of employment and type of occupancy. If a person lives or works—or plays—in a high–crime area, whether white or nonwhite, he or she is more likely to be a victim of crime because he or she *is there,* not because of the color of his or her skin. If a store or other place of business has cash or property of value, it is more likely to be stolen if the occupancy is in a high–crime area solely on the basis of accessibility. Merchants in such areas have been robbed as often as five times in a week, and thieves have returned for nocturnal looting to stores and warehouses in these areas with an equal frequency. It is the accessibility of cash or valuable property that

7. Einstadter, "The Social Organization of Armed Robbery," pp. 64–83.
8. Gerald D. Wolcott, *A Typology of Armed Robbers* (unpublished Master's Thesis, Sacramento, Calif.: Sacramento State College, 1968), p. 48.

identifies these victims. They are *targets of opportunity*, and they are not selected because the merchant or businessman happens to be white or nonwhite.

In a California study of the habit patterns of armed robbers, the most common premises attacked were grocery stores, off–premises liquor stores, bars, and gasoline stations. When these armed robberies were unplanned—the criminals cruising a neighborhood for a target of opportunity—the favorite premises attacked were liquor stores.[9]

Age and sex are factors in determining who will become victims of crime, but such factors are relevant only to crimes against the person (murder, non-negligent manslaughter, aggravated assault, child molestation, and rape).

The Genovese case in Forest Hills, New York, is a classic example of this type of crime and the manner in which chance determined the victim's identity; and the opportunity factor provided the offender with a victim for the necessary doer-sufferer relationship. Twenty-eight-year-old Catherine (Kitty) Genovese lived alone in a small apartment on the second floor of a two–story building with ground–floor business occupancies. She worked as a hostess in a bar–restaurant in New York's theater district. Kitty Genovese's work day ended at about 2:00 A.M. on March 31, 1964. She drove home, parking in a parking lot at the end of her apartment house, arriving about 3:00 A.M. Kitty's attacker caught up with her between the parking lot and her home. The first stabbing of Kitty was on the street. Her assailant slashed and stabbed and ran away. Kitty staggered about 50 yards and fell on the sidewalk outside her home. Her attacker came back, stabbed her again, and fled in a car. Kitty walked and fell to the stairway leading up to her second story apartment. The attacker returned and searched the area for his victim. He found Kitty on the stairs, a few feet from the door of her home and he killed her. Kitty's killer was arrested and convicted of this murder; police investigators reported he had never met his victim prior to the attack. (The screams of Kitty Genovese did not go unheard during this chance encounter and attack. Other residents turned on their lights, went to their windows, and shouted at the attacker—but no one of the 38 witnesses called police to destroy the 35 minutes of opportunity for this crime).[10]

A 1967 study of the offender–victim relationship by sex, age, race and place of occurrence in major crimes against the person (homicide, aggravated assault, and forcible rape) and robbery, authorized by the National Commission on the Causes and Prevention of Violence, revealed patterns based on a study of police records in 17 cities. This nationwide survey supports the data of more local studies as to the

9. Wolcott, *A Typology of Armed Robbers*, pp. 31–32.
10. A. M. Rosenthal, *Thirty–Eight Witnesses* (New York: McGraw-Hill Book Co., 1964).

place of occurrence, and relates data as to sex, race and age. In this survey, the leading combinations for the five crimes studied were: *Homicide:* male offender, male victim; black offender, black victim; 26–year–old and older offenders, same age group victims; and the general place of occurrence was outside, more specifically, alley and street. (Note: The place of 39 percent of these homicides was in the residence category.) *Aggravated Assault:* male offender, male victim; black offender, black victim; 26-year–old and upward offenders, same age group victims; and the place of occurrence was outside, in the alley and street area. *Rape* (force): offender–victim relationship classic male–female; offender and victim, black; victim and offender in 18–25 age group; and the residence was the place of occurrence, with the bedroom appropriately predominating as the specific place for rape. *Armed Robbery:* offender–victim relationship male–male; black–white; 18–25 age group offender, 26–year–old and upward victim; and these crimes took place outside, with alley and street as the specific place. *Unarmed Robbery:* male offender, male victim; black offender, white victim; victim and offender in 0–17 age group; and the place of occurrence was the residence area, with the specific locale designated as basement, hall, elevator or garage.

Victim Distribution: Victim–precipitated Crime

Victim–precipitated crime refers to criminal acts in which the victim is either the direct or a contributory cause of the crime, setting in motion the chain of circumstances spelling out the crime. When the victim is an active partner in the circumstances leading to the event classified as a crime, his contribution to the dynamics of the situation justifies investigation of his role. It is because so many victims can describe these precrime circumstances that police investigators probe the background of the victim–offender relationship in all crimes. The classic avenues of inquiry are usually structured by the following queries:

1. Did the victim know the offender? Is there any relationship?

2. Was the victim armed?

3. Is the victim known to be aggressive?

4. Has the victim been "field interrogated?" Are there any "connect–ups" with the victim and reports of other crimes?[11]

A previous relationship of victim and offender doesn't suggest a victim's active participation in the precrime circumstances, but it does

11. Paul B. Weston and Kenneth M. Wells, *Criminal Investigation: Basic Perspectives* (Englewood Cliffs, N.J.: Prentice–Hall, 1970), p. 91.

reveal a potential for contributing to the crime event. Children may make an unknowing contribution to crime against them by relatives and friends. Women contribute to a crime because some of their interrelationships suddenly move from normal to abnormal. A previous relationship often leads offenders to victims, such as children or women, the dull normals and mental defectives,[12] and the aged.

Friendships of the victim and the offender may also make an overt contribution to the dynamics of a crime when the victim is depressed, emotionally disturbed, or lonesome. These persons seek new friends and liaisons among chance drinking partners, prostitutes, homosexual pick-ups, and hitchhikers. These are the *night-people* victims of crime, and their provocative conduct and circle of acquaintances among hustlers, pimps, bartenders, and taxi drivers is the stage setting for sex crimes, crimes of violence, and crimes against property.

When a victim is armed at the time of a crime (carrying something for self-protection), or is known to be aggressive, there is a direct provocation for crime. To qualify as a crime determinant, however, an act is required beyond that of going into an area or place not likely to be frequented without arms or self-confidence. The necessary act is aggressiveness, or a combative response to threat, real or implied.

When a victim has been field interrogated or stopped and frisked by police, it is indicative of a predisposition to frequent high-crime areas or to be a night person, both invitations to crime. When a person has been victimized previously, the facts of the earlier crime or crimes may reveal a realtionship between the victim and one or more offenders. When a victim or his car is connected to a previous crime it may also reveal a course of conduct inviting crime.

It is in the fields of homicide and other crimes of violence that the most valid evidence of victims within the foregoing relationships acting provocatively to cause a crime are found. The crime-provoking function of the victim in such crimes has been thoroughly supported by major research. In a study of 588 criminal homicides in Philadelphia, 150 (26 percent) of these killings were classified as "V.P.": victim-precipitated. Many of these V.P. homicides in which the killer was provoked into the fatal attack showed a husband and wife relationship between victim and offender; or male victims killed by female offenders who had some previous relationship.[13]

In Chicago, a study of the patterns of murder collected sufficient data about 311 killings to divide these homicides into VP and non-VP categories. A total of 118 of these 311 killings (37.9 percent) were classed as victim-precipitated. The victim-offender relationship in

12. Von Hentig, *The Criminal and His Victim*, pp. 415–19.
13. Marvin E. Wolfgang, *Patterns in Criminal Homicide* (Philadelphia: University of Pennsylvania, 1958), pp. 254–60.

these 118 homicides was found to be family or friend in 59 cases (50 percent).[14]

In a British study of crimes of violence in London, a survey of previous association between victims and offenders discovered many instances in which the victim was not free of some culpability in the crime committed. At least, this three–year study reveals that the majority of violent crimes in London during the survey years (1950, 1957, 1960) were not unprovoked attacks by offenders who were complete strangers to their victims. It was found that 27 percent of the victims had a previous family relationship or an interrelationship (sweetheart, friend or rival, fellow employee, club member, or neighbor) of some duration; and 20 percent had a previous business or casual relationship.[15] A subsequent study in America, based on interviews with victims of crime, validates the foregoing report. About 45 percent of all serious crimes against the person (homicide, forcible rape, robbery, and aggravated assault) were committed by someone familiar to the victim.[16]

In the 1967 survey of five major crimes against the person authorized by the National Commission on the Causes and Prevention of Violence, the collected data supports the concept of a previous relationship between offenders and their victims. Among the relationships predominating in this report were:

Homicide: Acquaintances; and family members other than husband, wife, or child.

Aggravated Assault: Acquaintances; husband and wife; close friends, including mistresses and homosexual partners.

Rape: Acquaintances; and family members other than husband and wife or child.

Armed Robbery: Little or no relationships found (less than 1 percent usually); strangers predominated (78.6 percent).

Unarmed Robbery: No relationship between offender and victim at family or other intimate levels; acquaintances and neighbors to a slight extent; strangers were the primary victim

Victim Distribution: Hardening the Target

Victims of crime are not unaware of its threat. Many possible victims of crime change their habits or *harden the target* so as to make them-

14. Harwin L. Voss and John R. Hepburn, "Patterns in Criminal Homicide in Chicago," *Journal of Criminal Law, Criminology and Police Science,* 59, no. 4, (December 1968): 499–508.

15. F. H. McClintock, *Crimes of Violence* (London: MacMillan & Co., 1963), pp. 36–39.

16. Ennis, *Criminal Victimization in the U. S.,* p. 30.

selves less available to persons intent on the commission of a crime. In a recent survey of things done to protect themselves against crime, several habit changes were reported by residents in Boston and Chicago. These changes were: (1) staying off the streets at night; (2) using private vehicles or taxicabs for nighttime transportation (not walking); and (3) not talking to strangers.[17] Additionally, the respondents in this study also reported hardening the target by the following means: (1) carrying a firearm, knife or club when out on the street; (2) placing locks on doors, and locks or bars on windows of their home or store; (3) lighting up the exterior area around a residence or place of business; and (4) keeping a dog or weapon in a residence or store for protection against intruders.

In Oakland, California, a local law requires the past victims of property crimes to upgrade the physical security of their premises. In San Francisco, Washington, D.C., and other major cities, bus and taxi drivers no longer carry large sums of money, and exact–fare rules and locked fare boxes further harden these popular targets of criminals. Car owners can now purchase sophisticated burglar alarms, wheel locks, and a quick–release catch for their stereotape decks.[18]

Bait money is now utilized in most banks. A record is kept at the bank of the serial numbers of the paper currency that is the bait, and banks use extensive photographic programs for the same purpose. Such methodology is a secondary means of hardening the target. Offenders are identified when the bait money is spent and traced, or their pictures identified.

The Complainant

The victim is legally an aggrieved party: a *complainant.* This is a person whose legal rights have been invaded by the criminal act which is the subject of the report (complaint) to police. Modern criminal jurisprudence affords little recognition to victims of crime. The community and its agents of justice discharge any moral obligation to victims of crime by the apprehension and prosecution of the offender.

The role of victim in modern criminal proceedings is primarily as a focus for the essential elements of the crime charged. However, trial procedures sometimes establish the complainant as an accuser, and to be a victim participating in a criminal procedure is sometimes a dis-

17. Albert J. Reis, Jr., "Public Perceptions and Recollections About Crime, Law Enforcement and Criminal Justice," in *Studies in Crime and Law Enforcement in Major Metropolitan Areas*, vol. 1 (Washington, D.C.: The President's Commission on Law Enforcement and Administration of Justice, 1967), pp. 102–14.
18. Mel Mandell, "Can You Outsmart the New York Car Thief?" *New York*, 19, April 1971, pp. 41–46.

turbing experience. This is especially true if a person is unfamiliar with
the role of the defense counsel and the court's objective to protect the
rights of an accused person. The U.S. Supreme Court in the 1933 case
of *Snyder v. Massachusetts*,[19] commented on the need in criminal
proceedings of some balance between offender and victim: "But
justice, though due the accused, is due to the accuser also."

Not all victims promptly report a crime to police and cooperate in
prosecution. The seriousness of the crime, in terms of personal injury
or the value of the property stolen, is a factor in reporting. Aggravated
assaults are reported more frequently than ordinary assaults; and the
victim of a grand larceny (substantial loss) is more likely to report the
theft than the victim of a petty theft. Crimes are not reported for the
following reasons:

1. Identification with the offender as opposed to police.

2. A belief the act was not a crime.

3. Fear of physical harm—reprisal by offender or friends and
   associates of offender.

4. Economic loss through usually increased insurance rates.

5. Unwillingness to get involved (because of adverse publicity).

6. Loss of faith in police effectiveness.[20]

Of course, in cases of crimes without victims (abortion, homosexuality, prostitution, illegal gambling, and drug abuse) and some frauds
there is a real failure to report crimes to police, or for police to discover the crime. The girl who seeks an abortion, the two consenting adults
of the same sex, the whore and her customer, the person who bets on
the outcome of some game of chance, and the user of dangerous and
addicting drugs, do not report their criminal acts. They do not view
themselves as victims of a crime. Moreover, there is the doctrine of
volenti non fit injuria which holds that a person who consents to an act
cannot receive an injury.

Frauds are often based on the exploitation of an inherent dishones-
ty in the victim; and the victim's silence is guaranteed by his belief that
he is involved in a criminal act. There is a general ignorance among
fraud victims as to their criminal responsibility—a state of mind useful
to criminals seeking to silence the victims of various frauds.[21]

19. 291 U.S. 97 (1933).

20. Ennis, *Criminal Victimization in the United States*, pp. 41–44.

21. A *confidence game* or *con game* is any type of fraud or swindle in which the mark (victim)
is allowed to profit by dishonest means, then is induced to make a large investment and
is fleeced. *See* David W. Maurer, *The Big Con—The Story of the Confidence Man and the
Confidence Game* (Indianapolis and New York: Bobbs–Merrill Co., 1940).

Restitution and Compensation for Crime Victims

Restitution for victims of crime has an ancient origin. It is an act of restoration of property to the rightful owner, or of giving the equivalent in cash or merchandise. It is also the making of a payment to the victim or his family as an equivalent for death or injury.

Originally, restitution was a form of personal reparation by the offender or his kin to the victim or the victim's family. It stemmed from the primitive blood–feud (a sort of private war) and was a settlement between the family of the murder victim and the offender and his family. Later, the government participated in the arrangements. The amount of money paid by the offender as compensation (or satisfaction) for an offense varied with the status of the victim (royalty, nobility, clergy, freedman, slave), and the money was apportioned between the sovereign (loss of a subject), the Hundred or earlier community in which the victim resided (loss of a member), and the victim's family (loss of a relative).

Courts may allow restitution in an agreement between victim and offender to *compromise* a minor criminal action. This type of settlement requires a situation in which the victim has a cause for civil action arising from the crime, and the victim acknowledges that restitution has been made (satisfaction for the injury). If the court has no reason in its discretion or in the public interest (i.e., the crime was committed riotously; was against a public officer; or the offender's intent was to commit a felony) to deny the restitution as an effective settlement, then it is allowed.

Courts may also order restitution as part of the sentence of a convicted offender. These cases usually involve vandalism, malicious mischief, arson, or larceny. It is financial restitution for the costs of damage done to property, or a reasonable amount related to the current market value of stolen property.

In contemporary law, there is a strong belief that restitution is more properly a civil action for damages against an offender by the victim or his family. Any schedule of payments for injuries are in the area of *torts*—private or civil wrongs for which a civil action can be justified. However, victims without funds cannot hire attorneys to pursue their claims in court. In addition, most criminal offenders are without assets, and court judgments against them are worthless.

Probably a combination of indigent offenders and victims led to the concept of compensation for victims of crime. In 1964, Great Britain and New Zealand enacted similar legislation to relieve the poor victim of the costs of his injury and loss of income during the resultant disability period, if any. Such law making is within the obligation of a government to its citizens. Modern government accepts responsibility for the protection of citizens against criminals by its vast budgets for law enforcement and criminal justice. Failure to afford such protection makes the government (as representative of the whole community) to some extent liable for injuries to innocent victims—and there is some rationale for spreading the costs of treatment for injured victims to the whole community.[22]

There must be some level of maximum compensation: a ceiling on payments in any scheme for reimbursing victims of violent crime. However, when payments are keyed to wages (wage earners) and the value of lost services (housewife), the victim's inability to sustain the cost of treatment without help develops a welfare level compensation. This is unfair. It requires victims to exhaust minimal financial resources to qualify for victim's compensation.

State victim–compensation systems should be administered to refer claims to an attorney in the community in which the crime occurs. He would investigate and determine the award to the victim within the wages–services and out–of–pocket expenses framework, but without regard for the victim's ability to pay. Compensation would be immediate for out–of–pocket costs, and weekly or monthly for lost wages or services.[23]

Compensation for victims of crime should be extended to provide funds to cover injuries received by innocent bystanders or citizens who have rushed to the defense of a crime victim. This may overcome the existing reluctance of many citizens to get involved in an ongoing crime.

Restitution for the victims of crime by the government raises a rather different but important question in regard to innocent defendants being classed as victims. Should a defendant, having been found innocent, be reimbursed for his legal expenses, damages due to loss of wages or job loss while incarcerated, and the traumatic effect of jail life? Perhaps the jury or judge who acquits, or the judge who dismisses, might determine whether the defendant did or did not cause the victim's injury and was in fact sufficiently innocent of the charges to merit government reimbursment. In such instances, the innocent defendant may not be a crime victim, but he is a "victim" of the criminal justice process.

22. David J. Bentel, "Selected Problems of Public Compensation to Victims of Crime," *Issues in Criminology* 3, no. 2 (Spring 1968): 217–31.
23. Robert Childres, "The Victims," *Harper's*, April 1964, pp. 159–62.

Selected References

Books

Ennis, Phillip H. *Criminal Victimization in the United States.* Chicago, Ill.: National Opinion Research Center, University of Chicago, 1967; a report to the President's Commission on Law Enforcement and Administration of Justice.

Hentig, Hans von. *The Criminal and His Victim: Studies in the Sociology of Crime.* Hamden, Conn.: Archon Books, 1967; originally published in 1948 by the Yale University Press.

Wolfgang, Marvin E. *Patterns in Criminal Homicide.* Philadelphia: University of Pennsylvania Press, 1958.

Periodicals

Bentel, David J. "Selected Problems of Public Compensation to Victims of Crime." *Issues in Criminology* 3, no. 2 (Spring 1968): 217–31.

Childres, Robert "The Victims," *Harper's,* April 1964, pp. 159–62.

Einstaedter, Werner J. "The Social Organization of Armed Robbery" *Social Problems* 17, no. 1 (Summer 1969): 64–83.

Cases

Snyder v. Massachusetts, 291 U. S. 97 (1933).

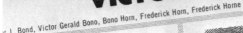

INTERSTATE F...

WANTED BY F

VICTOR JERALD BONO

...r J. Bond, Victor Gerald Bono, Bono Horn, Frederick Horn, Frederick Horne

CANCELLED

Victor

DESCRIPTION

AGE: 26, born July 29, 194...
   by birth records)
HEIGHT: 6' 2" to 6' 3"
WEIGHT: 195 to 210 pound...
BUILD: medium
HAIR: blond
OCCUPATIONS: firefight...
SCARS AND MARKS; ta...
middle finger left hand,
right hand.

CRIMINAL REC...

Bono has been convicted

CAUTION

BONO, WHO IS BEING
DERS OF FEDERAL
SIDER EXTREMELY D

...ederal warrant was issued on June 27, 1967, at Los Angeles, California, charging Bono with the murder of Federal Officers, as ...erformance of official duties (Title 18, U. S. Code, Sections 1114 and 111). A Federal warrant was also issued June 28, 196... ...erstate flight to avoid prosecution for narcotics (Title 18, U. S. Code, Section 1073).

Chapter V

Crime and Criminals

As communities organized for social control through law and its enforcement, the agents of criminal justice began to classify criminals into legal typologies. As the problem of crime developed over the centuries, scientists and scholars developed classification systems to *type* criminals for a better understanding of the one–time offender, the professional criminal, and the recidivist or repeating offender whose life history is primarily a criminal career.

Criminal or offender typologies categorize criminal behavior into *sets* (which can be identified by certain specific offender characteristics), and then use these individual categories: (1) to study the universe of criminal behavior and relate it to the known causative factors of such behavior, or to develop new theories of criminal behavior; and (2) to study individual offenders and classify them within the sets of a typology for an improved insight into the causative factors of their behavior for the purpose of treatment and rehabilitation.

There is a de facto division of criminals by police and other agents of criminal justice. It is a classification system with two major groups: (1) the professional criminal, whose criminality is a means of making a living, and (2) the accidental or occasional offender, whose criminality is a one–act aberration from his normal life style and pattern of behavior (despite the fact that the antisocial act may be repeated from time to time).

There is a legal division of criminals aligned with the seriousness of criminal acts or the grades of crime: misdemeanants and felons. This, however, is a very broad classification and of little scientific use in any attempt to secure greater knowledge about offenders. In addition, it is a classification based solely on the "thing done." A typology of offenders must be based on facts about the offender as a person. The nature and circumstances of the act that makes the behavior criminal is useful data in typing the offender, but no more so than other significant data.

For the purpose of these typologies the data base for studying offenders is the life history and criminal record of the individual, no less. In some of the offender typologies, life–history data is supplemented by interviews with the offender. The standardization of terminology used to describe criminal acts contributes a uniformity necessary to construct typologies and also to determine the appropriate category within a typology for a particular offender. Offender interviews add a new and significant dimension to our understanding. Not only do they afford an opportunity to observe the offender and ascertain how he sees himself in relation to others, but they offer a chance for reviewing reported factual information about his crimes.

The Professional vs. the Occasional Offender

The *"pro"* vs. the one–time offender has been a useful classification of criminals for police and other agents of criminal justice. It is directly related to the police apprehension process, to some of the judicial and legal concepts of sentencing, and to the work of probation, parole, and corrections generally. The professional criminal tends to concentrate on crimes in which there is a consenting victim; or the offender is unseen by, or unknown to, the victim. He is a two – to – seven – time offender; and is not usually an appropriate candidate for probation or release on parole after a short term of imprisonment. The accidental or occasional offender is usually identified by his victim or by his knowledge of, or access to, the victim of a crime or the place of occurrence. He is generally a first, or less serious offender; and is eligible for probation or parole after a short term of imprisonment.

Gabriel Tarde, a noted French criminologist, suggested a classification of criminals which would stress the identification of criminals whose major source of income came from crimes. He believed these individuals were criminals because of habit, and his measure of the professional criminal was whether the favored criminal activity was viewed as a trade. Criminals because of opportunity (accidental or occasional offenders) were to be classified separately as violaters of personal rights because of vengeance, or violaters of property rights in order to supplement a legal income at some honest trade.[1]

The first extensive classification along these lines was made by chief

1. Gabriel Tarde, *Penal Philosophy* (Boston: Little, Brown, and Co., 1912), pp. 265–68.

of detectives Thomas Byrnes in New York City.[2] Byrnes classified professional criminals only to show the trade of crime, rather than the acts of an occasional offender. These criminals were described by Byrnes as "clever in their own peculiar line," and as "intelligent and thoughtful rogues" who profited from their criminal activities.

In this classification of 204 professional criminals, a total of 11 categories were listed. The titles given each distinguishable group of criminals—whose photographs and criminal records were listed by Byrnes—in this contemporary classification are:

1. Bank burglars

2. Bank sneak thieves (daytime thefts by trick, speed, and stealth)

3. Forgers

4. Hotel and boardinghouse thieves

5. Sneak and house thieves

6. Store and safe burglars

7. Shoplifters and pickpockets

8. Confidence and bunco men (general swindling)

9. Receivers of stolen goods

10. Sawdust men (swindles involving the sale of alleged counterfeit money or bonds)

11. Dishonest horse dealers.[3]

A review of the case histories of these offenders reveals a mixed pattern of arrests in many instances, but in the majority of the criminal histories listed the offenders have a single pattern of arrests for the same kinds of crime.

In 1939, Dr. Arthur N. Foxe established a similar classification of criminals,[4] in which the professional criminals of Chief Byrnes' listing are grouped as repetitive criminals, and the occasional offender is subdivided into *situational* and *physical* categories.

In this typology of crime and criminals, the deeds of the repetitive criminal are listed as burglary, forgery, robbery, sexual crimes, swindling, and picking pockets. Dr. Foxe comments on this type of individual as follows: "His lack of maturation makes him commit the

2. Thomas Byrnes, *1886—Professional Criminals in America* (New York: Chelsea House Publishers, 1969, publication was approved by the New York Board of Police in 1886).
3. Ibid., pp. 1–51.
4. Arthur N. Foxe, "An Additional Classification of Criminals," *The Journal of Criminal Law and Criminology*, Volume 30, July-August 1939, pp. 232–236. (*Police Science* had not been added to the title of this periodical at that time.)

same crime with appalling consistency in his twenties, thirties, forties, and even fifties.[5]

Dr. Foxe rejects the term *accidental offender* since there is no evidence the thing done by the occasional offender is an accident. Foxe's occasional criminal is a person who has had a satisfactory adjustment to his life situation until some circumstance or series of events destroys that adjustment. These offenders may not be personally responsible for the events leading to the crime (victim–precipitated, possibly), but under the stress of certain circumstances they become criminals. Dr. Foxe's subdivision of the occasional lawbreaker is as follows:

1. Situational:

   a. Economic factor (problems).

   b. Life crisis (related to role of fiancée, father, spouse—such as frustration in love or infidelity of spouse—or reaction to an insult or a hostile act).

2. Physical:

   a. Alcoholic episode.*

   b. Venereal and other ego–destroying illness or injury (blow to vanity, pride, or capacity).

   c. Curable or incurable mental disease, syphilis, and the like.[6]

Professional Criminals in the Ghetto—The Hustler and the Drug Seller

Hustling is a form of criminal activity which not only has a distinguishable behavior pattern, but which also has some conflict relationship between the offender and the community. This is the activity and life–style of the hustler or the *cat.*

Hustling was once a deviant rather than criminal occupation limited to poolroom hustling.[7] The poolroom hustler made his living by betting and deceit. He would convince a stranger to play pool and wager small sums, but the hustler initially concealed his own skill at the game. When the wagered amounts were increased, the hustler used his skill to win back the money he had lost and the sums bet by the victim in anticipation of further winnings. The decline in poolrooms since the

5. Arthur N. Foxe, *Studies in Criminology* (New York: Nervous and Mental Disease Monographs, 1948) p. 105.
*Drug abuse episodes would be similar, although not common around 1939.
6. Ibid., p. 107.
7. Ned Polsky, *Hustlers, Beats and Others* (Chicago: Aldine Publishing Co. 1967), pp. 41–116.

first quarter of the century has led to economic disaster for the poolroom hustler.

The new breed of hustlers are still related to night hours, unsupervised occupations, and the thrill of working for part or all of the "action" rather than weekly or monthly wages. However, they now operate in ghetto areas and their hustle is diversified, profitable, criminal behavior: shoplifting, receiving stolen property, pimping,* numbers running (gambling agent), and selling narcotics or dangerous drugs.

Hustlers, in a strange shift from the all–man world of the traditional poolroom before midcentury, began to use—or misuse—women. Hustlers exploit women. Many attractive young females support a hustler in some luxury, by shoplifting and prostitution. Hustlers supervise the basic arrangements and operations, and the women dutifully hand over the proceeds. Additionally, the hustler sees himself as an operator with a scheme to avoid arrest because of an angle. His angle is to remain aloof from contact with stolen merchandise or the criminal conduct of prostitutes. Police find it difficult to gain probable cause for an arrest without evidence of active participation in crime.

Because the ghettos of a great many urban centers now have a considerable portion of black minority group citizens in their population, it is not surprising that many young black males have become hustlers. Since petty crime and street and tavern solicitation for prostitution have always been identified as a source of income in low–rent areas, it is not surprising that many of these black ghetto residents have seized this illegal opportunity for economic enrichment.

The black hustler is best characterized in a study of the Negro numbers man. The *numbers game* is a lottery in which the player bets small sums (ten cents to a dollar) and the outcome is determined by chance. In some areas, a specific procedure has been established for computing the day's winning number from the total payoffs reported in the day's pari–mutuel betting at a major horse–racing track. Numbers men were interviewed in this study and they admitted to the "fast–dollar" philosophy of the "angle boy," and observed that they did not think their work was in violation of the lottery laws (as a real criminal activity). These agents of a numbers ring (or bank) said their adolescent behavior was in the role of sport or big spender: and their chief adult recreation (*kick*) centered on betting on horses and sports events. However, both the juvenile police–encounter record and the adult arrest history of these numbers men were usually related to disorderly acts or gambling; there was no evidence of stealing or violence.[8]

*Securing prostitutes for customers, or vice versa.

8. Julian B. Roebuck, "The Negro Numbers Man as a Criminal Type: The Construction and Application of a Typology," *The Journal of Criminal Law, Criminology and Police Science* 54, no. 1 (March 1963): 48–60.

A modern variation on the black hustler in ghetto areas or urban population centers is the cat. Usually a drug user, each cat has his hustle (any nonviolent means of making money, usually illegal) to live without working for wages and his kick (any act usually tabooed by the community). The most popular kick is drugs, in some progression from marihuana to hard drugs and hallucinogens (heroin, methedrine, cocaine and acid—LSD).[9]

Drug selling is a type of crime that is popular with hustlers or cats hurrying to achieve upward social mobility. It is a fast route out of the slums, and out of the fields of petty theft and living off the proceeds of prostitution. It is a get–rich–quick scheme compared to the orderly and earned advancement of the numbers man from runner, to pickup man, to an executive role in the bank or counting room of a major gambling operation.

This is a rags–to–riches story of one hustler on the drug scene:

> If he could last six months selling narcotics he was a rich man. He owned part of a bar on 138th Street. He had excellent credit with bookies and gamblers. All of this because of money. He had all the money he wanted and everything that money could buy, and it came in every day. He controlled the major cutting of the heroin from its high purity state to the retail product at street level, and he took greater risks than the others in the drug–selling mob, but it was the risk–taking which accounted for his huge profits. He was the distributor, the supplier of the pushers who sold to the junkies.[10]

Once before, in the Roaring Twenties, a lucrative role in criminality had been held predominantly by the Irish, Italian, or German bootlegger, willing to risk arrest to bring his customers a supply of illegal whiskey and beer during America's Noble Experiment, the dry years. Of course, the harmful effects of drug selling is much greater than any harm from selling a fair quality of bootleg whiskey or beer, but the instant riches factor is quite similar.

The hustler in the ghetto of modern cities who specializes in the high–risk business of marketing illegal drugs will make money, but there is a lesser risk in the traditional hustler's role of pimp, thief, or numbers man. This is the new professional criminal in the ghetto: the drug bootlegger or the man with an angle.

Criminal Typologies

A recent system used to break up the universe of criminals combined the socio–psychological aspects of criminal behavior with the

9. Harold Finestone, "Cats, Kicks and Color," *Social Problems* 5, no. 1 (July 1957): 3–13.
10. Alvin Moscow, *Merchants of Heroin—An In-Depth Portrayal of Business in the Underworld* (New York: Dial Press, 1968), p. 225.

life-style of the criminal to create a typological classification system. The following factors are used to assign a criminal to one of the types of criminal behavior comprising this system:

1. Offense behavior (things done)
2. Interactional setting (crime scene; victim)
3. Role–career (life–style)
4. Offender's self–concept and attitudes
5. Family background, associates, and so forth.[11]

The descriptive titles given each distinguishable group of criminals in this array is more diversified than Byrnes' 1886 listing, ranging through the following role–careers in criminality:

1. Professional thief (confidence man, shoplifter, pickpocket)
2. Professional heavy (robber, burglar)
3. Professional fringe violator (doctors, attorneys, and other professional persons who violate laws)
4. Semiprofessional property criminal
5. White–collar criminal*
6. Forger (naive; checks)
7. Embezzler (dishonest employee)
8. Auto thief (joyrider)
9. Personal offender (assailant; one–time)
10. Property offender (one–time)
11. "Psycho" assailant
12. Sex offender—nonviolent
13. Sex offender—nonviolent (rape, statutory)
14. Sex offender—violent
15. Addict—heroin.[12]

11. Don C. Gibbons, *Society, Crime and Criminal Careers—An Introduction to Criminality* (Englewood Cliffs, N. J.: Prentice–Hall, 1968), pp. 215–42.
*A broad definition of white–collar criminality is: "The violation of criminal law by a person of high socio–economic status in the course of occupational activity." *See* Earl R. Quinney, "The Study of White Collar Crime: Toward a Reorientation in Theory and Research," *Journal of Criminal Law, Criminology and Police Science* 55, no. 2 (June 1964): 208–14.
12. Gibbons, *Changing the Lawbreaker*, pp. 96–128. (This typology of criminals was developed in association with Donald L. Garrity; *see* Don C. Gibbons and Donald L. Garrity, "Definition and Analysis of Certain Criminal Types," *Journal of Criminal Law, Criminology and Police Science* 53 (March 1962): 27–35.

While fashions in crime change over a half century, there is a remarkable similarity between this criminal typology and the prior classification of criminals by Tarde, the French criminologist, and Byrnes, the New York chief of detectives. There is a differentiation between groups of criminals where crime is a trade or major source of income (professional as opposed to semiprofessional and one-time criminals). The semiprofessional and one-time subdivisions in this typology of Gibbons and Garrity allows for classification of both the situational and physical occasional offenders described by Dr. Foxe.

One of the most recent criminal typologies constructed by American criminologists is a behavioral–cultural typology that uses not only the offender's criminal behavior as a criteria of classification, but also considers the interrelationships of individual human behavior with the behavior of others, both in the offender's social group and in the community. This brings the criminal deed and the offender into focus with the social context of the act and the perpetrator. This typology uses four major factors for analysis and classification:

1. Crime career

2. Support by offender's social group of the criminal behavior of offender

3. Relationship between the criminal behavior and noncriminal behavior in society generally

4. The reaction of the community (society) to the criminal behavior [13]

Marshall B. Clinard and Richard Quinney, the developers of this innovative behavioral–cultural typology, allow for eight types of offenders:

1. Violent criminals (murder, rape, aggravated assault)

2. Conventional criminals (robbery, burglary, theft)

3. Professional criminals (swindling, shoplifting, pickpocketing, counterfeiting, forgery)

4. Organized criminals (sale of narcotics and dangerous drugs, prostitution, gambling)

5. Occupational criminals (embezzlement, price fixing, fee splitting, black marketeering)

6. Occasional property criminals (auto theft, shoplifting, forgery—checks, vandalism)

13. Marshall B. Clinard and Richard Quinney, *Criminal Behavior Systems—A Typology* (New York: Holt, Rinehart and Winston, 1967), pp. 12–14.

7. Political criminals (treason, sedition, and protest defined as criminal)

8. Public order criminals (drunkenness, drug abuse or narcotic use, homosexuality, traffic violations) [14]

Criminal Careers

There is a cost to the entire community and its criminal justice system when a person becomes a criminal and begins a career in crime, which may be coterminous with his lifetime. There is a financial cost to victims of crime when money or property is stolen, an out–of–pocket cost when injuries or death are caused by crime, and the intangible social cost to the community of both criminal and victim. However, the most basic cost is the fiscal expenditure needed to process offenders in the criminal justice system from the beginning to the end of their criminal careers.

In a major study of offenders, it was reported that criminal career patterns of first arrests and subsequent rearrests revealed an average cost of $12,000 per individual. For instance, a sample of 1,000 offenders arrested initially for one of the FBI Index crimes (murder, nonnegligent manslaughter, forcible rape, robbery, aggravated assault, burglary, larceny of $50 or more, and auto theft) would build up to a total of 3,670 rearrests for Index crimes alone.[15]

In projecting crime–career costs, it was discovered that certain crimes could be identified with crime careers, which accounted for various segments of the community's crime–career cost:

1. Burglary (39 percent)

2. Theft—$50 and over (24 percent)

3. Automobiles (18 percent)

4. Aggravated assault (9 percent)

5. Robbery (7 percent)

6. Murder and nonnegligent manslaughter (2 percent)

7. Forcible rape (1 percent)[16]

In the rearrest crime–switch area of this study, it was reported that the professional or repetitive criminal was arrested three to four times

---

14. Clinard and Quinney, *Criminal Behavior Systems—A Typology*, pp. 14–19.

15. The Institute of Defense Analyses, *Task Force Report: Science and Technology* (Washington, D.C.: The President's Commission on Law Enforcement and Administration of Justice, 1967), pp. 59–65.

16. Ibid., p. 64.

in his life span of criminal behavior. For instance, a sample of 1,000 criminals arrested initially for robbery, during their collective lifetime would total:

1. Fifty arrests for murder

2. Seventy arrests for rape (forcible)

3. Eight hundred more arrests (in addition to the first arrests) for robbery

4. Two hundred and fifty arrests for aggravated assault

5. Fourteen hundred arrests for burglary

6. Seven hundred and thirty arrests for larceny of $50 or over

7. Three hundred and seventy arrests for auto theft [17]

While the FBI Index crimes are not representative of the universe of crimes committed, they are suggestive of crimes which can be classified as serious, and are commonly found in the American criminal justice process. Additionally, since the Index crimes do not include any offenses within the overreach of the criminal law, these patterns and their costs are for antisocial conduct justly termed criminal by law.

The reality of professional criminals whose recidivism develops into lifetime careers of repetitive criminal behavior indicates the importance of a classification system. This will aid and assist the judiciary in the sentencing dilemma, and aid and assist those responsible for custody and treatment in probation, institutional corrections, and parole. The continued development of offender typologies, both legal and behavioral, should have a much broader data base in the future. The information available from typical arrest reports (date, name, age, sex, offense, and physical characteristics) are insufficient for a basic typology of criminals that will meet the threefold needs of law enforcement and criminal justice (police, judiciary, corrections). The minimal data necessary for the construction of adequate typologies of criminals is: (1) educational achievement, (2) prior record (particularly while incarcerated or while on probation or parole), and (3) employment record and status.[18]

Data for Typologies

Ideally, a criminal typology should provide data about offenders in a fashion which would allow agents of criminal justice to better understand the offender as a person, and to better comprehend his criminal

17. Ibid., pp. 63–64.
18. Space–General Corporation, *A Study of the Prevention and Control of Crime and Delinquency* (El Monte, Calif.: Space-General Corporation, 1965), pp. 59–60.

behavior. Access to the following information would offer new horizons in this vital area:

1. Characteristics which are descriptive of criminals in each major category.

2. Similarities and differences in the characteristics of criminals in the major groupings of the typology.

3. The maturation factor, similarities and differences between early and later portions of criminal careers.[19]

Additionally, the organization of the collected data into offender classifications should be flexibile enough to accept the threat to legal typologies inherent in the overreach of morality laws; the penalty inconsistencies of politics–as–usual in such laws as those relating to drug abuse; and the threat to criminal typologies by the cultural conflict which develops new types of professional criminals such as the cats and hustlers.

The data collected by police and stored in their records identifies criminals and offers a primary source of information about offenders and their crimes. The universe of known criminal offenses listed in police recording systems establishes the boundaries of any legal typology of criminals. The data as to the disposition of each event in the life record of a criminal identifies the offender as a repetitive or occasional criminal. Rearrests and the switch from one crime to another reveals development in a criminal career, or some progression. When an offender repeats his crimes, there is likely to be an occupational upward mobility. Beginners in crime are handicapped by a lack of confidence in their ability, and have yet to meet older career criminals whose help beginners need to reach the top rungs of the criminal ladder.[20]

The three most important data elements in police records concerning the offender are those facts which will identify the offender in case of rearrest, describe the crime committed, and state the disposition of the arrest.

Identification Data—To enable the search of police files for a prior record, the minimum data required is usually name; sex; race; date of birth; height; local, state and federal (FBI) identification number (local police assign a number to a person on his first arrest and this procedure is carried out at other levels of government); fingerprints; and physical description. Fingerprint data begins with the standard classification of pattern types and subgroups, and includes data on missing fingers. Because of their identification potential, visible scars, marks, tatoos, amputations, or deformities are recorded by police.

19. Ibid., p. 64.
20. Byrnes, *1886—Professional Criminals in America*, p. 1.

Standardized Offense Terms—A massive research project at all levels of government concerned with data about crime and criminals has developed a uniform and standard list of criminal offenses in the United States.[21] While the laws of the federal and state governments differ, this listing allows a grouping of similar crimes, nationally or locally. The universe of crimes for police records systems is as follows:

1. Sovereignty (treason, espionage, sabotage, sedition)

2. Military (desertion)

3. Immigration (illegal entry, smuggled aliens, false citizenship)

4. Homicide (murder, manslaughter, manslaughter by vehicle)

5. Kidnapping

6. Sexual assault (forcible and statutory rape, sodomy)

7. Robbery

8. Assault (aggravated, simple)

9. Abortion

10. Arson

11. Extortion

12. Burglary (including "Burglar's Tools")

13. Larceny (pocket picking, purse snatching, shoplifting, thefts from vehicles, buildings, yards, coin machines, U.S. mail)

14. Stolen vehicle (includes airplanes)

15. Forgery (forging and passing forged checks, counterfeiting)

16. Fraud (confidence game, swindle, mail fraud, fraudulent credit cards, "Not Sufficient Funds" checks—own name, and false statements)

17. Embezzlement

18. Stolen property (receive, possess, transport, sell)

19. Property damage (vandalism—private or public property)

20. Dangerous drugs (hallucinogens, heroin, opium, cocaine, synthetic narcotics, narcotic equipment, marihuana, amphetamines, barbiturates)

21. Sex offenses (child molesting, indecent exposure, peeping Tom, bestiality, incest, homosexuality)

22. Obscene material

21. Project Search Staff, for *Electronic Analyses and Retrieval of Criminal Histories*—is a federal-grant project of the Law Enforcement Assistance Administration, the U.S. Department of Justice, and 10 participating states.

23. Family offenses (neglect, cruelty, nonsupport, bigamy, contributing to delinquency of minor)

24. Gambling (including possession and transportation of gambling devices, transmitting wagering information, tampering with sports events)

25. Commercial sex (brothel keeping, procuring, prostitution, homosexual prostitution)

26. Liquor (illegal manufacture, sale, possession; misrepresenting age)

27. Drunk

28. Obstruct police (resist officer, harbor fugitive, aid prisoner to escape, destroy evidence)

29. Flight—escape

30. Obstruct justice (perjury, contempt of court, obstructing court)

31. Bribery (give, offer, solicit, receive)

32. Weapon offense (includes "as" weapon, explosives, incendiary devices)

33. Public peace (anarchism, riot, unlawful assembly, false alarm, desecrate flag, disorderly conduct, loiter, disturb the peace, curfew)

34. Traffic offenses

35. Health and safety (adulterated or misbranded drugs, food, and cosmetics)

36. Civil rights

37. Invade privacy (trespass, eavesdrop, wiretap)

38. Smuggle (contrabrand, to avoid duty, prison contrabrand)

39. Election laws

40. Antitrust

41. Tax—revenue (income, sales, liquor)

42. Conservation (animals, fish, birds)

43. Vagrancy.[22]

Disposition Data—In the beginning there is an arrest, and what follows through court proceedings and correctional custody and treatment is disposition. Studies of individuals as offenders against the law

22. Project Search Staff, *Standardized Data Elements for Criminal History Files* (California Crime Technological Research Foundation, Sacramento, Ca., 1971), pp. E5–11.

of crimes will be facilitated by this all–inclusive definition of disposition. There is need for more than the finding of guilt or innocence and the length of a sentence following conviction for a crime. The major court outcome is important to a criminal history, but of even greater importance is data about each institutionalization and each release on probation or parole.

When such data is part of the police records system, future criminal typologies will be able to trace the role–careers of offenders from arrest to rearrest. Adequate data on how the criminal offender left the court–and–corrections phase of the criminal justice system, will allow the development of a matrix of "input" and "output" events in the life—and criminal history—of an offender.

Typologies of Delinquents

Classifications of juvenile and youthful offenders into criminal typologies include youngsters from 7 to 21 years of age. Children under seven are presumed incapable of committing crime, and the legal age of maturity is 21 years. To complicate the problem of constructing a typology of delinquency, the laws of many states have established the age of 18 as the age at which adolescence ceases and adulthood begins—and a few states have lowered this limit to the age of 16. At whatever age set within a state by statute law, a young person under 16, 18, or 21 is treated as a juvenile rather than as an adult and processed as a noncriminal by criminal justice agencies. Above the age established as the upper limit on juvenile delinquency, the young person is considered an adult with full criminal responsibility for his acts, and processed in an accusatory criminal proceeding.

To avoid a hasty conclusion that delinquency is only distantly related to criminality, it has been noted that there is an increased involvement of young people with violent and serious criminal behavior. The involvement of young people in real crimes is revealed in the official statistics of the FBI's uniform crime reports and the juvenile court reports of the Department of Health, Education and Welfare. These statistics reveal an increasing percentage of persons under the age of 18 arrested for the crimes of murder, aggravated assault, forcible rape, robbery, burglary, larceny–theft, and auto theft. Moreover, in recent years, the under–15 age group is a significant percentage of all age arrests for serious crimes.[23]

A typology of delinquency based mainly on sociological theory, and which uses the same criteria for classifying offenders as in categorizing

23. *Annual Report of Federal Activities in Juvenile Delinquency, Youth Development, and Related Fields,* (Washington, D.C.: U.S. Department of Health, Education, and Welfare, 1971), pp. 1–2.

adult criminal behavior, lists nine classes (types) of young persons in accordance with its four-dimensional criteria of: (1) offense behavior, (2) interactional setting, (3) selfconcept, and (4) offender attitudes (to community agencies). These nine types are:

1. Predatory (acquisitive or theft) gang delinquent
2. Conflict (fighting) gang delinquent
3. Occasional (casual) gang delinquent
4. Occasional (casual) non–gang delinquent
5. Auto thief—joy rider
6. Drug abuser
7. Overly aggressive delinquent
8. Female delinquent
9. Behavior problem delinquent.[24]

In the foregoing typology by Gibbons, heavy emphasis is placed upon group behavior in delinquency: *the gang.* Three of the nine classifications are assigned to gangs, either by the nature of the group or by the characteristics of the young person's membership. Three of the classifications are concerned with the occasional delinquent and the joy-riding auto thief who is not considered a real thief—whose intent is to steal property (the auto) rather than to temporarily use the property (for the ride). Another three classes of young offenders who appear to have a natural grouping are drug abusers, overly aggressive delinquents, and behavior problem delinquents. Certainly, the drug abuser and the overly aggressive youngster can be shown to have behavior problems. Lastly, the female offender group needs several subdivisions for clarification. They are often gang members in ghetto and barrio* areas. They are frequently drug abusers, and may be classed as behavior problem persons.

A typology of delinquency based on the viewpoints of psychology and psychiatry views delinquency as a complex pattern arising from individual problems, intrafamily problems, and situations conducive to delinquency. This typology is made up of four basic groups of identifiable delinquents. They are:

1. *Organic damage delinquents*—young persons with brain damage. There is usually an early history of birth trauma, early illness

24. Don C. Gibbons, *Changing the Lawbreaker* (Englewood Cliffs, N. J.: Prentice–Hall, 1965), pp. 74–97.

*Ghettos dominated by Spanish speaking residents: Mexican Americans (Chicanos) in the Southwest and Pacific Coast areas, and persons of Puerto Rican or Cuban origins along the East Coast.

(involving encephalitis)* or injury, and other difficulties in infancy. In childhood, there is a history of overactive (hyperkinetic) behavior, poor muscular coordination, and developmental retardations. These young people have serious difficulties beginning at puberty, and their behavior disorders in adolescence are usually a pattern of outbursts of temper and irrational or motiveless acts of crime and delinquency. There is some evidence that the behavior patterns of this group of young people result from brain damage or maldevelopment, epilepsy, and physiological immaturity; and there is also evidence that genetic defects, such as endocrine abnormalities and delayed or premature pubertal development, may account for such behavior.

2.   *Grossly deprived delinquents*—disadvantaged young persons with a history of illegitimacy or parental rejection at an early stage of their development, followed by nonparental care (foster homes, institutions) during infancy and childhood, and an early rejection by adults as the youngster reached adolescence. There is a pattern among these juveniles of a lack of love joined with hostility in all social relationships (increasing as the child grows); poor impulse control, a low threshold of frustration, and a need or tendency to immediate gratification of impulses.

3.   *Emotionally disturbed delinquents*—young people who are sick or verging on mental illness. There are three subgroups in this classification. They are:

a. The *neurotic reaction* juvenile who has a history of either deprivation, rejection, parental separation or disharmony, and hostility in social relationships in the early developmental years (sufficient to cause an early emotional disturbance). There is frequently a connection with parental relationships in the oedipal situation,** with difficulties at the time of puberty and some delay in psychosexual maturation. Guilt feelings and a need to emphasize identification with the sexual role are common and lead these delinquents to leave clues at the scene of their crimes so that detection and apprehension is inevitable.

b. The *psychotic reaction* juvenile and youth is a person with an early schizophrenic reaction (odd or bizarre behavior, irrational or motiveless delinquency, and withdrawal), or an

---

*Sleeping sickness; lethargica.
**Involving an early and primary attachment by a child with the parent of the opposite sex, and accompanied by hostility to the other parent.

individual with an early paranoid reaction (evidenced by feelings of persecution).

c. The *inadequate* delinquent is a youngster without personality damage due to organic causes or early deprivations, emotional disturbance, or neurotic or psychotic reactions, but with a personality inadequate to the demands of social relationships and adjustments—and the acts of delinquency arise from this inadequacy.

4. *Family problem delinquents*—juveniles and youths with average patterns of personality and development, and without any sign of emotional disturbance. The criminal and delinquent acts of these youngsters are a reaction to intrafamily tensions. The pathology of family situations are varied but some of the common situations leading to delinquency are:

a. Mother derives emotional satisfaction from son's delinquency and unconsciously encourages it.

b. An overstrict father gets satisfaction from his son's delinquency through some unconscious identification.

c. A mother is overtly hostile to daughter because of a father–daughter relationship at the daughter's time of puberty and the father's unconscious emotional involvement; or there is mother–daughter hostility from an early age which is marked by mother's rejection of daughter.[25]

K. R. H. Wardrop, the author of the foregoing typology of delinquency, presents four clear–cut types of adolescent delinquency. The first two groups of offenders (organic damage and grossly deprived delinquents) comprise a disabled population, while the remaining two groups are comprised of youngsters who are sick or verging on mental illness. This major division is evidenced by the concepts of sickness as opposed to disablement. Additionally, Wardrop constructs a fifth delinquent group to encompass youngsters who are nothing more than the products of their cultural background. These *situational delinquents* are generally described as young people with blocked goals who join aggressive or acquisitive gangs from the same cultural background. This subculture is marked by hostility to the rest of the community and its agencies, which often tolerate their violent behavior as the norm, and usually accept the acquisitive behavior of these neighborhood theft gangs as normal behavior.[26]

Both major typologies of delinquency, one with its origins in Ameri-

25. K.R.H. Wardrop, "Delinquent Teenage Types," *British Journal of Criminology* 7, no. 4 (October 1967): 371–80.
26. Ibid., p. 376.

ca and the other with its sources in Britain, reveal an ever-increasing stress on an *interactionist* theory of delinquency based on reaction to real–life situations. Both typologies strongly suggest that a heterogeneous mass of young persons interact with the circumstances of any given situation within a group of subcultural patterns of behavior determined by gang membership or ghetto residence.

Selected References

Books

Byrnes, Thomas. *1886—Professional Criminals in America.* New York: Chelsea House Publishers, 1969.

Clinard, Marshall B., and Quinney, Richard. *Criminal Behavior Systems—A Typology.* New York: Holt, Rinehart and Winston, 1967.

Foxe, Arthur, M.D. *Studies in Criminology.* New York: Nervous and Mental Disease Monographs, 1948.

Gibbons, Don C. *Changing the Lawbreaker—The Treatment of Delinquents and Criminals.* Englewood Cliffs, N.J.: Prentice–Hall, 1968.

Hall, Arthur Cleveland. *Crime in Its Relation to Social Progress.* New York: AMS Press, 1968.

Morris, Norval, and Hawkins, Gordon. *The Honest Politician's Guide to Crime Control.* Chicago and London: University of Chicago Press, 1969.

Polsky, Ned. *Hustlers, Beats and Others.* Chicago: Aldine Publishing Co., 1967.

Sellin, Thorsten. "Enrico Ferri, Pioneer in Criminology," in *The Positive School of Criminology: Three Lectures by Enrico Ferri.* Edited by Stanley E. Grupp, Pittsburgh, Pa.: University of Pittsburgh Press, 1968.

Periodicals

Wardrop, K.R.H. "Delinquent Teenage Types." *British Journal of Criminology* 7, no. 4 (October 1967): 371–80.

Chapter VI

Causative Factors In Criminal Behavior

As a human being grows, and wherever he goes, he is aware of being judged. The infant develops an awareness of whether a parent has a favorable or unfavorable reaction to some act. Young persons are particularly alert to social embarrassments and usually avoid actions likely to lead to humiliation. Older persons are very conscious of their social habits and tend to lessen any discomfort by adjusting habits to status in the social order. Judgment—approval or disapproval—turns upon interests shared by others, and the folkways and customs of the group. Social norms are established in the image of the group and its habits.

Social pressure to develop conformity among group members has two major forms: internal and external. Internal controls (conscience, superego, values, and beliefs) are the result of socialization by parents and other family members, school personnel, clergymen and church members, friends, and others in the community. They represent the first influence on the individual to adjust his behavior to conform to the behavior norms of the group, and to refrain from unacceptable behavior. External controls are the devices such as sanction laws which control antisocial behavior after it breaks the bounds of internal controls. The death penalty, banishment and deportation, and imprisonment are external controls capable of removing the offender from the community which failed to socialize him. Ostracism is a lesser and informal external control. It is related to other social controls associated with the stigma of being a criminal offender (the "ex–con" image), and it ranges from loss of job, of spouse and of friends, to the denial of public office or public employment, and the loss of civil rights (voting, jury duty, etc.).

However, conscious and unconscious wishes, urges, motives, interests, desires, and passions are continually in operation in all persons, serving as cues for intentional actions of an individual. This often leads to a conflict situation in which the outcome wished for or desired is blocked by either internal or external controls. Unfortunately, the conflict situation is frequently resolved in favor of the wished–for outcome. Social pressure does not always lead to thoroughgoing conformity.

In the nineteenth century the metaphysical world and the universe of theology began to interface with the emerging scientific disciplines of biology, psychiatry, psychology, and sociology in seeking the reasons for criminal behavior. Defective social controls encompassed the first theory of criminal behavior. Inherited traits or predispositions to criminality followed quickly as a contemporary explanation of crime and criminals, and this concept was promptly shelved for broader learning-theory concept: that criminal behavior was learned in the same manner as all behavior is learned.

In the following survey of the theories of crime causes, each theory of criminal behavior is identified with the scientist or scientists who contributed to its origin and development. Where possible, a relationship is shown between theories in the same major areas: (1) biological, (2) environmental, and (3) mental influences. Each theory is developed as if it were mutually exclusive and *could* be the single cause of criminal behavior. However, a multifactor theory of criminal behavior is discussed for the purpose of joining several theories, or all of them, as causative factors in criminal behavior.

The traditional theories of the origin of criminal behavior can be grouped into three broad areas by the major thrust of the theory itself or by the professional area of the theorist. These are:

Theory	*Professional Area*
1. Criminal behavior is inherited	Biology and Anthropology
2. Environment is the cause of criminal behavior	Sociology
3. Mental factors or conditions are the cause of criminal behavior	Psychiatry and Psychology

Classically, the connection between a single crime as an event and a theory of criminal behavior is the ever present problem of reducing the amount of crime in society. Researchers in this field are motivated in the search for knowledge and insight about the origins of criminal behavior for the purpose of preventing it and making a significant reduction in the crime rate. The research goal is to determine *why* persons of this kind (individuals with similar characteristics) commit such crimes, and why some individuals with like characteristics do not commit criminal acts. These are sizable dimensions for any research as crime ranges from the emotional outbursts of assailants and killers to the planned activities of professional thieves.

The earliest theory of criminal behavior was that each person had free will to decide whether to commit a crime. The rules of law and their sanctions against disobedience are aligned closely with this theory. Sanctions are those rules of the legal order that spell out the consequences of violating criminal law. Criminal punishment in sanction law is any disposition of an offender authorized by law for persons found guilty after a criminal trial.[1]

The next theory of criminal behavior developed the concept of determinism: a concept that is threaded through all subsequent theories of crime to date. This is that man is not a free agent, that various pressures and drives determine human behavior, and that the decision to commit a crime has little or no free will involved, but is determined by these forces acting upon a person at one place, and at one specific time.

The Classical and the Positive Schools* of Criminology

In the beginning there were man–to–man disputes and acts considered as threats or hazards to personal safety. Causes were factual and functional; the thing done was self–explanatory to the victim and his kin. It was a time of direct action and private revenge. In the later half of the eighteenth century, there were some changes for the better. Courts abandoned any concept of vengeance: punishment became a deterrent to crime rather than pure revenge, although punishment ranged from the death penalty, through various forms of mutilation, to flogging and prison sentences for long periods of time.[2]

Eighteenth–century penologists believed in the pleasure vs. pain principle in motivating human behavior and rational decision making. Individuals avoided acts that caused pain, and repeated acts that gave pleasure. When faced with the unknown consequences of an act, most persons would test for the pain–pleasure outcome, and adjust their subsequent action to secure as much pleasure and as little pain as possible.

Cesare Bonesana, Marchese de Beccaria was the first of a group now

1. Herbert L. Packer, *The Limits of the Criminal Sanction* (Stanford, Calif.: Stanford University Press, 1968), pp. 33–37.

*Criminology is a field in which dissent is common; the term school is used to indicate conceptual agreement among a group of criminologists.

2. Stephen Schafer, *Theories in Criminology—Past and Present Philosophies of the Crime Problem* (New York: Randon House, 1969), pp. 97–109.

known as the classical school of criminology to attempt modification of the overkill aspects of the severe sentences given criminals for minor crimes. In full support of the free will concept of decision making, and the pain–pleasure principle of motivation, Beccaria sought uniformity in sentencing offenders so that the punishment awarded for violation of a specific law would take cognizance of the seriousness of the offense and the proceeds or satisfaction gained by the offender. This theory would only make the punishment slightly more painful than the pleasure the offender could gain from the criminal act. Lengthy sentences—and the death penalty—would be cut back and tailored to the gain (pleasure) in crime as opposed to the loss when apprehended (pain), and not to the simplistic belief that the more severe the sentence, the greater the control of crime. The classical school of criminology based its scheme of criminality on the offense as the object of attention; the reaction to the offense as some punitive measure.[3]

In the late nineteenth century with the advance of scientific thought in other fields, a new school of criminology based on the doctrines of science set new directions for the study of criminal behavior. What is now known as the positive school of criminology suggested the scientific study of the origins of crime, and remedial action stressing rehabilitation, rather than punishment. The offender was the object of attention; the reaction to the offender was oriented to treatment.

The positivists originally viewed crime as a phenomenon in which the causative factors had roots in the anthropological criminal type. Later, the influence of environment was accepted by the positivists but always subordinated to the *born criminal* concept.[4] The positivists maintained that the offender was not the prime mover in criminality: the offender acted as a result of interaction between his personality and his environment. "In order to be a criminal it is rather necessary that the individual should find himself permanently or transitorily in such personal, physical and moral conditions, and live in such an environment, which become for him a chain of cause and effect, externally and internally, that disposes him to crime."[5]

The cofounders of the positive school of criminology were Cesare Lombroso and Enrico Ferri. Cesare Lombroso was educated in medicine and served as a physician in the Italian army. His first civilian practice was concerned with the mentally ill and he became interested in the problems of crime and insanity. This was a foreshadowing of his

3. *Ibid.,* pp. 105–37.
4. Thorsten Sellin, "Enrico Ferri, Pioneer in Criminology," in *The Positive School of Criminology: Three Lectures by Enrico Ferri,* edited by Stanley E. Grupp (Pittsburgh, Pa.: University of Pittsburgh Press, 1968), pp. 1–39.
5. Ferri, "Lecture I—Critique of the Classical School," in Sellin, *The Positive School of Criminology,* pp. 54.

pioneer work in criminal anthropology. His most important book, *L'Uomo Delinquente*, was first published in 1876. In this text, Lombroso theorized that crime resulted from the anthropological characteristics of the criminal. In later writings, however, he gave an increasing weight to social forces in the determination of criminal behavior.[6]

Yet, in 1909, in responding to a letter of notification that the new American Institute of Criminal Law and Criminology had selected his latest text for translation into English, Lombroso writes of the born criminal and his discovery of numerous atavistic* characteristics among them and links these physical characteristics to savage races (low cranial capacity, skull thickness, blunted affections, etc.). He also noted a relationship between criminals and epileptics which manifests itself in deterioration of the moral and emotional sensibilities—among other things. He describes a *criminaloid* as differing from a born criminal in the physical marks of criminality, but having some connection with atavism and epilepsy.[7]

Enrico Ferri was a student of Lombroso, and a contemporary in his adult years. Ferri was educated for the legal profession, and became a professor of criminal law at several universities in Italy. Ferri supported Lombroso's concept of an anthropological criminal type, but his writings stress the application of the discipline of sociology to the problem of criminal behavior. Ferri's five types of criminal offenders include the born criminal.* He qualified his belief in this congenital predisposition to crime by pointing out that many born criminals were law abiding when their environment was favorable and did not offer a temptation to crime.[8]

Ferri's sociological orientation foreshadowed the present concepts of crime causation which cite environmental factors as the major force in determining criminal behavior. However, in maintaining some linkage with the Lombrosian doctrine of hereditary criminality, the positivist school is in harmony with recent research on predispositions to criminal behavior which have sometimes been validated in studies of physique and temperament, chromosomal makeup, and pathological criminality.

---

6. Marvin E. Wolfgang, "Pioneers in Criminology: Cesare Lombroso (1835–1909)," *Journal of Criminal Law, Criminology, and Police Science*, 52, no. 4 (November–December 1961): 361–91.

*Lombroso's theory of atavism was based on personal confidence in his discovery of a marked resemblance between the typical criminal and the savage or prehistoric man.

7. Cesare Lombroso, *Crime—Its Causes and Remedies* (Montclair, N.J.: Patterson Smith, 1968; originally published in 1911, Little Brown & Co., translated by Henry P. Horton), pp. 363–76.

*Others were: the *insane criminal*, the *habitual criminal*, the *occasional criminal*, and the *passionate criminal*.

8. Enrico Ferri, *Criminal Sociology* (New York: Agathon Press, 1967), pp. 138–67.

The Theory of Differential Association

What will probably be known as the American school of criminology in future years has reached some agreement on the influence of environment on crime causation. The major theory accepted to date is the theory of differential association advanced in 1939 by Professor Edwin H. Sutherland. Sutherland's theory is that persons become criminals because of exposure to an overabundance of associations with criminal behavior patterns, as opposed to associations with anticriminal behavior patterns.[9]

Differential association is essentially a process of learning. As a process, Sutherland's theory is:

1. Criminal behavior is learned.

2. Learning is in the interaction with others and the inherent two–way communication between self and others.

3. Person–to–person contacts and communications among friends, relatives, associates, neighbors, acquaintances are more significant to this learning process than mass communications and its media.

4. Learning criminal behavior involves tutoring in operating techniques of crime, and a reorientation of attitudes, rationalization drives, and motives. (Specific direction of attitudes, motives, and drives is learned in orientation to definitions of law. In some groups, majority opinion favors obedience to law; in other groups, the majority favors violation of law.)

5. An individual's behavior becomes criminal because of an excess of definitions favorable to criminal action rather than anticriminal definitions.

6. Differential associations vary in priority, frequency, duration, and intensity (early influences may be as significant to learning as lengthy and repeated high intensity influences), and the process of learning criminal behavior involves all the mechanisms involved in other learning processes.

7. Criminal behavior is also an expression of general needs and values, but these general needs and values cannot be explained as a cause of crime (the same needs and values drive men to seek employment and to work hard).[10]

---

9. Edwin H. Sutherland and Donald R. Cressey, *Criminology*, 8th ed. (Philadelphia: J. P. Lippincott Co. 1970; originally published in 1924 with Edwin H. Sutherland as sole author), pp. 78–79.

10. Sutherland and Cressey, *Criminology*, pp. 75–77.

The Social Reality Theory

In a theory of crime related to Sutherland's differential association concept, criminal behavior is viewed as a product of the social process (continuing actions leading to a specific result), conflict between persons and groups, power (the ability of persons and groups to determine the conduct of others), and social action. This later term, social action, is defined as implying that human behavior is goal oriented and crime occurs with an awareness of its consequences.

The core area of this theory of the social reality of crime is: 1. Criminal definitions describe (and limit) behavior in conflict with behavior approved by those groups in the community which have the power to control or shape public policy. 2. Criminal definitions (and sanctions) are applied by, or in response to pressure from these community groups. 3. Behavior patterns are structured within the various segments of society in relation to criminal definitions, and persons engage in actions that may be defined as criminal. 4. Conceptions of crime are constructed and diffused by many means of communication, usually in response to the power segments of a community's population.[11]

An initial basis for this theory of crime as a social reality is that legislatures *create* crime. There's no doubt that sin–as–crime, and the other areas of crime without victims covered in the overreach of the criminal law, has created criminals. Moreover, because Sutherland's theory of differential association is assumed or incorporated within this theory of the social reality of criminal behavior, it has support for one of its major propositions: that behavior patterns are behavior learned in the environmental setting of the individual.

Anomie—The Goals–and–Means Theory

Life chances in the opportunity structure differ with the race, residence, education, and socioeconomic background of a person. Normal behavior can be classed as behavior aligned with prescribed, permitted, or preferred behavior, or behavior that contributes to stability in the social system. Historically, *anomie* refers to the breakdown of norms. More recently, it refers to the conflict between the community culture and that of a subgroup; and the growth of illegal or illicit success may enlarge the degree of anomie.[12]

There is always the possibility that one or more youngsters from a minority group, ghetto home, dropout centered education, or family

11. Richard Quinney, *The Social Reality of Crime* (Boston, Mass.: Little, Brown and Co. 1970), pp. 8–24.

12. Helen L. Witmer and Ruth Kotinsky, ed., *New Prespectives for Research on Juvenile*

with little or no financial resources will move from the subculture of his family and neighborhood to the subculture of the Ivy League college, the tennis club, and Wall Street. It doesn't happen too often. Most people who die poor were born poor.[13]

Success is the broad goal of upward mobility. It means different things to persons from various socioeconomic and racial subgroups. In America, success is hinged to occupational status and money. There is a pressure to outdo competitors, despite the cliché that there is plenty of room at the top. There is also pressure from within a family group, usually because parents want a better life for their children, and this upgrading is generally equated with success.

The goals–and–means segments of a community's social structure is severely strained, however, when some individuals are socially disadvantaged in the competitive struggle to move upward occupationally and socioeconomically. Honesty and noncriminal employment are viewed by some of the disadvantaged as limitations on the opportunity and means to success. This strain exerts pressure on disadvantaged persons to achieve success by any means available.

Society, and its social structure for the control of behavior identified as criminal, forbids criminal activity regardless of goals. There is the pressure of law upon persons to conform, rather than to engage in nonconforming conduct. Living in accordance with the rules of the game or the norms of prescribed conduct blocks the goal of success to many minority group persons with little education and no resources. Deviating from this, an individual loses his cultural anchorage of winning under the rules of the game, and is adrift in the rules of *normlessness:* win at any cost, but win.

Anomie is the term used to describe this social phenomenon. It is cultural chaos to the individual because it is the pull–and–push of conflicting values. A climate of anomie exists when common values are subordinated to private interests and there is an end–means reversal of the cultural norm. The exaltation of the end justifies almost any means to achieve goals. Anomie is the result of the American community's espousal of the good life, common success goals for the entire population, and a social structure that restricts or blocks the approved means of reaching such goals for considerable segments of the population. In turn, anomie is linked to criminal behavior by the fact that crime does pay under some circumstances and at some time. There is both a promise and a reward of high income from burglary, robbery, drug selling, and organized crime. Because of availability, the pressure for success leads to the use of illegitimate expedients to reach a life

Delinquency (Washington, D. C.: U.S. Department of Health, Education and Welfare, 1955), pp. 24–49.

13. Alvin L. Schorr, *Poor Kids—A Report on Children in Poverty* (New York: Basic Books, 1966), pp. 23–48.

goal. This strain toward anomie and deviant behavior (often criminal) breaks down the normal regulatory structure guiding human behavior as it develops a situation in which the approach–avoidance conflict is a simple weighing of two values: (1) calculation of personal advantage, and (2) fear of punishment.[14]

The utility of criminal behavior for breaking out of the ghetto has always been known to the immigrants and minority groups who reside in these low–rent and high–crime areas. To some youngsters the route of upward mobility is either theft, or the rackets of organized crime.[15]

A ghetto or slum area usually has two occupational styles which its young residents can emulate as role objects: (1) the low–income, unskilled but law–abiding laborer; or (2) the high–income worker in vice and crime. Prostitution is a local neighborhood operation for both the girls and the operators; the clerks and dealers in the neighborhood gambling centers are primarily recruited from among local residents; and the shylocks and loan sharks of the usury racket have developed a neighborhood business of small loans at high interest to the local "illegit" residents, so identified by local agents who know they "belong." Ghetto crime primarily consists of the side-actions made possible by the influx of visitors willing to pay for the services of prostitutes or to participate in various games of chance. There is robbery and theft, and the motive is gain. Since the entire neighborhood is keyed to victimize suckers, rather than to reward unskilled–but–honest labor, the favored role objects are the persons who can "take a sucker" and thrive on the income from this criminal behavior.[16]

Anomie is a complex of poverty, limited opportunities, and a shared system of success symbols.[17]

The New School of Criminal Anthropology

The concept of grouping humanity in types by using anthropological methods of measurement emerged from investigations in psychiatry. Investigations into the build of the body by experts in medicine and psychiatry were planned to probe the problem of the human constitution: the whole physical makeup of the individual, which comprises the individual's inherited qualities as modified by the environment. The

14. Robert K. Merton, *Social Theory and Social Structure* (New York: Free Press, 1957), pp. 131–60.

15. Irving Speigel, *Racketville, Slumtown and Haulberg—An Exploratory Study of Delinquent Subcultures* (Chicago, Ill.: University of Chicago Press, 1964), pp. 30–38, 47–53.

16. Joseph D. Lohman. "The Participant Observer in Community Studies," *American Sociological Review* 2, no. 6 (December 1937): 890–97.

17. Robert K. Merton, "Social Structure and Anomie," *American Sociological Review* 3, no. 5 (October 1938): 672–82.

landmark researcher in this field, Ernst Kretschmer, worked out a *constitution scheme* to record his investigations. Its major sections are:

1. *Measurement*—height, weight, length (legs, arms), breadth (shoulders, pelvis), circumference (chest, stomach, hips), and skull.

2. *Description of face and skull*—shape, profile, frontal outline (various shapes), height proportions (middle face, chin), and nose.

3. *Description of physique*—bones, musculature, fat; neck, shoulders, chest, stomach, pelvis, extremities (especially length), hands, and feet.

4. *Hair*—color and where located on body, and skin condition.

5. Glands—thyroid, mammary, testicles, genitalia, and sexual anomalies.

6. *Temporal*—commencement of mental disease, puberty, fattening, emaciation and certain physical diseases.[18]

Kretschmer's position was that any constitutional types must include the whole of mankind, physically and psychically, and would have biological significance only when relations were discovered between types of physique and psychic types. To secure the necessary "typical" values in his investigation, Kretschmer presorted photographs of many subjects and then superimposed the photos of selected subjects so that the characteristics which fit over one another were sharply outlined, and thus became an average value or typical.

Three ever–recurring principal types of physique surfaced from these studies: (1) asthenic, (2) athletic, and (3) pyknic. Briefly, the descriptive data on each of these types and a fourth nontypical group is:

1. The male *asthenic* type is a lean man who appears taller because of a deficiency in the thickness development of his body. Asthenic women are not only thin, but also very short.

2. The male *athletic* type is medium to tall in height, has a well–developed physique, a superb chest, firm stomach, good legs and a v-shaped trunk, tapering from shoulders to pelvis. The female athletic type corresponds to her male counterpart, but she is fatter, although the fat is in good proportion and distributed in a feminine rounded figure.

3. The *pyknic* type male is a person of middle height with a rounded figure, a soft–looking broad face on a short and thick

18. Ernst Kretschmer, *Physique and Character—An Investigation of the Nature of Constitution and of the Theory of Temperament,* 2nd ed. (New York: Humanities Press, 1951), pp. 3–16.

neck, a merging vaulted chest and potbelly stomach and a main covering of fat round the trunk area. Pyknic women are smaller than pyknic men, with the same general body build, except that the main covering of fat is concentrated around the breasts and hips.

4. *Dysplastic* types are representative of several small groups of individuals who differ among themselves and from the three major types listed above. They are the rare type, and not the average specimen.[19]

Kretschmer reports the findings based on his research were "surprising and of great biological importance." He had uncovered a correlation betwen bodily makeup and the two major forms of mental illness or emotional instability. His reported results are:

1. There is a clear biological affinity between manic–depressive individuals and the pyknic body type; and only a weak affinity between schizophrenics and pyknics.

2. There is a clear biological affinity between the schizophrenic and the asthenic and athletic types; and only a weak affinity between manic–depressives and the two types of asthenic, and athletic physique.[20]

In other words, the medium height, soft–looking pyknic was most often a manic–depressive person; and the thin, lean asthenic and the well–developed athletic was most likely to be a schizophrenic—a person with a split personality syndrome of mental illness.

This German scientist particularly disagreed with Lombroso's isolation of "petty peculiarities." In Kretschmer's physique and temperament study, a single characteristic was only significant for its contribution to the broad form of bodily makeup. Kretschmer rejected any "symptoms of degeneracy" such as the so–called "criminal ear," and credited such details as only one of the parts of a person's physique.[21]

Kretschmer's basic research was followed by the in–depth studies of William H. Sheldon, who developed an array of *somatotypes** and a theory of behavior based on physique. Apparently, Lombroso's theory of the biological factor in criminal behavior has a phoenix–like characteristic, rising again after being discredited by earlier researchers who had reviewed Lombroso's born criminal concept of criminality.

19. Kretschmer, *Physique and Character*, pp. 17–35.
20. Ibid., pp. 36–37.
21. Ibid., pp. 39–40.
*A quantification of the three primary components determining the morphological structure of an individual, using a series of numerals. *See* William H. Sheldon, *Atlas of Men* (New York: Harper & Row, 1954).

The three somatotypes of Sheldon are: (1) *endomorphic* (round; soft); (2) *mesomorphic* (heavy; hard); and (3) *ectomorphic* (thin). In this scheme of behavior projection, each somatotype was identified with various temperaments.[22] In the three dimensions of physique and temperament, endomorphy is visceral development and is usually associated with viscerotonic temperament (comfort, sociability); mesomorphy is muscular development and frequently correlates with somatotonic temperament (assertiveness, competitiveness); and ectomorphy is related to the linear structure of a person's physique and is generally aligned with a restrained and sensitive temperament. Sheldon concluded that mesomorphy was the physique most favorable to criminal behavior. Mesomorphs were high on activity, and vigorous and bold action people without too many inhibitions as individuals.[23]

It is not easy to devise reliable experiments and plan valid research for the study of physique and temperament. The reported results of the studies of physique and behavior are likely to be contaminated by research procedures. In fact, some of Sheldon's reported correlations between physique and temperament are unbelievably large and suggest that some of the temperament variables are aspects of physique rather than independent of it.[24] Despite the longtime rejection of some correspondence between criminal behavior and inherited characteristics, there is some valid (uncontaminated) research to support a theory of relationship between body build and criminal behavior. Since many of the factors governing body build are inherited, any suggestion that one body build is presidposed to criminality is a throwback, more or less, to Lombroso and his born criminal concept of criminal behavior.

Support for the viewpoint of the "New School of Criminal Anthropology" was developed during independent research into the causative factors of delinquency. In a study of 500 delinquent children and 500 nondelinquent children, the delinquents as a group were found to be physically distinguishable from the nondelinquents as they were essentially mesomorphic in bodily makeup (solid, muscular). Among the delinquents, 60.1 percent were mesomorphs, and twice the proportion of mesomorphs were found in the delinquent group as compared to the nondelinquent group. In subsequent research review it was found that the reason for the excess of mesomorphs among the delinquent group was that this physique type is more highly characterized by the presence of traits suitable to the commission of aggressive

22. Sheldon, *Varieties of Human Physique* (New York: Harper & Row, 1949), pp. 234–39.
23. William H. Sheldon, *Varieties of Delinquent Youth* (Darien, Conn.: Hafner Publishing Co., 1970; originally published in 1949, New York: Harper & Row), vol. 1, pp. 14–30; vol. 2, p. 762.
24. Ephraim Rosen and Jan Gregory, *Abnormal Psychology* (Philadelphia: W. B. Saunders Co., 1965), pp. 113–21.

acts, and the absence of many inhibitions.[25]

In summing up, Kretschmer's and Sheldon's research findings do not predict whether an individual will become a criminal on the basis of physique, but do hold that the forms of criminal behavior which might emerge will be related to an individual's physique. The research done by Sheldon and Elizabeth Glueck indicates that one type of physique (as isolated and identified by William Sheldon) was predominant among the juvenile delinquents of their research population.

A fast–breaking research finding related to the work of Lombroso, Kretschmer, and Sheldon surfaced during the investigation of a psychotic murderer. The breakthrough was the genetic finding that the presence of an extra Y chromosome makes boys and men unusually aggressive. It is a finding that appears to offer a genetic base for the Lombrosian concept that some men are born criminals.

Linkage between the chromosomal constitution of an individual and criminal behavior was discovered in 1965 in Scotland. A research team found seven out of 197 mentally abnormal male prison inmates were discovered to be XYY types; and this incidence of XYY males in a prison population far exceeded the precentage in the general population (approximately 1.3 in 1,000 live births). Therefore, it was a highly significant finding.

A human life begins as a single cell containing 46 chromosomes. Heritage has its beginning in a sperm cell (and there are millions in every drop of seminal fluid), and its union with an egg. At conception, the father's role in the child's heredity is encompassed in his sperm. Each single sperm carries 23 microscopic bodies called chromosomes (exactly half of the father's 46 chromosomes). The mother's role in her child's heredity is providing the egg into which the sperm enters. Each egg has a nucleus with 23 microscopic chromosomes, and a host arrangement for releasing the mother's 23 chromosomes (exactly half of her 46 chromosomes) when the father's sperm enters the egg and releases its chromosomes. These 46 chromosomes are the two sets of heredity factors that comprise the biological heritage of any child. By a process of division and redivision the chromosomes provide the new individual with genes. Genes are the ultimate factors in heredity; each gene has a definite function in the creation and development of every person.

Genes are living units, and there are both dominant* and *recessive***
genes. In addition, there are freak genes and supplementary genes. A confusing array, but the limitless combinations of genes are the origin

25. Sheldon Glueck and Elizabeth Glueck, *Physique and Delinquency* (New York: Commonwealth Fund, 1950), pp. 7–15, 217–27.

*Presence in father *or* mother establishes an equal (50–50) risk of appearance (of effect or defect) in child.
**Presence in *both* parents establishes a risk of appearance (of effect or defect) in child.

of the varieties of human life. The color and shape of eyes, the color of hair, skin color, facial structure, size and shape, and the other less visible parts of the human organism are determined by genes.

The XYY individual is produced during formation of the sperm. Normal division of the sex chromosomes leads to sperm of two kinds: X chromosome and Y chromosome. Female children are the result when an X chromosome fertilizes a normal ovum. (A normal female child is an XX individual.) Male children are the result when a Y chromosome fertilizes a normal X ovum. (A normal male child is an XY person.) The ordinary aggressiveness of a normal XY male is apparently doubled in the XYY male. While this doesn't always imply criminal behavior, it does suggest that the inherited genes must be influenced by a favorable environment if the XYY person is not to become overly aggressive and possibly engage in criminal behavior.[26]

Chromosomal deviations offer some promise for effective research in the biological basis of criminal behavior. Such deviations have been found and identified in the areas of the mentally ill, mentally retarded, homosexuals, and criminals.

It is the extra male chromosome (Y) that is the primary factor in this theory of behavior. In reviewing several years of research, the following findings have been substantiated:

1. The physique of an XYY person is taller and thinner than persons in the control groups—the average XYY individual is over 6 feet tall.

2. The personality structure of XYY individuals was found to be defective (often verging on psychopathy); and the XYY person was found to be more aggressive, and more often exhibited disturbed behavior.

3. The violent crime rate of XYY persons was high.

4. The XYY youngster began his criminal career at an early age (10–13 as opposed to 18).

5. The chance that a criminal is an XYY person is 60 times greater than that of the general population.[27]

Pathological Criminality

The advances made in psychiatry and psychology by mid century have provided criminologists with many research findings about path-

26. M. F. Ashley Montagu, "Chromosomes and Crime," *Psychology Today* 2, no. 5 (October 1968): 42–49.
27. Menachem Amir and Yitzchak Berman, "Chromosomal Deviation and Crime," *Federal Probation* 34, no. 2 (June 1970): 55–62.

ological criminals (persons whose behavior exhibits varying degrees of abnormality) and mental illness as it relates to criminal behavior.

In a 1931 report to the president of the United States, the National Commission on Law Observance and Enforcement (the "Wickersham Commission," named for its chairman, George W. Wickersham) reported that after extensive investigation into the causes of crime, it had been unable to determine to what extent defective intelligence or any other mental abnormality was present in the nation's criminal population. Even when defective intelligence was disclosed among criminals, it could not be isolated and identified as a cause of crime.[28]

In 1952, however, it was reported that the normal criminal was a myth, and that refined methods of examining criminals (other than the occasional, accidental, or one–time offender) was likely to disclose that all delinquents and criminals suffer from some form of mental disorder: either a psychosis, neurosis, character disorder, or some other form of emotional disturbance.[29]

Some mental disorders may originate in the transmissibility of a predisposition to criminality. If one believes in psychological heredity and the inheritance of tendencies and attitudes, then there are grounds for belief in the possibility of transmitting tendencies and attitudes predisposing or promoting criminal behavior. A predisposition to criminal behavior is a joinder of hereditary and acquired organic or psychological conditions which, by releasing aggressive forces and withholding inhibitory forces, lowers the threshold to criminal behavior. It also includes a heightened receptivity to criminality. The particular characteristics which make an individual receptive to external conditions leading to criminal behavior are an essential element of predisposition to criminal conduct.[30]

Psychological predispositions established early in childhood are based on experiences in the formative years (infancy, latency). An individual develops a pattern of expectancies and they become part of his self–concept. Untroubled or successful development leads to a healthy and mature self–concept. Early experience is of vital importance in the growth of a person and his personality. For normal personality growth, children require a close friendship with parents or parent substitutes. Any parental attitude that indicates rejection (overt rejection, perfectionism, inconsistency, overdominance) increases the

28. *Wickersham Commission Reports, No. 13, Report on the Causes of Crime*, vol. 1 (Montclair, N.J.: Patterson Smith, 1968; originally published in Washington, D.C., U. S. Government Printing Office, 1931), pp. 60–61.
29. David Abrahamsen, *Who Are the Guilty? A Study of Education and Crime* (New York: Holt Rinehart and Co., 1952), p. 125.
30. Benigno DiTullio, *Horizons in Clinical Criminology* (New York: New York University Criminal Law Education New York: New York University Criminal Law Education and Research Center, 1969), pp. 59–60, 66–67.

likelihood of emotional disorders. Severe or lengthy episodes of stress outside of the parent–child relationship can also alter a personality at any time, but they are particularly destructive when they occur early in life. Serious illness or injury, shortage of food, isolation by associates, war combat, threatened or actual economic loss, unemployment, divorce, rejection in love, death of a relative or close friend, and drastic loss of self–esteem are examples of nonfamilial stress situations.[31]

Basic personality patterns and traits such as aggressiveness, mental alertness, and tendencies to smile, laugh, and make other interrelational responses, are governed by heredity, childhood experiences, and the environment of home, neighborhood and school. To date, there has been no proof of the existence of behavior or personality genes. However, the genes that determine size, shape, and general appearance have some influence on the life experiences of a person because other persons react to the cues of size, shape, and appearance.

The child's personality heritage from its parents is probably a wide ranging personality potential which is shaped into a narrower pattern by environmental influences during the child's growth. In regard to the various factors influencing personality, and—to some extent—behavior, hereditary factors may be classified as:

1. *Hereditary influence likely:* intelligence, reaction time, motor skills, sensory discrimination.

2. Hereditary influence possible: Temperamental attributes—emotional balance, mood, activity, inactivity.

3. *Hereditary influence unlikely:* attitudes, values, beliefs.[32]

The psychological processes that underlie human behavior motivate a person's attitude and reaction to a prevailing situation. A person's behavior corresponds to his whole personality. The personality of a person is the total individual expressing himself: integration of individual thinking, willing, and acting out. Personality consists of four layers or levels: (1) the *anatomical* level of skeleton, muscles, and organs; (2) the *physiological* level or normal functioning of the organs, their interrelationship, and capability to adjust to a person's needs; (3) the *psychological* level of a person's mind: the ability to recognize, integrate, remember, and discriminate; and (4) the *social* level or behavior output. Personality is a dynamic unit; behavior depends on how it functions in a particular person. The riddle of human conduct generally, and criminal conduct specifically, must be searched for in the personality.[33]

31. Ephraim Rosen and Ian Gregory, *Abnormal Psychology* (Philadelphia: W. B. Saunders Co., 1965), pp. 64–65, 141–49.

32. Amram Scheinfeld, *Your Heredity and Environment* (Philadelphia: J. B. Lippincott Co., 1965), pp. 490–91.

33. David Abrahamsen, *Crime and the Human Mind* (New York: Columbia University Press, 1944), pp. 19–24.

Multiple Causation of Crime

It is unwarranted to assume that the causation of crime can be attributed to any single–factor theory of criminal behavior. Many of the causative factors in the foregoing theories are too remote from the operational mechanism of human behavior to be useful. The nexus between these causative factors of criminality and the physical and mental makeup of any particular individual must be determined. What distinguishes what kind of person (as one or more of these causative factors becomes more and more operational) will become a criminal? Why do some individuals *not* become criminals despite the influence of one or more of the causative factors listed in the theories of criminologists about criminality? A general theory of the causation of crime and delinquency should be composed of individual differences and social forces. The amount of crime at any time and in any society depends upon the extent of the social force pressure and the makeup of the persons subjected to it.[34]

A simple joining of the three major areas of the foregoing theories offers a multiple causation theory of some validity. This theory would be developed along these lines: 1. There is a biological base for criminal behavior in some inherited predisposition. 2. There is an environmental force or influence on this predisposed individual. 3. There is a mental condition or illness which spurs on the actual commission of a crime or fails to block the operation of the first two causative factors.

A multiple causation theory of criminal behavior is related to the direct causative factors, or indirect factors, with a cautious eye to the offender's most recent crime. Such a theory can be developed around the three following major factors:

1. The want or gain factor, the need for the act or the results of crime.

2. The opportunity or event factor, the place and the time of the crime and the situation that tempts or makes possible the crime as an event.

3. The restraint factor—or more properly, the lack of restraint —which inhibits the noncriminal population from committing the same act when confronted with an opportunity for crime and when there is a conscious or subliminal surfacing of the want or gain factor.

Additionally, a theory of delinquency has introduced another major

---

34. Sheldon Glueck, *Crime and Correction: Selected Papers* (Reading, Mass.: Addison–Wesley Press, 1952), pp. 4–12.

factor suitable for inclusion in any multiple causation theory of criminal behavior: the mental attitude that criminal conduct is right and proper. This is supportive of the lack of restraint factor, or an extension of it in the form of justification for criminal behavior. These techniques of neutralizing a young person's internal inhibitions may take one or more of the following four forms:

1. The denial of responsibility.

2. The denial of injury to the victim's person or property. ("He asked for it." "He can afford the loss." "We only borrowed it.")

3. The denial of the victim (in property crimes, attacks on premises in which the owner is absent, in crimes against the person, and against store employees who do not own the stolen money).

4. Condemnation—the denial of wrongdoing by accusing the accusers (store proprietors are dishonest, police are corrupt and brutal, and the judiciary is biased and prejudice).[35]

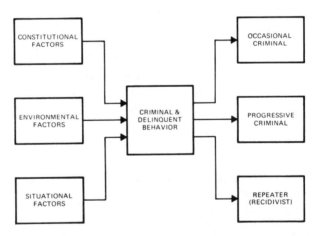

The multiple-factor theory of crime. Criminal and delinquent behavior is caused by constitutional defects or deficiencies, environmental influences, and response to a situation—in some combination. The result may be an occasional crime, progressive criminal behavior, or a confirmed repeating criminal—the recidivist. Occasional criminals may be one-time offenders; some will move to progressive criminality. From this plateau many become recidivists.

---

35. Gresham M. Sykes and David Matza, "Techniques of Neutralization—A Theory of Delinquency," *American Sociology Review* 22, no. 6 (December 1957): 664–70.

Many persons may become criminals because of any single causative factor. Two or more factors may result in a like—or greater—number of individuals committing criminal acts. There is no possible rank order for the causative factors of criminal behavior. Each person, each social group, and each neighborhood acts as a different host for the actions of one or more of the factors. However, criminal behavior is in response to one or more of these causative factors.

Delinquency

The same multiple causation of crime accounts for the acts of juveniles which would have been criminal if committed by adults. Whether the youngster goes on to a career in adult crime has its origin in one or more of the theories of criminality, coupled with the motivational thrust that led to delinquency.

Strangely, the element of free will occurs again and again in contemporary theories of delinquency. The concepts of Beccaria are expressed almost in totality. According to one formulation, the will, desire, or intent to engage in delinquency develops under two kinds of circumstances: (1) when the young person is able to manage the technical skills needed to perform the crime and is capable of controlling the fear or apprehension associated with it; and (2) when a sense of unfairness and desperation (being pushed around) enhances the delinquent act itself by providing the youngster with a means of demonstrating his potency. The situation leading to an act of delinquency is simply a two–factor situation: the strength of the temptations vs. the strength of the controls.[36]

Some juveniles are easily discouraged from acts of delinquency because they feel inadequate about the technical skills of breaking–and–entering and the taking–and–selling of stolen property. Others find the unknown and unusual aspects of delinquency frightening and avoid it because of this apprehension component. Still others lack the self–doubt which fosters desperation as a causative factor in delinquency. The young persons who commit delinquent acts are victims of drift, a force midway between effective social control and freedom to act antisocially. They respond in turn to the temptations of delinquency and the demands of convention (a drifting between criminal and conventional behavior).[37]

36. President's Commission on Law Enforcement and Administration of Justice, *Task Force Report: Juvenile Delinquency and Youth Crime* (Washington, D.C.: U.S. Government Printing Office, 1967)

37. David Matza, *Delinquency and Drift* (New York: John Wiley & Sons, 1964), pp. 27–30, 184–91.

Other studies of juveniles and crime have resulted in theories of delinquency closely associated with each of the major theories of criminality: from inherited traits or predispositions, through blocked goals and resultant anomie, to differential association and pathological criminality. Every typology of juvenile delinquents includes one or more categories labeled as maladjusted. This aligns with the theory of criminality that blames one cause of crime on personality disturbances. A major problem encountered by criminologists researching the etiology of delinquency is that one theory quite satisfactorily explains the conduct of young persons in the lower socioeconomic brackets of the ghetto or barrio areas. However, it falls short of the target in explaining the conduct of youngsters in the middle–class socioeconomic brackets who reside in suburban areas or in the better neighborhoods. Conversely, a theory that is explanatory of middle–class delinquency does not account for the conduct of youthful hustlers and cats with their origins in lower–class neighborhoods.

No single cause has been identified and isolated as the prime mover in delinquency. However, based upon a developing consensus in this field, a scheme or pattern of delinquency has been developed for the average delinquent among lower class young persons who are not maladjusted. This scheme or pattern of delinquency is:

1. The community has a limited ability to provide opportunities for young persons to achieve in accordance with middle–class values.

2. The young person's family has limited ability to maintain external controls.

3. The young person developed in a family using only limited child rearing techniques which lead to ineffective internal controls.[38]

A similar theory of delinquency applicable to middle–class and upper–class young people can be dovetailed with the psychological and psychiatric theories which trace criminality to a breakdown in the identification process during preadult years. This would be applied to middle–class delinquent males as follows:

1. Middle–class boys who are less attracted to their community are more likely to engage in delinquency.

2. The less middle–class boys are attracted to their fathers, the more likely they are to engage in delinquency.

---

38. *Task Force Report,* pp. 210–11.

3. Middle–class boys who do less well in school are more likely to engage in delinquent behavior (apprehensive of failure when seeking employment in postschool years).[39]

From the above, it appears that delinquency among young persons from families in the lower socioeconomic levels have a subcultural origin, while the delinquency of young people from families in the middle and upper socioeconomic levels are a contracultural phenomenon.

The Criminality Idea

There is an instinctive reaction to crime and criminals in any community: the arrested and convicted person is regarded as among a class of persons separated from the remaining population (assumed to be law–abiding) by some strange or mystical difference. In tracing this general tendency to place criminals in a group apart from the law–abiding segment of society, its origin, most likely, is in the criminal law itself and the development of the concept of an abstract penalty, rather than the very personal revenge for a wrong or evil. Of course, early theological and ecclesiastical traditions established mental images of right as opposed to wrong, and revenge or vengeance was aligned with this ethical idea of right and wrong, or good vs. evil. However, the concept of penalty in sanction law went beyond personal retaliation for a wrong or evil, and possibly even beyond the concept of abstract justice. It verges on an extension of God's wrath. The relationship between the words of early criminal law and biblical terminology is supportive of this belief. The similarity between the penalties suggested by early religious writings and the penalties of sanction law are also noteworthy.

In setting criminals, as a group, apart from the law–abiding, the criminal became an antagonist of the other noncriminal members of the community, an outcast. The early English concept of outlawry spelled this out, and it was carried to the new states in America. For over a century the westward thrust of the frontier stigmatized the criminal as an outlaw, a person to be hunted down. The posse comitatus of early England was also carried to America, and this "entire body of inhabitants liable to be summoned by the sheriff" became the sheriff's posse of the frontier and hunted down outlaws. The hue and cry of modern computer technology and microsecond communications across America searches for the FBI's "Ten Most Wanted Criminals" and lesser offenders, continuing the concept of outlawry and describing a criminal group in American society.

39. Jerome G. Miller, "Research and Theory in Middle-Class Delinquency," *British Journal of Criminology*, 10, no. 1, (January 1970): 33–51.

On the other hand, there is good and sufficient evidence that the conduct of criminals has the same motivational thrust as the conduct of so–called normal human beings. Despite the fact that criminals are alleged to be born to criminality and to have a classic criminal ear and other anomalies not found in normal persons; alleged to be set apart from others by chromosomal differences, types of physiques, mental instability or emotional disturbance; or alleged to exist as the victims of an adversely conditioning environment, criminal acts are more properly viewed as common behavioral possibilities. The criminal should not be thought of as a special class of person, but as a person properly considered to be a normal human being.

In 1913, in a well–known text rebutting the Lombrosian concept of a born criminal, Dr. Charles Goring wrote:

> Using the word "criminal" not necessarily in description of moral defectiveness, but merely to designate, in legal terminology, the fact that an individual has been imprisoned—using "criminal" in this sense implies a hypothetical character of some kind, a constitutional proclivity, either mental, moral or physical, present to a certain degree in all individuals, but so potent in some, as to determine for them, eventually, the fate of imprisonment. [40]

In this same text, Dr. Goring makes a strong case for a theory of "original equality." He asserts, "In view of the intricate nature of the mind of man, and of the mutability and complexity of environmental influences, it is impossible to state dogmatically, on *a priori* grounds, whether the criminal is born or made. . . . All we can assume, and what we must assume, is the *possibility* that constitutional as well as environmental factors, play a part in the production of criminality."[41]

Selected References

Books

Abrahamsen, David. *Who Are the Guilty? A Study of Education and Crime.* New York: Holt Rinehart and Co., 1952.
DiTullio, Benigno. *Horizons in Clinical Criminology.* New York: New York University Criminal Law Education and Research Center, 1969.
Ferri, Enrico. *Criminal Sociology.* New York: Agathon Press, 1967.
Glueck, Sheldon. *Crime and Correction: Selected Papers.* Cambridge, Mass.: Addison-Wesley Press, 1952.
— and Glueck, Elizabeth. *Physique and Delinquency.* New York: The Commonwealth Fund, 1950.

40. Charles Goring, *The English Convict: A Statistical Study* (London: Darling and Son, Ltd., for His Majesty's Stationery Office, 1913), pp. 26–27.
41. Ibid., p. 26.

Kretschmer, Ernst. *Physique and Character—An Investigation of the Nature of Constitution and of the Theory of Temperament.* 2d ed. New York: The Humanities Press, 1951.
Matza, David. *Delinquency and Drift.* New York: John Wiley & Sons, 1964.
Merton, Robert K. *Social Theory and Social Structure.* New York: Free Press, 1957.
Packer, Herbert L. *The Limits of the Criminal Sanction.* Stanford, Cal.: Stanford University Press, 1968.
President's Commission on Law Enforcement and Administration of Justice. *Task Force Report: Juvenile Delinquency and Youth Crime.* Washington, D.C.: U.S. Government Printing Office, 1967.
Quinney, Richard. *The Social Reality of Crime.* Boston, Mass.: Little, Brown and Co., 1970.
Schafer, Stephen. *Theories in Criminology—Past and Present Philosophies of the Crime Problem.* New York: Random House, 1969.
Sheldon, William H. *Varieties of Human Physique.* New York: Harper & Row Publishers, 1949.
Speigel, Irving. *Racketville, Slumtown and Haulberg—An Exploratory Study of Delinquent Subcultures.* Chicago: University of Chicago Press, 1964.
Sutherland, Edwin H., and Cressey, Donald R. *Criminology.* 8th ed. Phila., Penn.: J. P. Lippincott Co., 1970.

Periodicals

Amir, Menachem, and Berman, Yitzchak. "Chromosomal Deviation and Crime." *Federal Probation* 34, no. 2, (June 1970): 55–62.
Miller, Jerome G. "Research and Theory in Middle-Class Delinquency." *British Journal of Criminology,* 10, no. 1 (January 1970): 33–51.
Montague, M. F. Ashley. "Chromosomes and Crime." *Psychology Today* 2, no. 5 (October 1968): 42–49.
Sykes, Gresham M., and Matza, David. "Techniques of Neutralization—A Theory of Delinquency." *American Sociology Review* 22, no. 6 (December 1957): 664–70.
Wolfgang, Marvin E. "Pioneers in Criminology: Cesare Lombroso (1835–1909)." *Journal of Criminal Law Criminology, and Police Science* 52, no. 4 (November–December 1961): 361–91.

Chapter VII

Individual Rights vs. State Power

The Constitution of the United States and its amendments serve as a buffer in the conflict between the political states and the individual citizen: the conflict between order and liberty. The Constitution is the basic law of our country, and it contains guidelines delineating the rights of citizens and the limits of state power.

The Constitution should be judged by its survival as the supreme law of the land.[1] It foreshadowed a progressive form of government at a time when the democratic ideal was as yet little developed, and it has served as a framework for a democratic national government in the twentieth century. This document of 1787 now functions in a populous nation, with an urban–industrial environment and economy. The value of this written Constitution lies in the way it stabilizes a government in which frequent popular elections peacefully oust one set of officials and select their successors.

In its provision for judicial review, the Constitution places limitations on both legislative and executive action. A document such as the Constitution is nothing but empty words if it cannot be enforced by court action. The people of the United States enacted a written Constitution in which the theme is limitations on government power. Determination of the constitutionality of laws and government action is the

---

1. U. S. Constitution, Article VI, Paragraph 2: This Constitution, and the Laws of the United States which shall be made in Pursuance thereof; and all Treaties made, or which shall be made, under the Authority of the United States, shall be the supreme Law of the Land; and the Judges in every State shall be bound thereby, any Thing in the Constitution or Laws of any State to the Contrary notwithstanding.

essential element of judicial power under our Constitution. The doctrine of the supremacy of law dominated the thinking of the founders of the new nation, and this dominance probably accounts for the failure to specifically spell out the concept of judicial review in the Constitution. At that time, judicial review was the essence of government of laws and not of men, and was part of the legal tradition.[2] Judicial power, vested in a Supreme Court with tenure and salary protection which would insure an independent judiciary, was spelled out in Section 1, Article III, of the Constitution:

> The Judicial Power of the United States, shall be vested in one supreme Court, and in such inferior Courts as the Congress may from time to time ordain and establish. The Judges, both of the supreme and inferior Courts, shall hold their Offices during good Behaviour, and shall, at stated Times, receive for their Services, a Compensation, which shall not be diminished during their Continuance in Office.

The unamended Constitution provided for judicial review, and an adequate and speedy legal remedy in cases of illegal imprisonment by providing that the writ of *habeas corpus* should not be suspended except for public safety in time of war or rebellion.[3]

However, the document lacked a "bill of rights" for its citizens. This listing of the rights of an individual was delayed by the amending procedure[4] until 1791.

The absence of a bill of rights was justified initially because: (1) the new government was one of specific and enumerated powers and possessed no authority except in those spheres where it had received a grant of power; (2) an enumeration of the rights of the people as against the new government was by implication restrictive; and (3) in any attempt to enumerate the rights of the people, the enumeration must be complete, because everything not expressly mentioned will be presumed to be purposely omitted.[5] Criticism of the absence of a bill

2. Bernard Schwartz, *A Commentary on the Constitution of the United States, Part I: The Powers of Government* (New York: Macmillan Co., 1963), pp. 17–23.

3. U. S. Constitution, Article I, Section 9, Clause 2: The Privilege of the Writ of Habeas Corpus shall not be suspended, unless when in Cases of Rebellion or Invasion the public Safety may require it.

4. U. S. Constitution, Article V: The Congress, whenever two thirds of both Houses shall deem it necessary, shall propose Amendments to this Constitution, or, on the Application of the Legislatures of two thirds of the several States, shall call a Convention for proposing Amendments, which, in either Case, shall be valid to all Intents and Purposes, as Part of this Constitution, when ratified by the Legislatures of three fourths of the several States, or by Conventions in three fourths thereof, as the one or the other Mode of Ratification may be proposed by the Congress; Provided that no Amendment which may be made prior to the Year One thousand eight hundred and eight shall in any Manner affect the first and fourth Clauses in the Ninth Section of the first Article; and that no State, without its Consent, shall be deprived of it's equal Suffrage in the Senate.

5. Alfred H. Kelly and Winfred A. Harbison, *The American Constitution*, (New York: W. W. Norton & Co., 1963), pp. 152–53.

of rights led to a drive for the adoption of such legislation by amendment once the new government set up business.

The Bill of Rights

The first ten amendments to the Constitution are known as *The Bill of Rights*. They were proposed by Congress and ratified by the legislatures of the states in accordance with Article V of the original Constitution. The provisions of these ten amendments went into effect on December 15, 1791. They are as follows:

I. Congress shall make no law respecting an establishment of religion, or prohibiting the free exercise thereof; or abridging the freedom of speech, or of the press; or the right of the people peaceably to assemble, and to petition the Government for a redress of grievances.

II. A well regulated Militia, being necessary to the security of a free State, the right of the people to keep and bear Arms, shall not be infringed.

III. No Soldier shall, in time of peace be quartered in any house, without the consent of the Owner, nor in time of war, but in a manner to be prescribed by law.

IV. The right of the people to be secure in their persons, houses, papers, and effects, against unreasonable searches and seizures, shall not be violated, and no Warrants shall issue, but upon probable cause, supported by Oath or affirmation, and particularly describing the place to be searched, and the persons or things to be seized.

V. No person shall be held to answer for a capital, or otherwise infamous crime, unless on a presentment or indictment of a Grand Jury, except in cases arising in the land or naval forces, or in the Militia, when in actual service in time of War or public danger; nor shall any person be subject for the same offence to be twice put in jeopardy of life or limb; nor shall be compelled in any criminal case to be a witness against himself, nor be deprived of life, liberty, or property, without due process of law; nor shall private property be taken for public use, without just compensation.

VI. In all criminal prosecutions, the accused shall enjoy the right to a speedy and public trial, by an impartial jury of the State and district wherein the crime shall have been committed, which district shall have been previously ascertained by law, and to be informed of the nature and cause of the accusation; to be confronted with the witnesses against him; to have compulsory process for obtaining witnesses in his favor, and to have the Assistance of Counsel for his defence.

VII. In Suits at common law, where the value in controversy shall exceed twenty dollars, the right of trial by jury shall be preserved, and no fact tried by a jury, shall be otherwise re–examined in any Court of the United States than according to the rules of the common law.

VIII. Excessive bail shall not be required, nor excessive fines imposed, nor cruel and unusual punishments inflicted.

IX. The enumeration in the Constitution of certain rights shall not be construed to deny or disparage others retained by the people.

X. The powers not delegated to the United States by the Constitution, nor prohibited by it to the States, are reserved to the States respectively or to the people.

In tracing the history of these amendments to our Constitution there is a direct relationship to the English "Bill of Rights." In 1215, the Magna Charta was signed by King John of England. This document was a written agreement in which the sovereign granted to the people certain rights. Later, after James II fled England in early 1689, the English Parliament offered the crown conditionally to William and Mary. The condition was that the new rulers accept a declaration of the rights of the people. It was so agreed and the English Bill of Rights of 1689 became a written compact between rulers and subjects.

This compact is reported in full to permit comparison with the content of the first ten amendments to the U. S. Constitution. It reads:

1. That the pretended power of suspending of laws, or the execution of laws, by regall authority, without consent of Parlyament is illegall.

2. That the pretended power of dispensing with laws, or the execution of laws, by regall authoritie, as it hath beene assumed and exercised of late, is illegall.

3. That the commission for erecting the late Court of Commissioners for Ecclesiasticall Causes, and all other commissions and courts of like nature, are illegall and pernicious.

4. That levying money for or to the use of the Crowne by pretence of prerogative, without grant of Parlyament for longer time or in other manner than the same is or shall be granted, is illegall.

5. That it is the right of the subject to petition the King, and all commitments and prosecutions for such petitioning are illegall.

6. That the raising or keeping a standing army within the kingdome in time of peace, unless it be with consent of Parlyament, is against law.

7. That the subjects which are Protestants may have arms for their defence suitable to their conditions, and as allowed by law.

8. That election of members of Parlyament ought to be free.

9. That the freedome of speech, and debates or proceedings in Parlyament, ought not to be impeached or questioned in any court or place out of Parlyament.

10. That excessive baile ought not to be required nor excessive fines imposed; nor cruell and unusuall punishments inflicted.

11. That jurors ought to be duely impannelled and returned, and jurors which passe upon men in trialls for high treason ought to be freeholders.

12. That all grants and promises of fines and forfeitures of particular persons before conviction, are illegal and void.

13. And that for redresse of all grievances, and for the amending,

strengthening, and preserveing of the lawes, Parlyament ought to be held frequently.

14.   And they doe claime, demand, and insist upon all and singular the premisses, as their undoubted rights and liberties; and that noe declarations, judgments, doeings or proceedings, to the prejudice of the people in any of the said premisses, ought in anywise to be drawne hereafter into consequence or example.[6]

A comparison of the foregoing text indicates that the English Bill of Rights and the first ten amendments of our Constitution are remarkably similar and point to the former as the major source of the latter.

In 1833, the Supreme Court's decision in *Barron* v. *Baltimore*[7] rejected a claim that the Fifth Amendment guarantee of due process was applicable to the actions of state governments. Chief Justice John Marshall wrote the opinion in which the Bill of Rights was interpreted as placing limitations on the federal government only, and not upon the state governments.

The reasoning expressed in the opinion of the Court was based on its recollection of the Constitutional Conventions:

It is a part of the history of the day that the great revolution which established the Constitution of the United States was not effected without immense opposition. Serious fears were extensively entertained that those powers which the Patriot Statesmen who then watched over the interests of our country, deemed essential to union and to the attainment of those invaluable objects for which union was sought, might be exercised in a manner dangerous to liberty. In almost every convention by which the Constitution was adopted, amendments to guard against the abuse of power were recommended. These amendments demanded security against the apprehended encroachments of the general government—not against those of the local government. In compliance with a sentiment thus generally expressed, to quiet fears thus extensively entertained, amendments were proposed by the required majority in Congress, and adopted by the states. These amendments contain no expression indicating an intention to apply them to the state governments. This court cannot so apply them.[8]

The Fourteenth Amendment and the Bill of Rights

It is sometimes difficult to understand how a constitutional amendment, conceived as a device to make citizens of the nation's black population, has served to guarantee to all citizens, black or white, that state governments would not take away the rights to life, liberty, or property guaranteed by the Bill of Rights without due process of law.

6. Theodore F.T. Plucknett, *A Concise History of the Common Law*, 5th ed. (Boston: Little, Brown and Company, 1956), pp. 59–60.

7. 7 Peters 243 (1833).

8. Barron v. Baltimore, 7 Peters 243 (1833).

The original Constitution protected slavery in states in which it had taken root, set up a formula for counting slaves in apportioning congressional representation, and prohibited Congress from interfering with the importation of slaves before 1808. In 1857, the Supreme Court's opinion in the *Dred Scott* case[9] stated that Negroes were not included under the word citizen in the Constitution and, therefore, could not claim any of the rights and privileges of the Constitution provided for and secured to citizens of the United States.

In 1865, after a divisive war on the issue of slavery between the North and the South, slavery was abolished. A year later, Congress drafted the Fourteenth Amendment, and by 1868 the necessary three–fourths of the states had ratified it. The Fourteenth Amendment, in effect, reversed the Supreme Court's opinion in the *Dred Scott* case by amending the Constitution, and returned to the central government the powers that the *Dred Scott* decision had given to the states.[10]

The framers of the Fourteenth Amendment intended to remedy the absence of a citizenship clause in the Constitution; to confer citizenship upon Negroes; to guarantee individual rights against interference through the power of state governments; and to warn the states (the equal protection clause) not to discriminate against Negroes.[11]

While the Fourteenth Amendment was only one part of a comprehensive action plan of reconstruction, the main purpose of the 1866 Radical Republican majority in Congress was to establish the citizenship of free Negroes and to certify beyond doubt that all persons, black as well as white, who were born or naturalized in the United States, are U. S. citizens.

The Fourteenth Amendment reads as follows:

Section 1. All persons born or naturalized in the United States, and subject to the jurisdiction thereof, are citizens of the United States and of the State wherein they reside. No State shall make or enforce any law which shall abridge the privileges or immunities of citizens of the United States; nor shall any State deprive any person of life, liberty, or property, without due process of law; nor deny to any person within its jurisdiction the equal protection of the laws.

Section 2. Representatives shall be apportioned among the several States according to their respective numbers, counting the whole number of persons in each State, excluding Indians not taxed. But when the right to vote at any election for the choice of electors for President and Vice President of the United States, Representatives in Congress, the Executive and Judicial officers of a State, or the members of the Legislature

9. Dred Scott v. Sanford, 19 Howard 393 (1857).
10. Michael J. Hindelang, "Equality Under the Law," *Journal of Criminal Law, Criminology and Police Science,* 60, no. 3 (September 1969): 306–13.
11. Kelly and Harbison, *The American Constitution,* pp. 460–61.

thereof, is denied to any of the male inhabitants of such State, being twenty–one years of age, and citizens of the United States, or in any way abridged, except for participation in rebellion, or other crime, the basis of representation therein shall be reduced in the proportion which the number of such male citizens shall bear to the whole number of male citizens twenty–one years of age in such State.

Section 3. No person shall be a Senator or Representative in Congress, or elector of President and Vice President, or hold any office, civil or military, under the United States, or under any State, who, having previously taken an oath, as a member of Congress, or as an officer of the United States, or as a member of any State legislature, or as an executive or judicial officer of any State, to support the Constitution of the United States, shall have engaged in insurrection or rebellion against the same, or given aid or comfort to the enemies thereof. But Congress may by a vote of two–thirds of each House, remove such disability.

Section 4. The validity of the public debt of the United States, authorized by law, including debts incurred for payment of pensions and bounties for services in suppressing insurrection or rebellion, shall not be questioned. But neither the United States nor any State shall assume or pay any debt or obligation incurred in aid of insurrection or rebellion against the United States, or any claim for the loss or emancipation of any slave; but all such debts, obligations and claims shall be held illegal and void.

Section 5. The Congress shall have power to enforce, by appropriate legislation, the provisions of this article.

In this amendment, the rule of citizenship is delineated in section 1; the loss of political representation is itemized in section 2 as a means of gaining voluntary compliance by the states; and the fact of only one victor is suggested strongly in section 3. There is also a reassurance that the federal government would survive and pay its just debts, but there would be no reimbursement in any fashion to the Confederacy or any persons who had owned slaves. Lastly, section 5 specifies that the federal government intends to enforce the amendment and delegates this power to Congress.

In the half century following the passage of the Fourteenth Amendment there was only limited judicial recognition of the rights of citizens as opposed to the power of government:

1. In an 1886 case the Supreme Court criticized the federal government and its agents for its methods of collecting evidence, stating in its opinion: "It is the duty of courts to be watchful for the Constitutional rights of the citizen, and against any stealthy encroachments thereon.[12]

2. In a 1914 case, the decision of the Court forbid any illegal search by federal government agents and warns that such

12. Boyd v. U.S., 116 U.S. 616 (1886).

evidence could not be used against the person whose privacy had been unlawfully invaded. In its opinion the court stated: "The Fourth Amendment was a limitation and restraint upon the actions of the Federal courts and officials, and the use of evidence seized by Federal authorities in violation of the Fourth Amendment was a denial of the Constitutional rights of the accused."[13]

Moreover, in both of the foregoing cases, the Court acted under its authority to supervise the federal courts. In both cases, federal agents were accused of questionable conduct and both trials were conducted in federal courts. Neither of the cases presented a question of constitutionality to the courts: the action of the state agents deprived a citizen of his constitutional right without due process of law.

Applicable to the States By Reason of the Due Process Clause of the Fourteenth Amendment

Fifty–six years after the ratification of the Fourteenth Amendment, the Supreme Court merged the rights of a citizen under the Fourteenth Amendment with those of the Bill of Rights. This was accomplished by the decision in the case of *Gitlow* v. *New York*.[14] Gitlow was indicted and convicted under New York law on a charge of advocating the overthrow of government by unlawful acts. The main evidence at the trial was a series of writings published by Gitlow. The major argument presented by counsel for Gitlow was on the constitutional question that the liberty protected by the Fourteenth Amendment included the liberties of speech and of the press, and that deprivation of such liberty of expression by state courts way a violation of the due process clause of the Fourteenth Amendment. In its opinion in this case, the Court affirmed Gitlow's conviction on the grounds that it was a fundamental and long–established principle that the freedom of speech and of the press which is secured by the Constitution does not confer an absolute right to speak or publish without responsibility, and does not prevent the punishment of those who abuse this freedom. However, in a landmark "assumption," the Court stated:

> For present purposes we may and do assume that freedom of speech and of the press—which are protected by the First Amendment from abridgment by Congress—are among the fundamental personal rights and "liberties" protected by the due process clause of the Fourteenth Amendment from impairment by the States.

13. Weeks v. U.S., 232 U.S. 383 1914).
14. 268 U.S. 652 (1924).

The *Gitlow* doctrine was affirmed six years later in the 1930 case of *Stromberg* v. *California*.[15] It was another First Amendment "freedoms" case, and concerned a conviction under a California advocating–revolution law. Counsel for Stromberg claimed the law was vague and indefinite. The Court's opinion noted that it had been previously determined in the *Gitlow* case that the concept of liberty under the due process clause of the Fourteenth Amendment embraced the right of free speech, but that this right was not absolute and a state could punish those who incited to violence and crime and threatened the overthrow of organized government by unlawful means. However, the court reversed Stromberg's conviction because the California law was found to be so vague and indefinite as to threaten the right of free speech and was, therefore, repugnant to the guaranty of liberty contained in the Fourteenth Amendment.

It was not until 1937 that the United States Supreme Court clarified the issue of just how many of the rights guaranteed by the Bill of Rights were protected against state action by the due process clause of the Fourteenth Amendment. This was the case of *Palko* v. *Connecticut*.[16] Palko applied to the high court for a legal remedy as the result of an unusual Connecticut law which permitted appeals by the prosecutor from the verdict of a trial jury. Palko had been found guilty of murder in a jury trial and sentenced to life imprisonment, but the indictment had specified murder in the first degree and the jury had reduced this charge in their verdict to second degree murder. The prosecutor appealed, the Connecticut Supreme Court of Errors reviewed the case, and ordered Palko retried on the first degree murder charge. He was tried again, and his counsel made timely objections that the new trial placed Palko twice in jeopardy for the same offense and, in so doing, violated his constitutional rights under the Fourteenth Amendment. The objections were overruled, and Palko was convicted of murder in the first degree.

The following extracts from the Court's opinion in the Palko case develop the concept of "ordered liberty" and "fundamental freedoms and rights":

> The due process clause of the Fourteenth Amendment may make it unlaw-ful for a state to abridge by its statutes the freedom of speech which the First Amendment safeguards against encroachment by the Congress; or the like freedom of the press; or the free exercise of religion; or the right of peaceable assembly, without which speech would be unduly trammeled; or the right of one accused of crime to the benefit of counsel. In these and other situations, immunities that are valid as against the federal govern-ment by force of the specific pledges of particular amendments (Amend-

15. 283 U.S. 359 (1930) pp. 368–69.
16. 302 U.S. 319 (1937).

ment I and VI) have been found to be implicit in the concept of ordered liberty, and thus, through the Fourteenth Amendment, become valid as against the states.

Our survey of the cases serves, we think, to justify the statement that the dividing line between them, if not unfaltering throughout its course, has been true for the most part to a unifying principle.

The line of division may seem to be wavering and broken if there is a hasty catalogue of the cases on the one side and the other. Reflection and analysis will induce a different view. There emerges the perception of a rationalizing principle which gives to discrete instances a proper order and coherence.

The right to trial by jury and the immunity from prosecution except as the result of an indictment may have value and importance (Amendment VI and V). Even so, they are not of the very essence of a scheme of ordered liberty. To abolish them is not to violate a principle of justice so rooted in the traditions and conscience of our people as to be ranked as fundamental. Few would be so narrow or provincial as to maintain that a fair and enlightened system of justice would be impossible without them. What is true of jury trials and indictments is true also, as the cases show, of the immunity from compulsory self–incrimination (Amendment V).

On which side of the line the case made out by the appellant has appropriate location must be the next inquiry and the final one. Is that kind of double jeopardy to which the statute has subjected him a hardship so acute and shocking that our polity will not endure it? Does it violate those fundamental principles of liberty and justice which lie at the base of all our civil and political institutions?

The conviction of appellant is not in derogation of any privileges or immunities that belong to him as a citizen of the United States.[17]

The unifying principle that comes through strong and clear in the *Palko* opinion is that freedom of speech, press, religion, and assembly, and the right to counsel are fundamental principles of liberty and justice implicit in the concept of ordered liberty. Additionally, to abolish them is to violate a principle of justice so rooted in the traditions and conscience of our people as to be ranked as fundamental. On the other side of the dividing line are the rights to jury trial, prosecution by indictment, and immunity from compulsory self–incrimination. These rights were classed by the Court as of value and importance, but not of the very essence of a scheme of ordered liberty.

The legislation that had been enacted primarily to make citizens of ex–slaves and guarantee them the rights of citizens against any state

17. Palko v. Connecticut, 302 U.S. 319 (1937) pp. 324–28. In 1969, in Benton v. Maryland (395 U.S. 784), the double jeopardy clause of the Fifth Amendment was made applicable to the states through the Fourteenth Amendment. The guarantee against double jeopardy is fundamental to the American scheme of justice.

denial, was now being utilized for the protection of all citizens against state government power. However, the words "nor shall any state deprive any person of life, liberty or property, without due process of law" was being limited in their application by the concept of ordered liberty and the fundamental freedoms and rights doctrine.

It was not until 1949 that the Court decided that the right to privacy (to be safe from unreasonable searches and seizures) was a citizen's right guaranteed against state infringement by the due process clause of the Fourteenth Amendment. This was the case of *Wolf* v. *Colorado*,[18] and while the Court's decision was noted for its reluctance to use any form of federal intervention upon state governments, the opinion of the Court did incorporate the Fourth Amendment right of privacy into the scope of the Fourteenth Amendment. The Court stated:

> We have no hesitation in saying that were a state affirmatively to sanction such police invasion into privacy it would run counter to the guaranty of the Fourteenth Amendment. Security of our privacy against arbitrary intrusion by the police is implicit in the concept of ordered liberty and as such enforceable against the states through the Due Process Clause.

A dozen years later, in 1961, in the landmark case of *Mapp* v. *Ohio*,[19] the Fourteenth Amendment was used to safeguard citizens against unreasonable searches and seizures. The Court ruled that all evidence obtained by searches and seizures in violation of the Constitution (Fourth Amendment) is inadmissible in a criminal trial in a state court.

The facts of this case are: Dolly Mapp was convicted of knowingly having had in her possession and under her control certain lewd and lascivious books, pictures, and photographs in violation of the laws of Ohio. The Supreme Court of Ohio found that her conviction was valid though based primarily upon the introduction in evidence of lewd and lascivious books and pictures unlawfully seized during an unlawful search of the defendant's home.

The Supreme Court reversed the Ohio courts, and the following extracts from the *Mapp* case clearly indicate the Court was no longer reluctant to use the inherent power of the Fourteenth Amendment to protect a citizen from the illegal use of state power:

> Since the Fourth Amendment's right of privacy has been declared enforceable against the States through the Due Process Clause of the Fourteenth, it is enforceable against them by the same sanction of-exclusion as is used against the Federal Government. Were it otherwise, then just as without the *Weeks* rule* the assurance against unreasonable federal

18. 338 U.S. 25 (1949).

19. 367 U.S. 643 (1961).

*The Court ruled in Weeks v. United States, 232 U.S. 383 (1914), that "in a federal prosecution the Fourth Amendment barred the use of evidence secured through an illegal search and seizure." (In *Weeks*, the Court used its supervisory authority over the federal courts to enforce its ruling, and not the Fourteenth Amendment.)

searches and seizures would be "a form of words," valueless and undeserving of mention in a perpetual charter of inestimable human liberties, so too, without that rule the freedom from state invasions of privacy would be so ephemeral and so neatly severed from its conceptual nexus with the freedom from all brutish means of coercing evidence as not to merit this Court's high regard as a freedom "implicit in the concept of ordered liberty."

Moreover, our holding that the exclusionary rule is an essential part of both the Fourth and Fourteenth Amendments is not only the logical dictate of prior cases, but it also makes very good sense. There is no war between the Constitution and common sense. Presently, a federal prosecutor may make no use of evidence illegally seized, but a State's attorney across the street may, although he supposedly is operating under the enforceable prohibitions of the same Amendment. Thus the State, by admitting evidence unlawfully seized, serves to encourage disobedience to the Federal Constitution which it is bound to uphold.

Having once recognized that the right to privacy embodied in the Fourth Amendment is enforceable against the States, and that the right to be secure against rude invasions of privacy by state officers is, therefore, constitutional in origin, we can no longer permit that right to remain an empty promise. Because it is enforceable in the same manner and to like effect as other basic rights secured by the Due Process Clause, we can no longer permit it to be revocable at the whim of any police officer who, in the name of law enforcement itself, chooses to suspend its enjoyment. Our decision, founded on reason and truth, gives to the individual no more than that which the Constitution guarantees him, to the police officer no less than that to which honest law enforcement is entitled, and to the courts that judicial integrity so necessary in the true administration of justice.[20]

The Fourteenth Amendment and Criminal Prosecutions

In the decade that followed, most of the rights guaranteed in the Bill of Rights relating to criminal prosecutions were made applicable to the states by the Fourteenth Amendment. This was a selective incorporation of individual rights within the scope of the due process clause of the Fourteenth Amendment. A selected chronological review of landmark cases concerned with the rights of persons accused of crime indicates the balancing of community interest in law enforcement with the Constitutional rights of the accused persons. Additionally, extracts from these court decisions are illustrative of the mechanics of selected

20. Mapp v. Ohio, 367 U.S. 643 (1961) at pp. 655–657.

incorporation of a Constitutional Amendment within the due process clause of the Fourteenth Amendment.

In 1962, the Eighth Amendment protection against cruel and unusual punishment was made applicable to the states by the Fourteenth Amendment. In this case, *Robinson* v. *California*,[21] the defendant Robinson had been prosecuted and convicted and sentenced to prison under a California law which made it a misdemeanor for any person to be addicted to narcotics. The California Supreme Court, on Robinson's appeal, affirmed the conviction on the grounds that this law made the "status" of narcotic addict a criminal offense for which the offender could be prosecuted at any time before he reformed, even though he had never used or possessed narcotics, or been guilty of any criminal behavior, in the state.

In its landmark decision involving this Eighth Amendment area, the Court indicated that the California law as used in this case was cruel and unusual punishment and violated Robinson's rights; and that the due process clause of the Fourteenth Amendment forbade this type of state action. Therefore, the law was unconstitutional.

The following extracts from the opinion of the Court, delivered by Mr. Justice Potter Steward, explain this decision:

> It is unlikely that any State at this moment in history would attempt to make it a criminal offense for a person to be mentally ill, or a leper, or to be afflicted with a venereal disease. A State might determine that the general health and welfare require that the victims of these and other human afflictions be dealt with by compulsory treatment, involving quarantine, confinement, or sequestration. But, in the light of contemporary human knowledge, a law which made a criminal offense of such a disease would doubtless be universally thought to be an infliction of cruel and unusual punishment in violation of the Eighth and Fourteenth Amendments.

> We cannot but consider the statute before us as of the same category. In this Court counsel for the State recognized that narcotic addiction is an illness. Indeed, it is apparently an illness which may be contracted innocently or involuntarily. We hold that a state law which imprisons a person thus afflicted as a criminal, even though he has never touched any narcotic drug within the State or been guilty of any irregular behavior there, inflicts a cruel and unusual punishment in violation of the Fourteenth Amendment.[22]

Mr. Justice William Douglas, in a concurring opinion,* sums up the selective incorporation of the Eighth Amendment with the Fourteenth Amendment in these words:

21. 370 U.S. 660 (1962).
22. Robinson v. California, 370 U.S. 660 (1962) pp. 666–67.
*Filed when a justice votes with the majority, but differs with the opinion of the court, and wishes to place his views in the record of the case.

The command of the Eighth Amendment, banning "cruel and unusual punishments," stems from the Bill of Rights of 1868. And it is applicable to the States by reason of the Due Process Clause of the Fourteenth Amendment.[23]

Despite the U.S. Supreme Court's decisions in *Palko* v. *Connecticut* and *Powell* v. *Alabama*,[24] which classified the Sixth Amendment right to legal counsel within "the concept of ordered liberty" and as a necessity when a defendant faces "the danger of conviction because he does not know how to establish his innocence," the 1942 case of *Betts* v. *Brady*[25] refused similar classification to the appointment of legal counsel for an impoverished state court defendant who wished to hire an attorney of his own selection. The Sixth Amendment right of a person accused of crime to have legal assistance had been recognized in the federal court system and the practice of appointing counsel for indigent defendants was standard in federal courts since 1938. The implementation of this Sixth Amendment right was formalized in 1946 by Rule 44 of the Federal Rules of Criminal Procedure.

Gideon v. *Wainwright*[26] is the landmark case in the Sixth Amendment right to legal assistance by any person accused of crime. The holding of the Court in *Gideon* was: The right of an indigent defendant in a criminal trial to have the assistance of counsel is a fundamental right essential to a fair trial, and petitioner's trial and conviction without the assistance of counsel violated the Fourteenth Amendment.

Gideon brought his case before the Supreme Court in a handwritten petition for habeas corpus which began with the words: "I, Clarence Earl Gideon, claim that I was denied the rights of the 4th, 5th and 14th amendments of the Bill of Rights." Gideon then went on to reveal the facts of his case. He had been charged in a Florida court with a non-capital felony, and had appeared without counsel. At this time, he informed the court that he was without funds and asked for appointed counsel. His request was denied by the court on the grounds that Florida law only permitted the appointment of counsel for defendants without funds to hire counsel in capital cases. Gideon conducted his own defense, and he was convicted and sentenced to imprisonment. The Florida Supreme Court denied Gideon's applications for relief.

The *Gideon* case is particularly unique in that it was a rerun of this question of appointing legal counsel for defendants who could not afford to hire such counsel. Back in 1942, in the case of *Betts* v. *Brady*,[27] the Supreme Court had ruled that the appointment of legal counsel for indigent defendants, in accord with the Sixth Amendment guarantee

23. Ibid., p. 675.
24. 302 U.S. 319 (1937); 287 U.S. 45 (1932).
25. 316 U.S. 455 (1942).
26. 372 U.S. 335 (1963).
27. U.S. 455 (1942).

of legal assistance, was not a fundamental right essential to a fair trial, and was not "made obligatory upon the states by the Fourteenth Amendment."

The following extracts from the Court's opinion in *Gideon* reveal the overruling of *Betts* v. *Brady* and the new doctrine of *Gideon*:

> The fact is that in deciding as it did—that "appointment of counsel is not a fundamental right, essential to a fair trial"—the Court in *Betts* v. *Brady* made an abrupt break with its own well–considered precedents. In returning to these old precedents, sounder we believe than the new, we but restore constitutional principles established to achieve a fair system of justice. Not only these precedents but also reason and reflection require us to recognize that in our adversary system of criminal justice, any person haled into court, who is too poor to hire a lawyer, cannot be assured a fair trial unless counsel is provided for him.

> The Court in *Betts* v. *Brady* departed from the sound wisdom upon which the Court's holding in *Powell* v. *Alabama* rested. Florida, supported by two other States, has asked that *Betts* v. *Brady* be left intact. Twenty–two States, as friends of the Court, argue that *Betts* was "an anachronism when handed down" and that it should now be overruled. We agree.

> The judgment is reversed and the cause is remanded to the Supreme Court of Florida for further action not inconsistent with this opinion.[28]

In 1963, in *Ker* v. *California*,[29] the Supreme Court supplemented the landmark *Mapp* decision by spelling out the standards of reasonableness in searches and seizures.

Having reason to believe that Ker or one of his associates was selling marihuana and had just purchased some from a person who was known to be a dealer, California police officers, without a search warrant, used a passkey to enter an apartment and arrested George and Diane Ker. It was argued at the trial that the arrest was made without probable cause and entry was made without notice, in violation of the defendants' constitutional rights under the Fourth Amendment. Both Kers were convicted and the California District Court of Appeal affirmed the convictions. The U.S. Supreme Court upheld the action of the California courts.

The following extracts from the Court's opinion in this case not only establish Fourth Amendment guidelines, but also highlight the incorporation of the Fourth Amendment with the Fourteenth Amendment's due process clause:

> In *Mapp* v. *Ohio*,[30] we followed *Boyd* v. *United States*,[31] which held that the Fourth Amendment, implemented by the self–incrimination clause of the

28. Gideon v. Wainwright, 372 U.S. 335 (1963) pp. 343–45.

29. 374 U.S. 23 (1963). For an application of reasonable standards where a search was conducted incident to a lawful arrest yet limited to the "within reach" area of the arrestee (when there is no search warrant), *see:* Chimel v. California, 395 U.S. 752 (1969).

Fifth, forbids the Federal Government to convict a man of crime by using testimony or papers obtained from him by unreasonable searches and seizures as defined in the Fourth Amendment. We specifically held in *Mapp* that this constitutional prohibition is enforceable against the States through the Fourteenth Amendment. This means, as we said in *Mapp*, that the Fourth Amendment "is enforceable against them (the states) by the same sanction of exclusion as is used against the Federal Government," by the application of the same constitutional standard prohibiting "unreasonable searches and seizures." We now face the specific question as to whether *Mapp* requires the exclusion of evidence in this case.

Preliminary to our examination of the search and seizures involved here, it might be helpful for us to indicate what was not decided in *Mapp*.

First, it must be recognized that the "principles governing the admissibility of evidence in federal criminal trials have not been restricted ... to those derived solely from the Constitution. In the exercise of its supervisory authority over the administration of criminal justice in the federal courts ... this Court has ... formulated rules of evidence to be applied in federal criminal prosecutions."[32] *Mapp*, however, established no assumption by this Court of supervisory authority over state courts, and, consequently, it implied no total obliteration of state laws relating to arrests and searches in favor of federal law. *Mapp* sounded no death knell for our federalism; rather, it echoed the sentiment of *Elkins* v. *United States*,[33] that "a healthy federalism depends upon the avoidance of needless conflict between state and federal courts" by itself urging that "federal–state cooperation in the solution of crime under constitutional standards will be promoted, if only by recognition of their now mutual obligation to respect the same fundamental criteria in their approaches."

Second, *Mapp* did not attempt the impossible task of laying down a fixed formula for the application in specific cases of the constitutional prohibition against unreasonable searches and seizures; it recognized that we would be met with recurring questions of the reasonableness of searches and that, at any rate, "reasonableness is in the first instance for the (trial court) ... to determine," thus indicating that the usual weight be given to findings of trial courts.

Mapp, of course, did not lend itself to a detailed explication of standards, since the search involved there was clearly unreasonable and bore no stamp of legality even from the Ohio Supreme Court. This is true also of *Elkins* v. *United States*,[34] where all of the courts assumed the unreasonableness of the search in question and this Court "invoked" its "supervisory power over the administration of criminal justice in the

30. 367 U.S. 643 (1961).
31. 116 U.S. 616 (1886).
32. McNabb v. United States, 318 U.S. 332 (1943).
33. 364 U.S. 206 (1960).
34. 364 U.S. 206 (1960).

federal courts," in declaring that the evidence so seized by state officers was inadmissible in a federal prosecution.

Implicit in the Fourth Amendment's protection from unreasonable searches and seizures is its recognition of individual freedom. That safeguard has been declared to be as of the very essence of constitutional liberty the guaranty of which is as important and as imperative as are the guaranties of the other fundamental rights of the individual citizen. While the language of the Amendment is "general," it forbids every search that is unreasonable; it protects all, those suspected or known to be offenders as well as the innocent, and unquestionably extends to the premises where the search was made.

This Court's long–established recognition that standards of reasonableness under the Fourth Amendment are not susceptible of Procrustean application is carried forward when that Amendment's proscriptions are enforced against the states through the Fourteenth Amendment. And, although the standard of reasonableness is the same under the Fourth and Fourteenth Amendments, the demands of our federal system compel us to distinguish between evidence held inadmissible because of our supervisory powers over federal courts and that held inadmissible because prohibited by the United States Constitution. We reiterate that the reasonableness of a search is in the first instance a substantive determination to be made by the trial court from the facts and circumstances of the case and in the light of the "fundamental criteria" laid down by the Fourth Amendment and in opinions of this Court applying that Amendment. Findings of reasonableness, of course, are respected only insofar as consistent with federal constitutional guarantees. As we have stated above and in other cases involving federal constitutional rights, findings of state courts are by no means insulated against examination here. While this Court does not sit as in *nisi prius** to appraise contradictory factual questions, it will, where necessary to the determination of constitutional rights, make an independent examination of the facts, the findings, and the record so that it can determine for itself whether in the decision as to reasonableness the fundamental—i.e., constitutional—criteria established by this Court have been respected.

The states are not thereby precluded from developing workable rules governing arrests, searches and seizures to meet the practical demands of effective criminal investigation and law enforcement in the states, provided that those rules do not violate the constitutional proscription of unreasonable searches and seizures and the concomitant command that evidence so seized is inadmissible against one who has standing to complain. Such a standard implies no derogation of uniformity in applying federal constitutional guarantees but is only a recognition that conditions and circumstances vary just as do investigative and enforcement techniques.

---

*Examination of issues of fact; trial courts, rather than appellate courts.

The 1964 case of *Malloy* v. *Hogan*,[35] is a landmark case in protecting the right to silence. Petitioner Malloy was arrested during a gambling raid in 1959 by the police of Hartford, Connecticut. He pleaded guilty to the crime of pool selling, a misdemeanor, and was sentenced to one year in jail and fined $500. The sentence was ordered to be suspended after 90 days, at which time he was to be placed on probation for two years. About 16 months after his guilty plea, petitioner was ordered to testify before a referee appointed by the Superior Court of Hartford County to conduct an inquiry into alleged gambling and other criminal activities in the county. The petitioner was asked a number of questions related to events surrounding his arrest and conviction. He refused to answer any question "on the grounds it may tend to incriminate me." The superior court adjudged him in contempt, and committed him to prison until he was willing to answer the questions. Petitioner's application for a writ of habeas corpus was denied by the superior court, and the Connecticut Supreme Court of Errors affirmed. The U. S. Supreme Court granted *certiorari.**

In this case the U. S. Supreme Court was asked to reconsider prior decisions holding that the privilege against self–incrimination is not safeguarded against state action by the Fourteenth Amendment: *Twining* v. *New Jersey,* 211 U. S. 78; *Adamson* v. *California,* 332 U. S. 46. (In both cases the question was whether comment upon the failure of an accused to take the stand in his own defense in a state prosecution violated the privilege. It was assumed, but not decided, in both cases that such comment in a federal prosecution for a federal offense would infringe the provision of the Fifth Amendment that "no person . . . shall be compelled in any criminal case to be a witness against himself.") The Court held that the Fourteenth Amendment guaranteed the petitioner the protection of the Fifth Amendment's privilege against self–incrimination, and that under the applicable federal standard, the Connecticut Supreme Court of Errors erred in holding that the privilege was not properly invoked, and reversed the lower court's action.

The court's opinion in *Malloy* is a fine review of the Fourteenth Amendment and the Bill of Rights. It indicates that some, but not all, of the amendments are made applicable to the states and their agents and courts. These extracts from the Court's opinion in *Malloy* are a running commentary that solidifies the Court's action in case after case:

> The extent to which the Fourteenth Amendment prevents state invasion of rights enumerated in the first eight Amendments has been considered in numerous cases in this Court since the Amendments' adoption in 1868.

35. 378 U.S. 1 (1964).
*Review.

Although many Justices have deemed the Amendment to incorporate all eight of the Amendments, the view which has thus far prevailed dates from the decision in 1897 in *Chicago, B. & Q. R. Co.* v. *Chicago,* 166 U.S. 226, which held that the Due Process Clause requires the States to pay just compensation for private property taken for public use.[36] It was on the authority of that decision that the Court said in 1908 in *Twining* v. *New Jersey,*[37] that "it is possible that some of the personal rights safeguarded by the first eight Amendments against National action may also be safeguarded against state action, because a denial of them would be a denial of due process of law."

The Court has not hesitated to reexamine past decisions according the Fourteenth Amendment a less central role in the preservation of basic liberties than that which was contemplated by its Framers when they added the Amendment to our constitutional scheme. Thus although the Court as late as 1922 said that neither the Fourteenth Amendment nor any other provision of the Constitution of the United States imposes upon the States any restrictions about "freedom of speech," three years later, *Gitlow* v. *New York,* 268 U. S. 652 (1925), initiated a series of decisions which today hold immune from state invasion every First Amendment protection for the cherished rights of mind and spirit—the freedoms of speech, press, religion, assembly, association, and petition for redress of grievances.

Similarly, *Palko* v. *Connecticut,* 302 U.S. 383 decided in 1937, suggested that the rights secured by the Fourth Amendment were not protected against state action, citing the statement of the Court in *Weeks* v. *United States,* 232 U.S. 383 that "the Fourth Amendment is not directed to individual misconduct of (state) officials." In 1961, however, the Court held that in the light of later decisions,[38] it was taken as settled that "the Fourth Amendment's right of privacy has been declared enforceable against the States through the Due Process Clause of the Fourteenth."[39]

Again, although the Court held in 1942 that in a state prosecution for a noncapital offense, "appointment of counsel is not a fundamental right,"[40] only last Term this decision was re-examined and it was held that provision of counsel in all criminal cases was "a fundamental right, essential to a fair trial," and thus was made obligatory on the States by the Fourteenth Amendment.[41]

---

36. In Barron v. Baltimore, 7 Peters 243 (1833), decided before the adoption of the Fourteenth Amendment, Chief Justice Marshall, speaking for the Court, held that this right was not secured against state action by the Fifth Amendment provision: "Nor shall private property be taken for public use, without just compensation."

37. 211 U.S. 78 (1908).

38. Wolf v. Colorado, 338 U.S. 25 (1949); Elkins v. United States, 364 U.S. 206 (1960).

39. Mapp v. Ohio, 367 U.S. 643 (1961).

40. Betts v. Brady, 316 U.S. 455 (1942).

41. Gideon v. Wainwright, 372 U.S. 335 (1963). *See also* Robinson v. California, 370 U.S. 660 (1962) which, despite prior decisions, made applicable to the States the Eighth Amendment ban on cruel and unusual punishments.

We hold today that the Fifth Amendment's exception from compulsory self–incrimination is also protected by the Fourteenth Amendment against abridgment by the States.

The Fourteenth Amendment secures against state invasion the same privilege that the Fifth Amendment guarantees against federal infringement—the right of a person to remain silent unless he chooses to speak in the unfettered exercise of his own will, and to suffer no penalty, as held in *Twining*, for such silence.

This conclusion is fortified by our recent decision in *Mapp* v. *Ohio*,[42] overruling *Wolf* v. *Colorado*,[43] which had held "that in a prosecution in a State court for a State crime the Fourteenth Amendment does not forbid the admission of evidence obtained by an unreasonable search and seizure." *Mapp* held that the Fifth Amendment privilege against self–incrimination implemented the Fourth Amendment to make the exclusionary rule obligatory upon the States.

A 1965 case, *Pointer* v. *Texas*,[44] was a landmark Sixth Amendment case of the right granted to an accused to confront witnesses against him. The Court's holding in this case was: The right granted to an accused by the Sixth Amendment to confront the witnesses against him, which includes the right of cross–examination, is a fundamental right essential to a fair trial and is made obligatory on the States by the Fourteenth Amendment.

Pointer and his crime partner were arrested in Texas and taken before a state judge for a preliminary hearing (in Texas called the examining trial) on a charge of: robbery by assault, or violence, or by putting in fear of life or bodily injury, in violation of the Texas penal code. At this hearing an assistant district attorney examined witnesses, but neither of the defendants, both of whom were laymen, had a lawyer. The robbery victim, a man named Phillips, gave his version of the robbery in detail, identifying Pointer as the man who had robbed him at gunpoint. Pointer did not cross–examine the victim, although it was said he tried to cross–examine some other witnesses at the hearing. Pointer was subsequently indicted on a charge of robbery. Some time before the trial was held the victim moved to California, and the State at the trial offered the transcript of the victim's testimony given at the preliminary hearing as evidence against petitioner. Petitioner's counsel immediately objected to introduction of the transcript, stating, "Your Honor, we will object to that, as it is a denial of the confrontment of the witnesses against the Defendant." Similar objections were repeatedly made by petitioner's counsel but were overruled by the trial judge. The Texas Court of Criminal Appeals, the

42. 367 U.S. 643 (1961).
43. 338 U.S. 25 (1949).
44. 380 U.S. 400 (1965).

highest state court to which the case could be taken, affirmed the petitioner's conviction, rejecting his contention that use of the transcript to convict him denied him rights guaranteed by the Sixth and Fourteenth Amendments. The U. S. Supreme Court granted certiorari to consider the important constitutional question involved in the case.

The extracts below from the Court's opinion in *Pointer* v. *Texas* reveals the basis for the incorporation of this Sixth Amendment right within the scope of the Fourteenth Amendment:

> The Sixth Amendment is a part of what is called our Bill of Rights. In *Gideon* v. *Wainwright*,[45] in which this Court held that the Sixth Amendment's right to the assistance of counsel is obligatory upon the States, we did so on the ground that a provision of the Bill of Rights which is "fundamental and essential to a fair trial" is made obligatory upon the States by the Fourteenth Amendment.

> We hold today that the Sixth Amendment's right of an accused to confront the witnesses against him is likewise a fundamental right and is made obligatory on the States by the Fourteenth Amendment.

> We are aware that some cases, particularly *West* v. *Louisiana*,[46] have stated that the Sixth Amendment's right of confrontation does not apply to trials in state courts, on the ground that the entire Sixth Amendment does not so apply. But of course since *Gideon* v. *Wainwright*, it no longer can broadly be said that the Sixth Amendment does not apply to state courts. And as this Court said in *Malloy* v. *Hogan:* "The Court has not hesitated to re-examine past decisions according the Fourteenth Amendment a less central role in the preservation of basic liberties than that which was contemplated by its framers when they added the Amendment to our constitutional scheme."[47] In the light of *Gideon, Malloy*, and other cases cited in those opinions holding various provisions of the Bill of Rights applicable to the States by virtue of the Fourteenth Amendment, the statements made in *West* and similar cases generally declaring that the Sixth Amendment does not apply to the States can no longer be regarded as the law.

> We hold that petitioner was entitled to be tried in accordance with the protection of the confrontation guarantee of the Sixth Amendment, and that that guarantee, like the right against compelled self-incrimination, is "to be enforced against the States under the Fourteenth Amendment according to the same standards that protect those personal rights against federal encroachment."

> Because the transcript of Phillips'* statement offered against petitioner at his trial had not been taken at a time and under circumstances affording

45. 372 U.S. 335 (1963).
46. 194 U.S. 258 (1903).
47. Malloy v. Hogan, 378 U.S. 1 (1964), p. 5.
*The victim in the robbery for which Pointer was indicted, tried, convicted, and sentenced.

petitioner through counsel an adequate opportunity to cross-examine Phillips, its introduction in a federal court in a criminal case against Pointer would have amounted to denial of the privilege of confrontation guaranteed by the Sixth Amendment. Since we hold that the right of an accused to be confronted with the witnesses against him must be determined by the same standards whether the right is denied in a federal or state proceeding, it follows that use of the transcript to convict petitioner denied him a constitutional right, and that his conviction must be reversed.[48]

Balancing the Conflict

The decade of the 1960s was indeed a decade of conflict. It defined the limits of governmental power, state and federal, more closely than at any time in our history. Court decisions since 1960 have been more concerned with individual liberty than at any time since the framing and adoption of the Constitution and its first amendments. All of this judicial review was done in an atmosphere of rising crime rates, increasing violence in the streets of our cities, and some deadly ambush attacks on the police.

Limiting the power of government as opposed to the rights of suspects and defendants in criminal cases was achieved despite the severest criticism of the courts by government officials and laymen, who were justifiably concerned about the crime and violence which was increasing in the nation. On the other hand, an extension of the power of government in this decade in reaction to crime and violence would have stripped citizens of the liberties preserved for nearly 200 years.

Edward Bennett Williams, attorney, author, and educator, believes we are in the midst of a social revolution, and offers his views as follows:

> It is the revolution of the young, the poor, the blacks, the social aliens of our society. It has created a crisis of authority, a crisis in which the authority of all our institutions is under challenge: the family, the university, the church, the judicial system, the economic system, and the very government itself.[49]

The problem of crime is a serious and emotional one. Perhaps the answer is not the abridgment of liberty, but rather an analysis of the entire system of justice. It certainly is easier and less expensive to blame the courts for crime than to give the police the men, the training, and the equipment needed to make the criminal realize he will get

---

48. Pointer v. Texas, 380 U.S. 400 (1965) pp. 403, 406–7.
49. Edward Bennett Williams, address to the California Bar Association; Los Angeles, September 17, 1970, *Journal of the State Bar of California* 45, no. 6 (November–December 1970): p. 819.

caught. It certainly is more popular to advocate the repeal of the Bill of Rights than to advocate an increase of taxes, or a sincere and well-funded program to combat ignorance, poverty, illiteracy, and racial discrimination. It would be a terrible paradox if we lost our freedom in an attempt to restore order.

Selected References

Books

Kelly, Alfred H., and Harbison, Winfred A. *The American Constitution,* 3d ed. New York: W. W. Norton and Co., 1963.

Schwartz, Bernard. *A Commentary on the Constitution of the United States, Part I: The Powers of Government.* New York: Macmillan Co., 1963.

Periodicals

Hindelang, Michael J. "Equality Under the Law." *Journal of Criminal Law, Criminology and Police Science* 60, no. 3 (September 1969): 306–13.

Cases

Gideon v. Wainwright, 372 U.S. 335 (1963).
Gitlow v. New York, 268 U.S. 652 (1924).
Ker v. California, 374 U.S. 23 (1963).
Malloy v. Hogan, 378 U.S. 1 (1964).
Mapp v. Ohio, 367 U.S. 643 (1961).
Palko v. Connecticut, 302 U.S. 319 (1937).
Pointer v. Texas, 380 U.S. 400 (1965).
Robinson v. California, 370 U.S. 660 (1962).

Chapter VIII

The Right to Counsel

In England, prior to 1836, the accused was not allowed legal counsel in felony cases unless the charge was associated with treason, but defendants in minor cases had legal right to appear with counsel. It was an incongruous practice as the accused was denied the assistance of counsel in cases where death was likely to be the most common penalty, yet was allowed counsel in cases involving a fine or, at most, short imprisonment. Judges, aware of the ironic circumstances, usually permitted counsel. Between 1836 and 1850, there was some legislative action for reform and, in 1850, Parliament specifically provided that all persons tried for felonies should be allowed, after the close of the case for the prosecution, to make full answer and defense to the prosecution's case, by counsel "learned in the law."[1]

In America, the colonists were aware that an accused, undefended by counsel, was at a serious disadvantage. After the Revolution, most states included a clause respecting the right to counsel in their state constitutions; and, in 1791, the right to the assistance of counsel became part of the Constitution as a clause in the Sixth Amendment's specification of the mode of criminal proceedings: ". . . and to have the assistance of counsel for his defense."

A defendant's need for a lawyer is nowhere better stated than in the moving words of Mr. Justice George Sutherland in *Powell* v. *Alabama:*

> The right to be heard would be, in many cases, of little avail if it did not comprehend the right to be heard by counsel. Even the intelligent and

1. William M. Beaney, *The Right to Counsel in American Courts* (Ann Arbor: University of Michigan Press, 1955), pp. 8–24.

educated layman has small and sometimes no skill in the science of law. If charged with crime, he is incapable, generally, of determining for himself whether the indictment is good or bad. He is unfamiliar with the rules of evidence. Left without the aid of counsel he may be put on trial without a proper charge, and convicted upon incompetent evidence, or evidence irrelevant to the issue or otherwise inadmissible. He lacks both the skill and knowledge adequately to prepare his defense, even though he have a perfect one. He requires the guiding hand of counsel at every step in the proceedings against him. Without it, though he be not guilty, he faces the danger of conviction because he does not know how to establish his innocence.[2]

While a defendant in a criminal proceeding also has a constitutionally guaranteed right to represent himself (to appear *pro se*) at trial, this right has long been aligned with the common saying that "a man who represents himself in the legal arena has a fool for a client." In fact, courts not only recognize the need for counsel by defendants without funds to employ their own lawyers, but also acknowledge the fact that many illiterate or uneducated inmates of correctional institutions do not have access to qualified attorneys. They may use their right to counsel to seek help from a knowledgeable fellow inmate who can prepare applications for habeas corpus and other legal remedies.

The right of an accused to legal assistance at trial has always been linked with the right to effective counsel, and courts have uniformly allowed time for retained or appointed counsel to prepare their cases prior to trial. Traditionally, appointed or assigned counsel are appointed early in the proceedings. This has always meant not later than the first judicial appearance. Appointment of counsel subsequent to this stage of criminal proceedings is considered an untimely appointment and creates a presumption that the defendant's rights were prejudiced, and this shifts the burden of showing the contrary to the state. Aligned with this time needed for preparation and the concept of effective counsel, recent decisions of the Supreme Court have extended the right of legal counsel to the pretrial period.

Three landmark cases[3] in the area of criminal procedure have established new horizons in the "time clock" of criminal justice. The Court's decisions in these cases have advanced the right to counsel to the time at which: (1) an investigation focuses upon one suspect; (2) a suspect is subjected to custodial interrogation; and (3) a suspect is made part of a lineup for identification by eyewitnesses. In addition to having advanced the time at which a person suspected or accused of a crime is entitled to legal counsel to the pretrial period necessary for preparation of the case for the defense, the Court has established an

2. Powell v. Alabama, 287 U.S. 45 (1932) pp. 68–69.
3. Escobedo v. Illinois, 378 U.S. 478 (1964); Miranda v. Arizona, 387 U.S. 436 (1966); United States v. Wade. 338 U.S. 218 (1967).

additional procedural safeguard in requiring the police to warn a suspect or accused person of his constitutional rights to silence *and* legal counsel.[4]

The Indigent Accused

The right to counsel is never a problem when the accused has sufficient funds to retain a lawyer of his own choosing. Even prior to the ratification of the Sixth Amendment, legislation was enacted stating that every person indicted for treason or other capital crime would be allowed to make a full defense by counsel. In felony cases less serious than capital crimes, some members of the judiciary made a practice of appointing lawyers to defend accused persons without funds, but it was not a common practice.

Over many, many years, however, an emerging belief developed for the right to counsel by indigent defendants in all criminal proceedings. In 1963, a convict in Florida finally achieved this goal. Clarence Earl Gideon sent a handwritten appeal to the U.S. Supreme Court, along with a written motion to proceed in *forma pauperis* (as a person without funds for an attorney or formal documents), and papers showing that the Florida Supreme Court had denied his application for a writ of habeas corpus (an order to free him because he was unjustly imprisoned). Gideon claimed his trial for a felony without an attorney deprived him of the due process of law.[5]

The high court responded to Gideon's appeal for a legal remedy and in the landmark case of *Gideon* v. *Wainwright*[6] they reversed his conviction and ordered a new trial. The essence of the U.S. Supreme Court's decision in this case was that America was a country in which a person accused of crime would be capably defended no matter what his financial circumstances, and that the lawyer representing an indigent defendant would do so with pride and a knowledge that all of the support necessary to prepare an adequate defense would also be available. The Court held that every defendant in a criminal proceeding who desires a lawyer should have one (even if legal counsel had to be appointed at state expense for indigent defendants). This was guaranteed by the Sixth Amendment right to counsel.

Some of the key language of the *Gideon* majority opinion indicates

4. Miranda v. Arizona, 387 U.S. 436 (1966), and Escobedo v. Illinois, 378 U.S. 478 (1964).

5. Anthony Lewis, *Gideon's Triumph* (New York: Random House, 1964), pp. 3–10, 205–10.

6. 372 U.S. 355 (1963).

the court's viewpoint about the right to counsel for indigent persons accused of crime. For instance:

1. Reason and reflection require us to recognize that any person haled into court, who is too poor to hire a lawyer, cannot be assured a fair trial unless counsel is provided for him.

2. Lawyers in criminal courts are necessities, not luxuries.

3. This noble ideal (fair trial) cannot be realized if the poor man charged with crime has to face his accusers without a lawyer to assist him.

The right to appointed counsel cannot logically be based on the name given a crime. It is simply impossible to draw a distinction between the right to counsel in misdemeanor, high misdemeanors, and felony cases merely because of terminology. The possible loss of liberty to an innocent person charged with a misdemeanor, who does not know how to defend himself, is too important a right to be sacrificed on the altar of expedience. A community that can afford a professional prosecuting attorney to prosecute these lesser crimes can also assume the burden of providing adequate defense counsel for accused persons financially unable to employ counsel, so that the innocent accused will not be convicted because of an inadequate defense.

The President's Commission on Law Enforcement and Administration of Justice made the following recommendation:

> The objective to be met as quickly as possible is to provide counsel to every criminal defendant who faces a significant penalty, if he cannot afford to provide counsel himself. This should apply to cases classified as misdemeanors as well as those classified as felonies.[7]

It is the duty of counsel appointed to represent an indigent defendant to respond to the needs of this client as he responds to the needs of other clients who retain him, and to remain in the case until prosecution is terminated or until other counsel is assigned in the trial court. His duties include informing any succeeding counsel, by way of a brief report, of all action previously taken and of any information relevant to the defendant's case.

The Public Defender

Los Angeles County, California, began its public defender system in 1913, the first in the United States. It is now a complex organization with a central office and branch offices. From that early beginning, the

7. The President's Commission on Law Enforcement and Administration of Justice, *The Challenge of Crime in a Free Society* (Washington, D.C.: U.S. Government Printing Office, 1967), p. 150.

public defender concept has spread throughout California and, in other forms, throughout the nation. This system for providing legal counsel for indigent defendants is now providing qualified lawyers for accused persons in both felony and misdemeanor cases, and for juveniles appearing in juvenile court on petitions of delinquency. In addition, counsel is provided for hearings in relation to insanity, such as sexual psychopath proceedings and mental illness hearings. Its services range from implementation of the *Miranda* rule (police interrogations) and release on personal recognizance in lieu of bail, through the preliminary hearings and trial on the issue of guilt or innocence, to appeals. For an accused person to be eligible for the services of a defender he must be financially unable to employ legal counsel. Courts can appoint counsel for indigent defendants, but such appointments are coordinated with the public defender's office to make certain the additional cost is justified. To insure full use of the public defender system, county officials or local agencies only approve payment to appointed counsel when the public defender cannot supply an attorney, or there is a conflict of interest.

In 1960, a state agency was established to perform similar services throughout Massachusetts: The Massachusetts Defenders Committee. In 1967, a new statewide public defender system was established in New Jersey. In various forms, this concept of a public or voluntary agency that serves as a central supply of attorneys to represent indigent defendants is spreading at either county or state levels.

The public defender system is more economically valuable to the community than the old system of appointing lawyers from a pool of attorneys willing to accept such work, and paying appropriate fees for each case. It is claimed that it is better than a system based on a pool of lawyers who volunteered in the public interest (or were coerced into volunteering by a local court) and who were paid no more than token fees, if anything. Public defenders offer every indigent defendant an established competency and experience in legal services, and the support of an office well-staffed with clerical and stenographic help and competent investigators. In the past, some appointed attorneys could ill afford the necessary time to defend an indigent client. In the public defender system, all of the time of a public defender is spent on behalf of indigent clients, just as all of the time of a prosecuting attorney is spent on prosecuting accused persons.

Success in the defense of any client accused of crime depends upon many things and various circumstances—as well as the competency of defense counsel. There is a belief throughout the country that the public defender system is less costly to government and better serves the interests of indigent defendants than past systems which appointed legal counsel for indigent defendants.

Counsel *Pro se*

When a person accused of crime intelligently waives his right to legal counsel and asks that the court permit him to represent himself, he appears *pro se:* in his own behalf. In some county jails in California, *pro se* defendants who have been unable to arrange release on bail or personal recognizance, are given cells in which telephones are installed. They can then conduct their defense adequately despite confinement prior to trial.

While a defendant has the right to defend himself without the assistance of counsel, and an equal right to discharge his attorney and defend *pro se* prior to commencement of his trial, a trial court must have a basis for allowing the defendant to represent himself. In addition, once a trial has begun, the defendant has no absolute right to discharge his attorney and defend himself. To allow such action, a trial court must be convinced that to do otherwise would be to prejudice the rights of the defendant.

The defendant must fully understand his right to retained or assigned counsel, and the court must ascertain whether the waiver of counsel is made intelligently and with full knowledge of the duties of legal counsel. The court must also be assured by the defendant's background (education or experience) that he has the capability of representing himself adequately, and be assured by the defendant's actions and attitudes that there will be no undue interference with the orderly procedure of the trial. It is reversible error by the trial court if a person appearing *pro se* is grossly ineffective in this role or acts in a violent and abusive manner during court proceedings.

Counsel—When a Case Focuses

The 1964 case of *Escobedo* v. *Illinois*[8] was the landmark case which established the right of counsel when a police investigation is no longer a general inquiry into an unsolved crime, but has begun to focus on a particular suspect already in police custody.

Police arrested Escobedo for the homicide of his brother–in–law, but he made no statement, and secured an attorney. His counsel filed for habeas corpus in a state court and Escobedo was ordered released. About ten days later, police again arrested Escobedo and took him to police headquarters for interrogation. Escobedo now made several requests to see his lawyer, who, though present in the building, and despite persistent efforts, was refused access to his client. Petitioner was not advised by the police of his right to remain silent and, after

8. 378 U.S. 478 (1964).

persistent questioning by the police, made a damaging statement which was admitted at the trial. Convicted of murder, he appealed to the state supreme court, which affirmed the conviction.

When a police investigation ceases to be a general inquiry into an unsolved crime and begins to focus on a particular suspect in police custody, if that suspect has been refused an opportuntiy to consult with his counsel and has not been warned of his constitutional right to keep silent, then the procedures have been in violation of the Sixth and Fourteenth Amendments. No statement extracted by the police during the interrogation may be used against him at a trial.

The critical question in this case is whether, under the circumstances, the police refusal to honor the petitioner's request to consult with his lawyer during the course of an interrogation constitutes a denial of the assistance of counsel. This is in violation of the Sixth Amendment to the Constitution as made obligatory upon the states by the Fourteenth Amendment; and thereby renders inadmissible in a state criminal trial any incriminating statement elicited by the police during the interrogation.

The following are selected extracts from the court's majority opinion in *Escobedo:*

> The interrogation here was conducted before petitioner was formally indicted. But in the context of this case, that fact should make no difference. When petitioner requested, and was denied, an opportunity to consult with his lawyer, the investigation had ceased to be a general investigation of an unsolved crime. Petitioner had become the accused, and the purpose of the interrogation was to get him to confess his guilt despite his constitutional right not to do so. At the time of his arrest and throughout the course of the interrogation, the police told petitioner that they had convincing evidence that he had fired the fatal shots. Without informing him of his absolute right to remain silent in the face of this accusation, the police urged him to make a statement.

> It is argued that if the right to counsel is afforded prior to indictment, the number of confessions obtained by the police will diminish significantly, because most confessions are obtained during the period between arrest and indictment, and any lawyer worth his salt will tell the suspect in no uncertain terms to make no statement to police under any circumstances. This argument, of course, cuts two ways. The fact that many confessions are obtained during this period points up its critical nature as a stage when legal aid and advice are surely needed. The right to counsel would indeed be hollow if it began at a period when few confessions were obtained. There is necessarily a direct relationship between the importance of a stage to the police in their quest for a confession and the criticalness of that stage to the accused in his need for legal advice. Our Constitution, unlike some others, strikes the balance in favor of the right of the accused to be advised by his lawyer of his privilege against self-incrimination.

We have learned the lesson of history, ancient and modern, that a system of criminal law enforcement which comes to depend on the "confession" will, in the long run, be less reliable and more subject to abuses than a system which depends on extrinsic evidence independently secured through skillful investigation.

We have also learned the companion lesson of history that no system of criminal justice can, or should survive if it comes to depend for its continued effectiveness on the citizens' abdication through unawareness of their constitutional rights. No system worth preserving should have to fear that if an accused is permitted to consult with a lawyer, he will become aware of, and exercise, these rights. If the exercise of constitutional rights will thwart the effectiveness of a system of law enforcement, then there is something very wrong with that system.

We hold, therefore, that where, as here, the investigation is no longer a general inquiry into an unsolved crime but has begun to focus on a particular suspect, the suspect has been taken into police custody, the police carry out a process of interrogations that lends itself to eliciting incriminating statements, the suspect has requested and been denied an opportunity to consult with his lawyer, and the police have not effectively warned him of his absolute constitutional right to remain silent, the accused has been denied "the Assistance of Counsel" in violation of the Sixth Amendment to the Constitution as "made obligatory upon the States by the Fourteenth Amendment," *Gideon v. Wainwright,* 372 U.S., at 342, and that no statement elicited by the police during the interrogation may be used against him at a criminal trial.

Nothing we have said today affects the powers of the police to investigate an unsolved crime by gathering information from witnesses and by other proper investigative efforts. We hold only that when the process shifts from investigatory to accusatory—when its focus is on the accused and its purpose is to elicit a confession—our adversary system begins to operate, and, under the circumstances here, the accused must be permitted to consult with his lawyer.

The facts of this case, the Court's holding, and the selected extracts from the majority opinion signify a new alertness on the part of the nation's high court to insure the preservation of the intrinsic value of the constitutional guarantee of the right to legal assistance: that it should be helpful to the person accused of a crime and not negated by pretrial procedures.

Counsel—When a Suspect is Interrogated

The many decisions of the U.S. Supreme Court that are known as "the confession cases"[9] (a long history of correcting individual viola-

9. Beginning with Brown v. Mississippi, 297 U.S. 278 (1936).

tions of a suspect's rights during pretrial interrogation sessions), culminated in a landmark decision with a definitive majority opinion that established the time of police interrogation as a time when a suspect was entitled not only to legal counsel, but also to a warning about his right to silence.

In each of these cases[10] the defendant, while in police custody, was questioned by police officers, detectives, or a prosecuting attorney in a room in which he was cut off from the outside world. None of the defendants was given a full and effective warning of his rights at the outset of the interrogation process. In all four cases the questioning elicited oral admissions—and in three of them, signed statements as well—which were admitted at their trials. All defendants were convicted.

Ernesto Miranda was arrested at his home, taken in custody to a Phoenix police station, identified by the complaining witness, then taken to an interrogation room in the detective bureau. There he was questioned by two police officers. Miranda was not advised that he had a right to an attorney present. Two hours later, the officers emerged from the interrogation room with a written confession signed by Miranda. At the top of the statement was a typed paragraph stating that the confession was made voluntarily, without threats or promises of immunity and "with full knowledge of my legal rights, understanding any statement I make may be used against me."

At his jury trial, the written confession was admitted into evidence over the objection of defense counsel, and the two officers testified to the prior oral confession made by Miranda during the interrogation. Miranda was found guilty of kidnapping and rape. The U.S. Supreme Court reversed the trial court's action, ruling that Miranda's constitutional rights were violated. The statements of guilt being obtained under circumstances that did not meet constitutional standards for protection of the privilege against self-incrimination.

The following are selected extracts from the court's majority opinion in *Miranda:*

> We start here, as we did in *Escobedo*, with the premise that our holding is not an innovation in our jurisprudence, but is an application of principles long recognized and applied in other settings. We have undertaken a thorough re-examination of the *Escobedo* decision and the principles it announced, and we reaffirm it. That case was but an explication of basic rights that are enshrined in our Constitution—that "No person . . . shall be compelled in any criminal case to be a witness against himself," and that "the accused shall . . . have the Assistance of Counsel"—rights which were put in jeopardy in that case through official overbearing. These precious rights were fixed in our Constitution only after centuries of

10. Miranda v. Arizona, Vignera v. New York, Westover v. United States, and California v. Stewart 387 U.S. 436 (1966). usually cited as *Miranda* v. *Arizona,* 387 U.S. 436 (1966).

persecution and struggle. And in the words of Chief Justice Marshall, they were secured "for ages to come, and ... designed to approach immortality as nearly as human institutions can approach it," *Cohens v. Virginia*, 6 Wheat. 264, 387 (1821).

Over 70 years ago, our predecessors on this Court eloquently stated:

"The maxim *nemo tenetur seipsum accusare** had its origin in a protest against the inquisitorial and manifestly unjust methods of interrogating accused persons, which (have) long obtained in the continental system, and, until the expulsion of the Stuarts from the British throne in 1688, and the erection of additional barriers for the protection of the people against the exercise of arbitrary power, (were) not uncommon even in England. While the admissions or confessions of the prisoner, when voluntarily and freely made, have always ranked high in the scale of incriminating evidence, if an accused person be asked to explain his apparent connection with a crime under investigation, the ease with which the questions put to him may assume an inquisitorial character, the temptation to press the witness unduly, to browbeat him if he be timid or reluctant, to push him into a corner, and to entrap him into fatal contradictions, which is so painfully evident in many of the earlier state trials, notably in those of Sir Nicholas Throckmorton, and Udal, the Puritan minister, made the system so odious as to give rise to a demand for its total abolition. The change in the English criminal procedure in that particular seems to be founded upon no statute and no judicial opinion, but upon a general and silent acquiescence of the courts in a popular demand. But, however adopted, it has become firmly embedded in English, as well as in American jurisprudence. So deeply did the iniquities of the ancient system impress themselves upon the minds of the American colonists that the States, with one accord, made a denial of the right to question an accused person a part of their fundamental law, so that a maxim, which in England was a mere rule of evidence, became clothed in this country with the impregnability of a constitutional enactment. *Brown v. Walker*, 161 U.S. 591, 596–597 (1896)."

In these cases, we might not find the defendants' statements to have been involuntary in traditional terms. Our concern for adequate safeguards to protect precious Fifth Amendment rights is, of course, not lessened in the slightest. In each of the cases, the defendant was thrust into an unfamiliar atmosphere and run through menacing police interrogation procedures.

It is obvious that such an interrogation environment is created for no purpose other than to subjugate the individual to the will of his examiner. This atmosphere carries its own badge of intimidation. To be sure, this is not physical intimidation, but it is equally destructive of human dignity. The current practice of incommunicado interrogation is at odds with one of our Nation's most cherished principles—that the individual may not be compelled to incriminate himself. Unless adequate protective devices are employed to dispel the compulsion inherent in custodial surroundings,

---

*No one is bound to accuse himself.

no statement obtained from the defendant can truly be the product of his free choice.

We have recently noted that the privilege against self–incrimination—the essential mainstay of our adversary system—is founded on a complex of values. All these policies point to one overriding thought: the constitutional foundation underlying the privilege is the respect a government—state or federal—must accord to the dignity and integrity of its citizens. To maintain a fair state–individual balance, to require the government to shoulder the entire load, to respect the inviolability of the human personality, our accusatory system of criminal justice demands that the government seeking to punish an individual produce the evidence against him by its own independent labors, rather than by the cruel, simple expedient of compelling it from his own mouth. In sum, the privilege is fulfilled only when the person is guaranteed the right "to remain silent unless he chooses to speak in the unfettered exercise of his own will."

The circumstances surrounding in–custody interrogation can operate very quickly to overbear the will of one merely made aware of his privilege by his interrogators. *Therefore, the right to have counsel present at the interrogation is indispensable to the protection of the Fifth Amendment privilege under the system we delineate today.** Our aim is to assure that the individual's right to choose between silence and speech remains unfettered throughout the interrogation process. A once–stated warning, delivered by those who will conduct the interrogation, cannot itself suffice to that end among those who most require knowledge of their rights. A mere warning given by the interrogators is not alone sufficient to accomplish that end.

*Thus, the need for counsel to protect the Fifth Amendment privilege comprehends not merely a right to consult with counsel prior to questioning, but also to have counsel present during any questioning if the defendant so desires.** Accordingly we hold that an individual held for interrogation must be clearly informed that he has *the right to consult with a lawyer and to have the lawyer with him during interrogation** under the system for protecting the privilege we delineate today.

On the important issue of guilt or innocence, a careful review of the two foregoing decisions dictates the conclusion that an accused's statement procured either after failure to give him an opportunity to consult with his counsel, failure to warn him of his right to remain silent, or in the absence of police attempts to advise the accused person of his constitutional rights, cannot be employed at trial.

Counsel—When a Suspect is Placed in Police Lineup

In the case of *United States* v. *Wade*,[11] the U.S. Supreme Court moved the right to counsel forward in the time clock of a criminal proceeding, to the time of a pretrial police lineup.

*Emphasis added.

11. 388 U.S. 218 (1967).

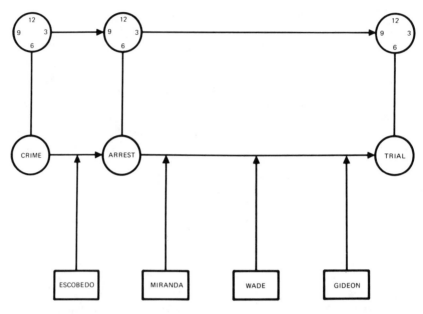

The right to legal counsel. Shown here is the extension of this right to a time earlier than the time of trial (Gideon), to police lineups (Wade), to any custodial interrogation (Miranda), and to the time between the crime and the arrest when the police investigation focuses on a particular suspect (Escobedo).

A federally insured bank was robbed by a man with a small strip of tape on each side of his face. He pointed a pistol at the female cashier and the vice-president, the only persons in the bank at the time, and forced them to fill a pillowcase with the bank's money. The robber then drove away with an accomplice who had been waiting in a stolen car outside the bank. After an investigation, during which the two eye witnesses selected Wade's mug-shot photograph from among others presented to them by FBI agents, an indictment was returned against Wade for conspiring to rob the bank, and for the robbery itself. Wade was arrested and counsel was appointed to represent him.

Fifteen days later an FBI agent, without notice to Wade's lawyer, arranged to have the two bank employees observe a lineup made up of Wade and five or six other prisoners and conducted in a courtroom of the local county courthouse. Each person in the line wore strips of tape such as allegedly worn by the robber and upon direction each said something like "put the money in the bag," the words allegedly uttered by the robber. Both bank employees identified Wade in the lineup as the bank robber. At trial, the two employees, when asked on direct examination if the robber was in the courtroom, pointed to

Wade. The prior lineup identification was then elicited from both employees on cross-examination. At the close of testimony, Wade's counsel moved for a judgment of acquittal or, alternatively, to strike the bank employees' courtroom identifications on the ground that conduct of the lineup, without notice to and in the absence of his appointed counsel, violated his Fifth Amendment privilege against self-incrimination and his Sixth Amendment right to the assistance of counsel. The motion was denied, and Wade was convicted.

The court's ruling in *Wade* was:

1. Neither the lineup itself nor anything required therein violated respondent's Fifth Amendment privilege against self-incrimination since merely exhibiting his person for observation by witnesses and using his voice as identifying physical characteristic involved no compulsion of the accused to give evidence of a testimonial nature against himself which is prohibited by that Amendment.

2. *The Sixth Amendment guarantees an accused the right to counsel not only at his trial but at any critical confrontation by the prosecution at pretrial proceedings where the results might well determine his fate and where the absence of counsel might derogate from his right to a fair trial.**

3. *The post-indictment lineup* (unlike such preparatory steps as analyzing fingerprints and blood samples) *was a critical prosecutive stage at which respondent was entitled to the aid of counsel.**

   a. There is a great possibility of unfairness to the accused at that point, (1) because of the manner in which confrontations for identification are frequently conducted, (2) because of dangers inherent in eyewitness identification and suggestibility inherent in the context of the confrontations, and (3) because of the likelihood that the accused will often be precluded from reconstructing what occurred and thereby obtaining a full hearing on the identification issue at trial.

   b. This case illustrates the potential for improper influence on witnesses through the lineup procedure, since the bank employees were allowed to see respondent in the custody of FBI agents before the lineup began.

   c. *The presence of counsel** at the lineup will significantly promote fairness at the confrontation and a full hearing at trial on the issue of identification.

4. In–court identification by a witness to whom the accused was exhibited before trial *in the absence of counsel** must be excluded unless it can be established that such evidence had an independent origin or that error in its admission was harmless. Since it is not clear that

*Emphasis added.

the Court of Appeals applied the prescribed rule of exclusion, and since the nature of the in–court identifications here was not an issue in the trial and cannot be determined on the record, the case must be remanded to the District Court for resolution of these issues.

Selected extracts from the majority opinion in *Wade* are:

The fact that the lineup involved no violation of Wade's privilege against self-incrimination does not, however, dispose of his contention that the courtroom identifications should have been excluded because the lineup was conducted without notice to and in the absence of his counsel.

When the Bill of Rights was adopted, there were no organized police forces as we know them today. The accused confronted the prosecutor and the witnesses against him, and the evidence was marshalled, largely at the trial itself. In contrast, today's law enforcement machinery involves critical confrontations of the accused by the prosecution at pretrial proceedings where the results might well settle the accused's fate and reduce the trial itself to a mere formality. In recognition of these realities of modern criminal prosecution, our cases have construed the Sixth Amendment guarantee to apply to "critical" stages of the proceedings. The guarantee reads: "In all criminal prosecutions, the accused shall enjoy the right . . . to have the Assistance of Counsel *for his defense.*'* The plain wording of this guarantee thus encompasses counsel's assistance whenever necessary to assure a meaningful "defense."

As early as *Powell* v. *Alabama*,[12] we recognized that the period from arraignment to trial was perhaps the most critical period of the proceedings, during which the accused requires the guiding hand of counsel, if the guarantee is not to prove an empty right. That principle has since been applied to require the assistance of counsel at the type of arraignment—for example, that provided by Alabama—where certain rights might be sacrificed or lost: "What happens there may affect the whole trial. Available defenses may be irretrievably lost, if not then and there asserted." *Hamilton* v. *Alabama*, 368 U.S. 52.

The principle was also applied in *Massiah* v. *United States*, 377 U.S. 201, where we held that incriminating statements of the defendant should have been excluded from evidence when it appeared that they were overheard by federal agents who, without notice to the defendant's lawyer, arranged a meeting between the defendant and an accomplice turned informant.

The Government characterized the lineup as a mere preparatory step in the gathering of the prosecution's evidence, not different—for Sixth Amendment purposes—from the various other preparatory steps, such as systematized or scientific analyzing of the accused's fingerprints, blood sample, clothing, hair, and the like. We think there are differences which preclude such stages being characterized as critical stages at which the accused has the right to the presence of his counsel. Knowledge of the techniques of science and technology is sufficiently available, and the

*Emphasis added.
12. 287 U.S. 45 (1932).

variables in techniques few enough, that the accused has the opportunity for a meaningful confrontation of the Government's case at trial through the ordinary processes of cross-examination of the Government's expert witnesses and the presentation of the evidence of his own experts. The denial of a right to have his counsel present at such analysis does not therefore violate the Sixth Amendment; they are not critical stages since there is minimal risk that his counsel's absence at such stages might derogate from his right to a fair trial. But the confrontation compelled by the State between the accused and the victim or eyewitnesses to a crime to elicit identification evidence is peculiarly riddled with innumerable dangers and variable factors which might seriously, even crucially, derogate from a fair trial.

The vagaries of eyewitness identification are well-known; the annals of criminal law are rife with instances of mistaken identification. A major factor contributing to the high incidence of miscarriage of justice from mistaken identification has been the degree of suggestion inherent in the manner in which the prosecution presents the suspect to witnesses for pretrial identification. Suggestion can be created intentionally or unintentionally in many subtle ways. And the dangers for the suspect are particularly grave when the witness' opportunity for observation was insubstantial, and thus his susceptibility to suggestion the greatest.

The impediments to an objective observation are increased when the victim is the witness. Lineups are prevalent in rape and robbery prosecutions and present a particular hazard that a victim's understandable outrage may excite vengeful or spiteful motives. In any event, neither witnesses nor lineup participants are apt to be alert for conditions prejudicial to the suspect. And if they were, it would likely be of scant benefit to the suspect since neither witnesses nor lineup participants are likely to be schooled in the detection of suggestive influences. Improper influences may go undetected by a suspect, guilty or not, who experiences the emotional tension which we might expect in one being confronted with potential accusers. Even when he does observe abuse, if he has a criminal record he may be reluctant to take the stand and open up the admission of prior convictions. Moreover, any protestations by the suspect of the fairness of the lineup made at trial are likely to be in vain. The jury's choice is between the accused's unsupported version and that of the police officers present. In short, the accused's inability effectively to reconstruct at trial any unfairness that occurred at the lineup may deprive him of his only opportunity meaningfully to attack the credibility of the witness' courtroom identification.

What facts have been disclosed in specific cases about the conduct of pretrial confrontations for identification illustrate both the potential for substantial prejudice to the accused at that stage and the need for its revelation at trial. In sum, the principle of *Powell* v. *Alabama* and succeeding cases requires that we scrutinize any pretrial confrontation of the accused to determine whether the presence of his counsel is necessary to preserve the defendant's basic right to a fair trial as affected by his right meaningfully to cross-examine the witnesses against him and to have effective assistance of counsel at the trial itself. It calls upon us to analyze whether potential substantial prejudice to defendant's rights inheres in the particular confrontation and the ability of counsel to help avoid that prejudice.

Of course, nothing decided or said in the opinions in the cited cases links the right to counsel only to protection of Fifth Amendment rights. Rather those decisions no more than reflect a constitutional principle established as long ago as *Powell* v. *Alabama*. It is central to that principle that in addition to counsel's presence at trial, the accused is guaranteed that he need not stand alone against the State at any stage of the prosecution, formal or informal, in court or out, where counsel's absence might derogate from the accused's right to a fair trial. The security of that right is as much the aim of the right to counsel as it is of the other guarantees of the Sixth Amendment—the right of the accused to a speedy and public trial by an impartial jury, his right to be informed of the nature and cause of the accusation, and his right to be confronted with the witnesses against him and to have compulsory process for obtaining witnesses in his favor. The presence of counsel at such critical confrontations, as at the trial itself, operates to assure that the accused's interests will be protected consistently with our adversary theory of criminal prosecution.

Jail House Lawyers and Habeas Corpus

A strange extension of the right to counsel has developed because of the lack of attorneys available to prisoners confined in state prisons or local jails. In a few areas, there is a regular system of assistance by public defenders, or law-school students. In most areas one or more inmates advise, aid, or assist other inmates to prepare writs and other legal matters. Partly in the interest of limiting the practice of law to licensed attorneys, and partly to preserve prison discipline, jailhouse lawyers are often disciplined by prison or jail authorities, and forbidden to continue helping other inmates as substitutes for legal counsel. However, in the reality that is institutional life in American prisons and jails, if illiterate or poorly educated prisoners cannot have the assistance of a jailhouse lawyer to file habeas corpus petitions their possibly valid constitutional claims will never be heard in any court.

It is reasonable to control any propensity of prisoners to abuse both the giving and seeking of assistance in the preparation of applications for legal remedies related to their imprisonment. On the other hand, unless and until the administrator of a prison or jail provides a reasonable alternative to jailhouse lawyers—such as public defenders or voluntary legal assistance—to assist inmates in the preparation of petitions for postconviction relief, it does not serve the ends of justice to enforce a regulation barring capable prisoners from furnishing such assistance to other less capable inmates.

The jailhouse lawyer who assists other prisoners in seeking habeas corpus and other legal remedies is no less than an extension of the Sixth Amendment's right to counsel in a rudimentary form.

Selected References

Books

Beaney, William M. *The Right to Counsel in American Courts.* Ann Arbor: University of Michigan Press, 1955.
Lewis, Anthony. *Gideon's Triumph.* New York: Random House, 1964.

Cases

Escobedo v. Illinois, 378 U.S. 478 (1964).
Gideon v. Wainwright, 372 U.S. 355 (1963).
Miranda v. Arizona, 387 U.S. 436 (1966).
United States v. Wade, 388 U.S. 218 (1967).

Chapter IX

Criminal Proceedings: Prosecutor, Defense Counsel, Judge

The basic thrust of justice in the criminal courts of the United States is to accuse and prove at trial: accusatorial. The accusatorial method necessarily implies a conflict between the state (the people) and the person accused of crime. However, in this instance, conflict is not a destructive force; in the courts of America, conflict is a creative force. Our system of justice is called the adversary system, wherein the inherent conflict is a creative force for discovering truth. This is a system that pits one adversary against another to find the truth. It is a system in which the conflict is resolved at a trial: a criminal proceeding in which the accusation is tested on the issue of guilt or innocence.

This testing at trial of an accusation of crime involves a classic triumvirate in America's legal system: the prosecuting attorney, the counsel for the defense, and the trial judge. The prosecutor and counsel for the defendant are adversaries: the prosecutor advocating the side of the accuser, and the defense attorney advocating the side of the defendant. The judge's role is to insure that the issues are joined within the rules of the legal system for the trial of persons accused of crime. In the three–sided interaction of prosecutor, attorney for the defense, and the trial judge, the court becomes a place where a fair balance is struck between the rights of the state and the rights of the individual.

In the prosecution of persons accused of crime in American courts, the formality of the procedure depends upon the seriousness of the

161

crime. Lesser offenses, such as traffic violations, are disposed of by a magistrate in summary proceedings, although the accused person has the right to seek a postponement and formalize the most minor hearing. A variety of offenses, from violations of local laws about sweeping sidewalks to petty theft, are also disposed of by a magistrate in the majority of cases, after the defendant has waived a more formal prosecution. It is in the trial of major offenses that the adversary system comes into full flower. These are the crimes at the felony level: the serious crimes in which the victim may be killed or injured; and crimes against property such as burglary or thefts in which the value of the stolen property exceeds $50.00 (or other minimum value).

In the trial of such crimes the accused shall enjoy the right to a speedy and public trial, and he has the right to representation by counsel, as well as other rights designed to safeguard persons accused of crime from an arbitrary, abusive, or wrongful process of criminal justice. The major provision of the Constitution dealing with the rights of an accused person and the mode of criminal proceedings is the Sixth Amendment:

> In all criminal prosecutions, the accused shall enjoy the right to a speedy and public trial, by an impartial jury of the state and district wherein the crime shall have been committed, which district shall have been previously ascertained by law, and to be informed of the nature and cause of the accusation; to be confronted with the witnesses against him; to have compulsory process for obtaining witnesses in his favor, and to have the assistance of counsel for his defense.

In addition, there is the Fifth Amendment guarantee of notice and preliminary investigation ("No person shall be held to answer for capital or otherwise infamous crime unless on a presentment or indictment of a grand jury. . ."); protection against double jeopardy (". . . nor shall any person be subject for the same offense to be twice put in jeopardy of life or limb. . ."); and privilege against self–incrimination (". . . nor shall be compelled in any criminal case to be a witness against himself. . ."). These were enacted to insure the protection of an accused person from arbitrary charges of crime and criminal proceedings by state or federal agents.

The criminal proceeding is to be a fair trial before an impartial tribunal, and it is to be preceded by a preliminary investigation by the prosecutor to insure that the crime committed is one which should be prosecuted. Then, if warranted, appropriate action is taken by the prosecutor to bring the accusation of crime before or within the power of the proper tribunal. The accused person must be given adequate notice of the offense charged against him, and an opportunity to prepare for trial, procure witnesses, and make such investigation as deemed necessary—with legal counsel to assist him in this work. Lastly, there should be provision for a suitable appellate review of the case.[1]

Moreover, the concept of a fair trial before an impartial tribunal has been further enhanced by recent U.S. Supreme Court decisions. These have made applicable to the states and their agents and courts the provisions of the Fourteenth Amendment which forbid abridging the privileges or immunities of citizens or depriving any person of life, liberty, or property without due process of law.

Other legal systems throughout the world reject the adversary system and depend upon one with an inquisitorial thrust, often unimpeded by any guarantees of individual rights or the assistance of legal counsel. The trial itself is merely an appeal from an extensive pretrial investigation, or an appeal from a custodial interrogation.[2] In such jurisdictions, a speedy trial or the right to representation by counsel at trial are very hollow things. For all practical purposes, the conviction of guilty had been assured by the pretrial procedure permitted the government agents, the police, and the prosecutor.

The Prosecuting Attorney

The prosecuting attorney may be called the public prosecutor, the district attorney, the county prosecutor, the county attorney, or the state's attorney. Regardless of the terminology used to identify this agent of criminal justice, his role is essentially the same across the United States. It is the role of a lawyer representing the people of the state in a criminal proceeding. Sometimes, the role overlaps with some functions and duties in regard to civil law and the best interest of the county government, but the chief function of the prosecuting attorney is enforcement of the law against criminals of every kind, and prosecution of offenders before appropriate courts.

Prosecution by a public official educated in law developed rapidly in America. While the colonists adopted the English attorney general concept, there was a definite and early trend to creating local political offices for persons charged with the duty of conducting criminal prosecutions. The statewide attorney general may have been handicapped by transportation problems in the early years, but there is evidence the colonists preferred local control of this important role in government. They proceeded in its development with enthusiasm because of a wish to decentralize the office of attorney general in regard to local prosecutions. In many states, the first step was the designation of an assistant or deputy attorney general with local or limited territorial jurisdiction. Later, the office became one in which the prosecuting attorney was

1. William M. Beaney, *The Right to Counsel In American Courts* (Ann Arbor: University of Michigan Press, 1955), pp. 4–5.
2. Escobedo v. Illinois, 378 U.S. 478 (1963), pp. 487–488.

elected by the people of the jurisdictional district.

With the advent of county government, this area of jurisdiction became the county. The prosecutor has a role in county government as legal advisor to county and other local officials (possibly defending the interests of the county in civil litigation). To some degree he is under the control of county government because of the budgetary administration of the office of the prosecuting attorney. In this balkanization of the ancient role of attorney general, it was never intended that a board of supervisors, or other county legislative or executive agents, be permitted to interfere with, or control the management of criminal prosecutions by the prosecuting attorney. In his capacity as prosecutor, the prosecuting attorney is clearly the agent of the state government and its people. He is under no direct control as public prosecutor because he acts by the authority and in the name of the *people* of the state.

The prosecuting attorney is the key law enforcement officer in the particular area over which he has jurisdiction. In this area, the potentialities of the office are limited only by the intelligence, skill, and legal and political capacity of the incumbent. In the formidable list of duties often assigned to this public official, the interests of the state is almost entirely in his hands. He is a quasi–judicial officer who determines from his own investigation, or evidence submitted to him by police or others, whether a criminal offense has been committed, and upon grounds of public policy the prosecuting attorney enjoys an absolute immunity from civil liability for his official acts (similar to judges and grand juries). The public interest demands the prosecuting attorney to speak and act freely and fearlessly in the discharge of his important official functions and duties. The prosecuting attorney is expected to be the mainspring of law enforcement. If evidence of a crime is not available—and there is good reason to believe it might be secured—he is supposed to go out and get it.[3] The specific functions of the prosecutor are:

1. To serve as an agent (agency) of the executive branch of government particularly charged with the duty to see that the laws are faithfully executed and enforced in order to maintain the rule of law.

2. To accept the dual role of administrator of justice and advocate, and exercise sound discretion in the performance of this role.

3. To seek justice, not merely convictions.

---

3. Raymond Moley, *Politics and Criminal Prosecution* (New York: Minton, Balch and Co., 1929), pp. 48–62.

4. To know and be guided by the standards of professional conduct as defined in codes and cannons of the legal profession.[4]

In performing his functions, the prosecuting attorney has considerable discretion at many decision points in the administration of criminal justice. However, the most important area of this discretionary power is the power to charge—or not to charge—a person with a crime. The decision to charge requires the resolution of three related, but independent issues:

1. A determination as to whether there is sufficient probability of guilt to justify bringing the case to trial.

2. Whether prosecution is in the community interest.

3. Decision making as to the specific crime or crimes to charge in the accusatory pleading.[5]

Nonlegal aspects of a case may suggest a decision not to charge an individual. Many prosecuting attorneys avoid family disputes unless a trial is vitally necessary to force a husband to recognize his responsibilities for his children; others hesitate to prosecute in cases of crimes without victims, or to serve as a collection agency in insufficient funds fraud check cases. In addition, the nature of a crime (nonprofessional gambling, shoplifting, fraud checks) may indicate that a jury will not focus on the issue of guilt or innocence, but will exercise their decision-making power to acquit the defendant for reasons unrelated to evidence of his guilt.

Many aspects of the decision to charge rests on standard legal issues. For instance:

1. Has a crime been committed?

2. What crime has been committed, both by common name and statute designation, and by the circumstances of the crime?

3. Was the crime committed within the area served by the prosecuting attorney?

4. Do the presence of facts indicate all of the elements of this crime in the circumstances of its happening?

5. Has the suspect been connected to the crime by either direct or indirect (circumstantial) evidence, or by the suspect's own statement?

4. Advisory Committee on the Prosecution and Defense Functions, American Bar Association, *Standards Relating to the Prosecution Function and the Defense Function—Tentative Draft* (New York: Institute of Judicial Administration, 1970), p. 43.
5. Frank W. Miller, *Prosecution—The Decision to Charge a Suspect With a Crime* (Boston: Little, Brown and Company, 1969), pp. 3–5.

6. Are there any legal problems precluding the successful prosecution of the suspect: missing witnesses, tainted evidence, double jeopardy, and so forth?

In preparing a case for trial, the prosecuting attorney sifts the evidence, and plans his case along the following lines: (1) presentation of the case in court; (2) proper direct examination of the state's witnesses and cross–examination of defense witnesses; (3) preparation of instructions for the use of the trial judge in charging the jury; and (4) preparation of the oral argument of the prosecution.

Usually, the presentation of a case in court is based on preparation before trial. In filing an accusatory pleading, the prosecuting attorney reviews the crime (offense) report, the arrest record, the connect–up sheet revealing the suspect's tie–ins with other crimes, the evidence summary and report, and the criminal history sheet of the suspect. Often, he interviews the investigating officers and prosecution witnesses, examines evidence, and participates in querying the accused. Then, in presenting the case to the grand jury for an indictment, or participating in a preliminary hearing before a magistrate at which the issue is whether the accused should be held to answer (predates the filing of an information by the prosecuting attorney), there is a review of the circumstances of the crime, the criminal agency, and the linking of the suspect to the crime and criminal agency. All of this is preparation for trial, and in the larger offices of prosecuting attorneys one or more assistants may participate in the case at these pretrial levels, and still another actually prepare the case for trial and take over its prosecution in court.

Traditionally, the prosecutor may best present his case in court by creating, from the beginning of the proceedings, an atmosphere of sincerity, earnestness, and confidence in the righteousness of his cause. The prosecuting attorney is, like all lawyers, a partisan in litigation, but as a public official he cannot allow this partisanship to lead him to an unjust harassment of the person accused. He should be as concerned with giving the accused a fair trial as he is of obtaining a conviction. He is an officer of the court and should be fair, seeking a conviction only by legal means. However, he is still the attorney for the people (the state) and may properly use legal means to secure a conviction. The suppression of facts or the secreting of witnesses capable of establishing the innocence of the accused is highly reprehensible. However, he is not bound to use as witnesses for the people any person whom he believes is mistaken as to the facts or likely to commit perjury; or to call any witness whose testimony he does not believe to be relevent or which might confuse the issue in dispute.

In direct examination of his witnesses, the prosecuting attorney seeks to preserve their credibility by revealing their ability to observe and recall their positions when they viewed the crime or a related event; their business at this place at this particular time; and all the other factors that make witnesses credible and their stories worthy of belief. In cross-examination, the prosecuting attorney attempts to destroy belief in the stories of defense witnesses by attacks on the personal knowledge of the witnesses and their motivation to tell the truth.

In making his requests to charge to the trial judge, the prosecuting attorney seeks to bring the appropriate sections of law to the attention of the jury. The substance of these requests varies with the circumstances of a case, but inherent in the advocacy of the state's case is to bring before the jury at the end of the trial, instructions that will present law and legal theory favorable to the prosecution and its case.

The prosecuting attorney's closing argument presents his case and its strong points, and points out the weakness and lack of merit in the defense case. Then, when it becomes time to reply to defense counsel's argument, the prosecuting attorney must destroy the defense argument. In both instances, this oral argument by the prosecuting attorney must be a well–founded and logical presentation utilizing the type of argument that can be followed easily and which will lead to reasonable conclusions. It must reconcile evidence in conflict with the prosecution's theory of the crime and the evidence structure of the case, and must destroy any favorable impressions the defense case may have made upon the minds of the jurors.[6]

The Defense Counsel

In California, the duties of an attorney are specified in state statutes as follows:

1. To support the Constitution and laws of the United States and of this State.

2. To maintain the respect due to the courts of justice and judicial officers.

3. To counsel or maintain such actions, proceedings or defenses only as appear to him legal or just, except the defense of a person charged with a public offense.

4. To employ, for the purpose of maintaining the causes confided to him such means only as are consistent with truth, and never to seek to mislead the judge or any judicial officer by an artifice or false statement of fact or law.

5. To maintain inviolate the confidence, and at every peril to himself to preserve the secrets, of his client.

6. Manley J. Bowler, "Oral Argument in Criminal Prosecution," *The Journal of Criminal Law, Criminology and Police Science* 52, No. 2, (July–August 1961): 203–9.

6. To abstain from all offensive personality, and to advance no fact prejudicial to the honor or reputation of a party or witness, unless required by the justice of the cause with which he is charged.

7. Not to encourage either the commencement or the continuance of an action or proceeding from any corrupt motive of passion or interest.

8. Never to reject, for any consideration personal to himself, the cause of the defenseless or the oppressed.[7]

In contrast to the prosecutor who has an attorney's responsibility to the people of the state, the county, and the accused, the counsel for the defense is responsible to his client only, within the bounds of the ethics of his profession and state law. He is the classic opponent of the prosecutor, and the protection of his client's rights may require him to oppose the wishes of the judge on various matters. He does this respectfully at all times, even when he must appear unyielding and uncooperative. As an advocate of his client he performs his function within our adversary system. He does not impede the administration of justice because he challenges the prosecutor or resists the judge, but rather fulfills his role in the administration of criminal justice. Defense counsel's obligations are multiple and complex. His obligation to his client is that of counselor and advocate; toward the prosecuting attorney he is a professional adversary; and toward the court he is an advocate for his client and a counselor to the court.

The specific function and role of defense counsel are:

1. Serve as the accused's counselor and advocate with courage, devotion and to the utmost of his learning and ability, and according to law.

2. Serve as the professional representative of the accused, not his alter ego. He has no duty to execute any directive of the accused which does not comport with law or professional standards of conduct, and it is unprofessional conduct for a lawyer intentionally to misrepresent matters of fact or law to the court.[8]

A defense attorney retains for himself an independence of action and control over the defense case. All tactical and strategical decisions, such as which jurors to keep or excuse, what witnesses to call, how to conduct cross–examination, and which trial motions to attempt, should be made by the defense attorney after consulting with his client.

7. *California Business and Professional Code*, Chapter 4, Section 6068.
8. *Standards Relating to the Prosecution and Defense Functions*, p. 153.

As the defendant, the client must finally decide, after consultation with his legal counsel, what plea to enter, whether to waive jury trial, and whether to testify in his own behalf.

For effective representation, the defense counsel must achieve a lawyer–client relationship with the accused. He must get the complete candor of the accused about the crime charged and its circumstances, and full consent to control the legal aspects of the defense case. When the accused understands the defense attorney's obligation of confidentiality in relation to any disclosures (privileged communication), this confidential relationship between lawyer and client will foster candor, and candor plus control establishes the basis for an effective defense.

Accused persons as clients often withhold information from their lawyers, sometimes for reasons of their own, but quite frequently because they believe this is the lawyer's desire. To break down this reluctance to disclose all the known facts, it is not uncommon for an attorney serving as defense counsel to use the "hard sell" to induce candor: a warning that if the client fails to disclose all relevant facts he will find himself looking for a new lawyer, as withdrawal from the case would be logical upon discovery of this lack of trust. Possibly some comment will be added about the reality of a criminal trial It may be pointed out that nothing the client can disclose is likely to be as embarrassing or incriminating as a handicapped defense counsel attempting to locate witnesses, interview them, and investigate the facts of their stories, only to have the defense case set back at trial by surprise testimony or other evidence. At the very least, defense counsel should know as much about the case as his client.

Every man accused of a crime is entitled to have a lawyer to present a legal defense. But in this client–lawyer relationship, the client is not entitled to have a lawyer who will permit the client or a witness to testify to something which the lawyer knows is untrue. If a defense attorney knows his client or a defense witness is not telling the truth, he should not be a party to the perjury. In the client–attorney preparation of a case for trial, the attorney should probe vigorously into the evidence which corroborates or refutes the proposed testimony which is to be offered in court, and thus prevent his introduction of false testimony.[9] However, it is not the attorney's duty to judge the weight of the evidence and determine where truth lies when the evidence is in conflict. This is the function of the trial jury, or judge in a trial without a jury.

The relationship between the defendant and defense counsel does not require the attorney to be a "mouthpiece" for his client: a mere mechanical reproduction of the thoughts, words, and alibi of his client.

9. Emory Buckner, "The Trial of Cases," in *The Lawyer's Treasury*, edited by Eugene C. Gerhart (New York: Bobbs-Merrill Company, Charter Books, 1963), pp. 400–01.

The lawyer's obligation to client, court, and community does not include the presentation of false or improper testimony, nor does it justify untruthfulness and insincerity, but it does include service as an advocate who will present all the relevant facts and circumstances in his client's defense. In fact, despite any belief in the guilt of the defendant, the defense attorney has a duty to present the extenuating facts and circumstances on behalf of his client.[10] The defense attorney must represent his client's side when his evidence and that of the prosecution are different. It is not for him to decide who is telling the truth when each side claims truth.

A defense attorney must advise his client against unlawful conduct, and must refuse to be a party to illegal conduct in his service. The problem becomes critical when a defendant desires to testify falsely and informs his attorney of his resolve to take the stand as a witness. However, the absolute prohibition against subornation applies where the defendant himself wishes to testify. Therefore, the defense attorney should withdraw from the case rather than place himself in the position of offering a perjurious witness.

Sometimes, such a critical situation is aggravated by the fact that withdrawal will leave the defendant without counsel, and the court is likely to deny a request to withdraw. There are conflicting views as to whether an attorney should disclose any part of this conflict to the court, but it seems that the lawyer's duty to maintain confidentiality between client and attorney will not permit such a disclosure.

In this conflict between the obligation of an attorney and the defendant's absolute right to testify in his own behalf, a suggested solution is to counsel against such a course of action by the defendant and advise him that he (defense counsel) will not use such testimony in any way in his oral argument. When this fails, the defense attorney may: (1) allow the defendant to testify in narrative form and in his own words, but without direct examination in the conventional manner, and (2) avoid any reference to the defendant's testimony in conducting the remainder of the defense case. In this fashion, the defense attorney avoids participation in a fraud on the court.

A defense attorney cannot presume a client is guilty before guilt is established in accordance with due process: a verdict and judgment of guilty after a fair trial in a court of competent jurisdiction. However, what if the accused admits guilt or the attorney discovers direct evidence of it? So far as the accused is concerned, he is entitled to plead not guilty (placing the burden of proof of guilt on the prosecution), and maintains right to counsel. When his reputation, livelihood, freedom, and even life, are hazarded, some lawyer must take his case. One

---

10. A. S. Cutler, "Is a Lawyer Bound to Support an Unjust Cause?" in *The Lawyer's Treasury*, pp. 420–27.

of the controlling factors in the plea decision is often whether the accused realizes the fact that obviously guilty persons have little evidence upon which to build a defense, and that the most appropriate action may be an attempt to achieve some bargain with the prosecuting attorney in exchange for a plea of guilty.[11]

The prosecution has the burden of proof on the issue of guilt. In the absence of a voluntary plea of guilty by the defendant, the defense attorney need present nothing, reveal no confidences of his client, nor furnish any other information to help the prosecution's case. The public interest not to convict innocent persons accused of crime permits the defense attorney to put the state and its prosecuting attorney to its proof. Regardless of what he may think as to the issue of guilt or innocence, it is his job to put the prosecution's case in the worst possible light.

It is common defense strategy to plan along the lines of one or more of the following common defenses. These are:

1. The defendant did not commit the crime—the accused is the victim of mistaken identification, poor investigation, or coincidence.

2. The defendant did commit the crime, but it was excusable (self–defense; provocation), an accident, or the result of insanity or other factors diminishing the accused's capacity to develop intent or plan the crime.

3. No crime was committed—one or more essential elements of the crime charged cannot be proved, or there is insufficient evidence to prove the corpus delicti.[12]

As the preparation of the defense case proceeds, beginning with the first client–lawyer interview, the defense counsel must develop a theory upon which to base his preparation for trial. This is a marshaling of facts so that by appropriate emphasis and orderly assembly at trial, the defense counsel can present evidence capable of arousing doubt in the minds of the jurors as to the guilt of the accused.

Jurors usually accept their grave responsibility and realize they have taken an oath to try the accused on the evidence presented by the prosecution and the defense. However, the total impact of the defense case must convince the jury, as triers of fact, that the prosecution has failed to establish the accused's guilt beyond a reasonable doubt. As early in the trial as the jury selection period—and as late as the time for filing requests to charge pertinent aspects of law—the defense

11. Arthur Lewis Wood, *Criminal Lawyer* (New Haven, Conn.: College and University Press, 1967), pp. 242–45.
12. Paul B. Weston and Kenneth M. Wells, *Criminal Investigation—Basic Perspectives* (Englewood Cliffs, N.J.: Prentice–Hall, 1970), pp. 270–71.

counsel must define with simplicity and clarity the issues before the jury: the elements of the crime charged and the fact that the prosecution must prove each element beyond a reasonable doubt.

After all the evidence has been presented, the defense counsel's right to a closing argument for the defense is an important method by which he relates basic laws to the evidence presented. Of course, this is a partisan exposition in which the prosecution's case is stated or summed up to highlight its *improbabilities*, and the defense case presented as favorably as possible. After all, it is an "argument for the defense" (the prosecuting attorney is allowed time for *his* closing argument).

One of the strongest arguments likely to develop the necessary doubt in the jurors' minds, is the one based on improbabilities. The average juror is not a person trained in law or experienced in its enforcement, and tends to believe that which is in accord with his own experience and the recorded experience of others. He is reluctant to believe that which he considers improbable. This avenue of persuasion may be linked to subarguments based on what the prosecution has *not* proved: 1. The lack of motive (a classic ploy in murder trials is that more victims are killed by persons with some motive for killing them than by those who have no motive). 2. The good character of the accused 3. An attack on the value of circumstantial evidence and on the credibility of accomplice testimony as completely unreliable and untrustworthy (when appropriate). 4. A spirited defense of alibi witnesses who testify for the accused.[13]

Defense counsel often requests that specified instructions be given to the jury by the trial judge as he instructs them in the law, just prior to the jury's determination of the facts in their quest for a verdict.[14] (These "requests to charge" suggest the direction of major defense attacks on the prosecution's case.)

Jury instructions required by law or commonly requested by lawyers in criminal cases have developed some uniformity. The following illustrations are based on California case law, California statutory law, and Los Angeles County Superior Court instructions:

> *Presumption of Innocence, Reasonable Doubt, Burden of Proof*—A defendant in a criminal action is presumed to be innocent until the contrary is proved, and in case of a reasonable doubt whether his guilt is satisfactorily shown he is entitled to an acquittal, but the effect of this presumption is only to place upon the State the burden of proving him guilty beyond a reasonable doubt. Reasonable doubt is defined as follows: It is not a mere possi-

---

13. G. Arthur Martin, "Closing Argument to the Jury for the Defense in Criminal Cases," *The Journal of Criminal Law, Criminology and Police Science* 58, no. 1 (March 1967): 2–17.

14. Henry B. Rothblatt, *Successful Techniques in the Trial of Criminal Cases* (Englewood Cliffs, N. J., Prentice–Hall, 1961), pp. 189–225.

ble doubt; because everything relating to human affairs, and depending on moral evidence, is open to some possible or imaginary doubt. It is that state of the case which, after the entire comparison and consideration of all the evidence, leaves the minds of the jurors in that condition that they cannot say they feel an abiding conviction, to a moral certainty, of the truth of the charge.

Credibility of Witnesses—The jury are the sole and exclusive judges of the effect and value of evidence addressed to them and of the credibility of the witnesses who have testified in the case. Every person who testifies under oath is a witness. You are the sole and exclusive judges of the credibility of the witnesses who have testified in this case.

In determining the credibility of a witness you may consider any matter that has a tendency in reason to prove or disprove the truthfulness of his testimony, including but not limited to the following:

His demeanor while testifying and the manner in which he testifies;

The character of his testimony;

The extent of his capacity to perceive, to recollect, or to communicate any matter about which he testifies;

The extent of his opportunity to perceive any matter about which he testifies;

His character for honesty or veracity or their opposites;

The existence or nonexistence of a bias, interest, or other motive;

A statement previously made by him that is consistent with his testimony;

A statement made by him that is inconsistent with any part of his testimony;

The existence or nonexistence of any fact testified to by him;

His attitude toward the action in which he testifies or toward the giving of testimony;

His admission of untruthfulness;

His prior conviction of a felony.

A witness willfully false in one material part of his testimony is to be distrusted in others. You may reject the whole testimony of a witness who wilfully has testified falsely as to a material point, unless, from all the evidence, you shall believe the probability of truth favors his testimony in other particulars.

However, discrepancies in a witness' testimony or between his testimony and that of others, if there were any, do not necessarily mean that the witness should be discredited. Failure of recollection is a common experience; and innocent misrecollection is not uncommon. It is a fact, also, that two persons witnessing an incident or a transaction often will see or hear it differently. Whether a discrepancy pertains to a fact of importance or only to a trivial detail should be considered in weighing its significance.

You are not bound to decide in conformity with the testimony of a number of witnesses, which does not produce conviction in your mind, as against the testimony of a lesser number or other evidence, which appeals to your mind with more convincing force. [Testimony which you believe given by one witness is sufficient for the proof of any fact.] This does not mean that you are at liberty to disregard the testimony of the greater number of witnesses merely from caprice or prejudice, or from a desire to favor one side as against the other. It does mean that you are not to decide an issue by the simple process of counting the number of witnesses who have testified on the opposing sides. It means that the final test is not in the relative number of witnesses, but in the relative convincing force of the evidence.

Motive is not an element of the crime charged and need not be shown. However, you may consider motive or lack of motive as a circumstance in this case. Presence of motive may tend to establish guilt. Absence of motive may tend to establish innocence. You will therefore give its presence or absence, as the case may be, the weight to which you find it to be entitled.

Evidence of the defendant's character as to those traits which ordinarily would be involved in the commission of a crime such as that charged in this case is relevant to the question of the defendant's guilt or innocence because it may be reasoned that a person of good character as to such traits would not be likely to commit the crime of which the defendant is charged.

Evidence of good character may be sufficient to raise a reasonable doubt whether the defendant is guilty, which doubt otherwise would not exist.

If the evidence establishes that the defendant's character as to certain traits has not been discussed among those who know him, you may infer from the absence of such discussion that his character in those respects is good.

But if, after weighing all the evidence, you are convinced beyond a reasonable doubt that the defendant is guilty of the (a) crime charged against him in the information, your duty will be to find him guilty (of that offense), notwithstanding the testimony that he was or is a person of good character.

Direct and Circumstantial Evidence—The testimony of a witness, a writing, a material object, or anything presented to the senses offered to prove the existence or nonexistence of a fact is either direct or circumstantial evidence.

Direct evidence means evidence that directly proves a fact, without an inference, and which in itself, if true, conclusively establishes that fact.

Circumstantial evidence means evidence that proves a fact from which an inference of the existence of another fact may be drawn.

An inference is a deduction of fact that may logically and reasonably be drawn from another fact or group of facts established by the evidence.

It is not necessary that facts be proved by direct evidence. They may be proved also by circumstantial evidence or by a combination of direct evidence and circumstantial evidence. Both direct evidence and circumstantial evidence are acceptable as a means of proof. Neither is entitled to any greater weight than the other.

You are not permitted to find the defendant guilty of the crime charged against him based on circumstantial evidence unless the proved circumstances are not only consistent with the theory that the defendant is guilty of the crime, but cannot be reconciled with any other rational conclusion and each fact which is essential to complete a set of circumstances necessary to establish the defendant's guilt has been proved beyond a reasonable doubt.

Also, if the evidence is susceptible of two reasonable interpretations, one of which points to the defendant's guilt and the other to his innocence, it is your duty to adopt that interpretation which points to the defendant's innocence, and reject the other which points to his guilt.

The specific intent with which an act is done may be manifested by the circumstances surrounding its commission. But you may not find the defendant guilty of the offense charged in this case unless the proved circumstances not only are consistent with the hypothesis that he had the specific intent to commit the crime charged but are irreconcilable with any other rational conclusion.

Also, if the evidence as to such specific intent is susceptible of two reasonable interpretations, one of which points to the existence thereof and the other to the absence thereof, you must adopt that interpretation which points to its absence. If, on the other hand, one interpretation of the evidence as to such specific intent appears to you to be reasonable and the other interpretation to be unreasonable, it would be your duty to accept the reasonable interpretation and to reject the unreasonable.

Accomplice—An accomplice is one who is liable to be prosecuted for the identical offense charged against the defendant on trial.

To be an accomplice, the person must have knowingly and with criminal intent aided, promoted, encouraged, or instigated by act or advice, the commission of such offense.

A conviction can not be had upon the testimony of an accomplice unless it is corroborated by such other evidence as shall tend to connect the defendant with the commission of such offense.

Corroborative evidence is evidence of some act or fact related to the offense which, if believed, by itself and without any aid, interpretation or direction from the testimony of the accomplice, tends to connect the defendant with the commission of the offense charged.

However, it is not necessary that the corroborative evidence be sufficient in itself to establish every element of the offense charged, or that it corroborate every fact to which the accomplice testifies.

In determining whether an accomplice has been corroborated, you must first assume the testimony of the accomplice has been removed from the case. You must then determine whether there is any remaining evidence which tends to connect the defendant with the commission of the offense.

If there is not such independent evidence which tends to connect defendant with the commission of the offense, the testimony of the accomplice is not corroborated.

If there is such independent evidence which you believe, then the testimony of the accomplice is corroborated.

The corroboration of the testimony of an accomplice required by law may not be supplied by the testimony of any or all of his accomplices, but must come from other evidence.

Merely assenting to or aiding or assisting in the commission of a crime without guilty knowledge or intent is not criminal, and a person so assenting to, or aiding, or assisting in, the commission of a crime without guilty knowledge or intent in respect thereto, is not an accomplice in the commission of such crime.

It is the law that the testimony of an accomplice ought to be viewed with distrust. This does not mean that you may arbitrarily disregard such testimony, but you should give to it the weight to which you find it to be entitled after examining it with care and caution and in the light of all the evidence in the case.

The defendant in this case has introduced evidence tending to show that he was not present at the time and place of the commission of the alleged offense for which he is here on trial. If, after a consideration of all the evidence, you have a reasonable doubt that the defendant was present at the time the crime was committed, he is entitled to an acquittal.

The Judge

The judge is the person, educated in law, whose role in the administration of justice is to settle all kinds of legal controversy. These controversies may be civil questions of contracts, wills, personal injury involving a person's money, and they may be criminal issues, involving a person's life or liberty.

There is a continual search for ways and means to improve the quality of the judiciary through better selection and improved disciplinary procedures. The election of judges is the major method of selection, but pending an election, governors often make selections to fill vacancies. Such appointments are usually tantamount to permanent positions, because rarely does an incumbent judge have opposition, and even more rarely is an incumbent defeated. Discipline of judges is a delicate subject, and impeachment is much too cumbersome, expensive, and ineffective. Since the establishment of the federal courts, only eight judges have been impeached. Other disciplinary methods are by resolution,* recall,** and removal or discipline by the judiciary.

*Resolution of the legislature.
**Recall by popular vote.

New Jersey's supreme court has the power to discipline members of the state judiciary by its contempt power and its power to issue administrative orders.

A member of the judiciary can influence the actual enforcement of the laws by his own attitude toward particular crimes. If he regards an offense as so minor that it deserves no punishment, the prosecuting attorney becomes reluctant to prosecute, and policemen begin to close their eyes to this offense and concentrate available enforcement on other violations. While the prosecuting attorney has vast powers because of the discretion allowed him to make decisions to charge or not to charge an accused, the judge is influential because of the authority entrusted to him as the decision maker.

In the administration of criminal justice the government has the power to take a person's life or liberty in order to preserve an orderly society. This power is given to the trial judge to exercise. The trial judge is the center of the process which includes the victim, the accused, the prosecutor, the defense attorney, jurors (when appropriate), spectators (public trial), and himself. The decisions and actions of the others are governed in a large measure by the immediate rulings of the trial judge.

The public impression of our legal system is largely shaped by the impact of the trial judge on victim, juror, and spectator, His dignity and demeanor, his evenhanded control of the proceedings, his courtesy toward all involved, and his display of respect for the rules of evidence and other procedures and courts, are important factors in shaping the total image.

The judge is an arbiter, an umpire, and an advisor in the process of trying and determining the facts. If he is the trier of fact (trial without a jury), his is the final word on the credibility of witnesses and facts in dispute. His primary role, however, is to insure that the proceedings against the accused are conducted fairly and within the rules of the adjudicatory process: the judicial supervision over criminal proceedings requiring a decision by judge or jury. The trial of most serious offenses in the United States is by jury unless the defendant, and his counsel, waive a jury trial and place the entire adjudicatory process in the hands of the trial judge.

The trial judge also has supervision of the Sixth Amendment right to a speedy trial (enforceable against the states as one of the basic rights preserved by the constitution).[14] This constitutional guarantee is essential to protect the accused from: (1) undue and oppressive incarceration prior to trial, (2) anxiety and concern accompanying public accusation, and (3) long delays likely to impair the ability of the accused to defend himself. Initially, an accused who has not been

14. Klopfer v. North Carolina, 386 U.S. 213 (1968).

released on bail because of the nature of the charge, or an inability to post the required bail, has a problem keeping in touch with his counsel and with potential defense witnesses. When long delays prolong the pretrial period, the accused—in or out of prison—has a problem mitigating the corrosive effects of time: the disappearance of witnesses and evidence, memory failure, and a loss of perspective concerning past events.

The prosecuting attorney is often the prime mover in securing a speedy trial. The accused's right dates from the time he was first accused or held to answer for the crime charged. Usually, the trial of defendants in custody has first priority, but in scheduling cases for a court's calendar, the prosecuting attorney must advise the presiding judge of the relevant facts used to determine the order of cases to be scheduled, and his reasons for not scheduling past-due cases. Continuances which postpone the trial of a case are only granted by a court for good cause based on a triology of interests: the prosecution, the defense, and the public.

The selection of a jury is the first step in a criminal trial in which the right to jury is not waived. Under the trial judge's supervision, the qualifications of jurors called to serve are examined under oath. Each of the advocates, the prosecuting attorney and the defense counsel, seek the right people for a trial jury. (This is within the concept of the adversary system of justice and part of the role of attorney.) Challenges for cause (without limit) are used to get rid of those prospective jurors who indicate an inability or unwillingness to participate in a verdict based on the law as it will be explained by the trial judge, and the facts of the case as they will be presented in the trial. Each side is allowed a certain number of peremptory challenges (varies with state law, nature of charges, and number of defendants) to dismiss from the jury any person that attorney deems unsuitable, but whose responses did not establish grounds to challenge for cause.[15]

There is extensive judicial supervision of this jury selection process, despite the fact that the district attorney is an officer of the court and should be fair, seeking a conviction only by legal means. It is improper for a prosecutor to wilfully try to pack a jury or to attempt to place on the jury persons who are biased against the defendant to such a degree as to make them unfair jurors under the law. *Ex parte* * exclusion of potential jurors by a prosecutor (removing their names from the master jury list through the jury commissioner or other persons charged with the selection and formation of jury lists and panels) is also improper and calculated to thwart the objectives of justice. Trial by an impartial jury, not one composed from a list which consciously

15. Paul B. Weston and Kenneth M. Wells, *The Administration of Justice* (Englewood Cliffs, N.J.: Prentice-Hall, 1967), pp. 193–97.

*Of or from one side or party, without notice to the adverse party.

eliminated "pro-defense" jurors is guaranteed. Juries are not to be hand picked by prosecutors so that they may merely ratify indictments and information with verdicts of guilty.[16] Trial judges do make inquiry into the entire process of selecting jurors, but they also recognize the fact that the prosecuting attorney is still the lawyer for the people, and may in a legitimate way ascertain the character, standing, and integrity of jurors before they are sworn.[17]

When the jury has been selected, the trial judge administers the oath to the selected jurors and alternates. The actual trial begins with an opening by both sides, usually brief statements of what each attorney intends to prove in court. This is followed by the state's case—all the witnesses and other evidence assembled by police and prosecutor. When the prosecution rests, the defense has the opportunity to present their witnesses and assembled evidence. When the defense rests, the prosecution responds to the defense case (rebuttal), and this is followed by a defense answer to the latest attempt by the prosecutor to prove the accusation (surrebuttal). When the presentation of evidence is ended, opposing attorneys have a chance to request the trial judge to instruct the jury on various points of law, and each attorney has an opportunity to present a closing or oral argument to explain the case and its evidence to the jury.[18]

Criminal proceedings in all serious criminal cases require the participation of three independent agents of justice: (1) the prosecutor who initiates the accusation on behalf of the people; (2) the defense counsel (barring a valid waiver) who responds to the accusation on behalf of his client; and (3) a judge who will preside at the trial and supervise and instruct the jury (where appropriate, barring valid waiver).

In a jury trial, the court competent to hear and examine a criminal case is a tripartite entity made up of (1) prosecuting attorney, (2) defense counsel, and (3) the assigned judge and selected jury. In administering criminal justice the court is a cooperative effort in which the best results are obtained by the interaction of the minds of the trial judge and counsel.

The adversary system for the conduct of trials in our legal system is rigorously institutionalized with rigidly defined roles for the prosecuting attorney and defense counsel. The purpose of this contentious system is clear, its rules are known, and it is the watchful trial judge who depersonalizes this battle by forcing participants to follow the rules and attempt to achieve the adversary system's goal: truth.

One judicial problem in relation to any jury trial on the issue of guilt

16. Noland v State Bar 63 Cal. 2d 298 (1965).
17. People v Ruef 14 Cal. App 576 (1910).
18. Weston and Wells, *The Administration of Justice*, p. 185.

or innocence is that only one side can win. Part of the judicial role is to convey this fact to the jurors in the case, and to point out the collateral fact that their decision as to the winner should be based on the merits of the case as they see it through their evaluation of the evidence presented in the courtroom.

Many persons fail to realize the fervent love for the administration of justice that exists in the hearts of judges, jurors, and the counsel for both sides who fulfill the adversary system roles of prosecuting attorney and counsel for the defense. It is as American as the traditional apple pie, and the court in which these people work cooperatively is preserved by a calm, unemotional, and dignified management of criminal proceedings by men of loyalty and sincerity who "call them as they see them coming over the plate."[19]

Disparities in Justice and *Voir Dire*

From the preliminary hearing to verdict, there are disparities in the quality and measure of justice because of a defendant's age, sex, education, economic status, and race.

The age of a defendant acts to secure a young person a lighter sentence (usually on first offender rules), but disadvantages the youth since he is less likely to receive the procedural safeguards insuring fair trial and due process. The processes of justice have a standard sex orientation (chivalry) in favoring the female, but the large number of male criminals may account for this disparity. The less educated defendant is more likely to go to prison, either because he is unaware of his rights, docile about the denial of them, or because he is not believed to be a good risk for probation. The indigent defendant is found guilty upon trial, either because the poor are usually passive in their defense, or are more likely to have a prior record, or be guilty as charged, or both.

As a black or Spanish–speaking defendant, there is a greater likelihood of no release on bail, or representation by a court-appointed attorney, of trial without a jury, or conviction as a result of plea negotiations. This may not result from discrimination against minorities, but rather from the correlation between minority groups, poverty, and lack of education, plus a distrust of all-white or near-white juries.[20]

Disparity does not mean discrimination with its overt implication of being unfavored, nor does it mean any inequity because of gross unfairness. It does mean that the accused is disadvantaged in some way

19. Harold A. Medina, "Some Reflections on the Judicial Function," in *The Lawyer's Treasury*, pp. 481–89.

20. Stuart S. Nagel, *The Legal Process from a Behavioral Perspective* (Homewood, Ill.: Dorsey Press, 1969), pp. 88–112.

in the postarrest process. Since defendants from minority groups are likely to be disadvantaged because of their ethnic background, their poverty, their lack of education, and in some instances their youth, it is important that these defendants be protected against any disparity of justice.

In the final analysis the issue of guilt or innocence is in the care of the jury. If justice is to be obtained for a minority group defendant in our adversary system of trial, a good beginning must be in the careful selection of the jury. Therefore, to guard against any disparity of justice, defense counsel must be alert and work hard to screen out undesirable jurors at the pretrial *voir dire* * examination.

A general question does not single out the bigot, or the prejudiced. Simply asking a prospective juror if he (or she) harbors prejudice (that cannot be set aside for the purpose of a fair trial) on the subject of race, religion, or national origin does not probe and pry adequately. A probing series of questions is required. For instance:

Q: Mr. Smith, I suppose that you, like most of us, have certain feelings about members of the Negro race, blacks, that are different from our feelings about members of our own race?

Q: Do you personally know many blacks?

Q: Have you ever had a black in your home as a social guest?

Q: Have you ever been in a black person's home as a social guest?

Q: Do your children have close friends who are blacks?

Q: If the daughter of one of your close friends married a black, do you feel that would create problems for that girl and her family?

Q: (If the answer is "Yes") Why do you think such a marriage would create problems?

Q: When you indicate in your answer that it is because most people are prejudiced, do you think that applies to this jury panel also?

Q: Do you feel that those feelings would bias most jurors against my client, who is a Negro, a black?

Q: Do you share those feelings yourself?

Q: Would you have a difficult time setting aside those biases in fairly considering my client's case?[21]

These questions point up the real extent of the problem in finding

---

*Questioning to determine qualifications.

21. Herbert Hafis, "Adequate *Voir Dire*" *Journal of the California State Bar* 44, no. 6 (November–December 1969): 858–60.

jurors truly unbiased in a black defendant's cause, no matter in what part of the nation the trial is held.

The problem of bias is further complicated by the fact that the trial courts are not agreed on whether they will even allow such probing questions. In those trial courts which do allow the defense attorney to ask probing questions, a basis can be developed for the excusal of a juror for cause, or the defense attorney may excuse the prospective juror on a peremptory challenge.

There is a long journey yet to travel before bias and prejudice are finally completely excluded from our system of justice. However, it is happening more often, and in more and more areas. The court of judge, prosecutor, and defense counsel is a forum for justice, and justice is based on a fair trial before an impartial jury.

Selected References

Books

Advisory Committee on the Prosecution and Defense Functions, American Bar Association. *Standards Relating to the Prosecution Function and the Defense Function—Tentative Draft*. New York: Institute of Judicial Administration, 1970.

Miller, Frank W. *Prosecution—The Decision to Charge Suspect with a Crime*. Boston: Little Brown and Co., 1969.

Rothblatt, Henry B. *Successful Techniques in the Trial of Criminal Cases*. Englewood Cliffs, N.J., 1961.

Wood, Arthur Lewis. *Criminal Lawyer*. New Haven, Conn.: College and University Press, 1967.

Weston, Paul B., and Wells, Kenneth M. *The Administration of Justice*. Englewood Cliffs, N.J.: Prentice–Hall, 1967.

Periodicals

Hafis, Herbert "Adequate *Voir Dire.*" *Journal of the California State Bar* 44, no. 6 (November–December 1969): 858–60.

Chapter X

Plea Negotiations—Conviction Without Trial

At least 90 percent of all persons convicted of crime in the United States are convicted by their plea of guilty. Less than 10 percent of the persons arrested and accused of crime are convicted as a result of trial by either a judge or a jury.[1] Plea negotiations (or "deal" as it is often termed) are the means for maintaining a constant percentage of guilty pleas necessary to keep from swamping the courts with work, creating greater delays in the time between accusation and trial.

Trials take time and are costly. The courts throughout the country are usually staffed to offer trials to no more than 10 percent of the persons arrested and accused of crime. One may imagine what would happen to the machinery of justice if 20, 30, or 50 percent of the criminal cases went to trial. The courts which now are not in a workload chaos, live on the verge of one. Obviously, the present functioning of our courts is dependent upon this working arrangement: pleas of guilty save both the time of a court and the expense of a trial. Any legal system which must have this "back door" arrangement of plea negotiations to survive is in constant danger of sacrificing the accused for the goal of expediency; of trading fairness to the accused individual for perpetuation of a system that can only function efficiently because of plea negotiations.

The participants in plea negotiations are the prosecutor, the defendant, the defense counsel, and the judge. Because of the arcane

1. President's Commission on Law Enforcement and Administration of Justice, *The Challenge of Crime in a Free Society* (Washington, D.C.: U.S. Government Printing Office, 1967), p. 134.

methodology involved in plea negotiations, the defendant is an outsider to whom the nuances of plea negotiations and agreement are explained by his counsel. In a spin–off from the adversary system of trials in the American legal system, the antagonists in plea negotiations are the prosecuting attorney and the defense counsel. However, to make certain that cases come to trial without long delays, a judge of the trial court having jurisdiction over a case is an interested party. In fact, the sentencing judge has a strange role in plea negotiations. He has not only a vested interest in the number of cases that do *not* go to trial, but he also has to concur in the plea agreement—or there is no "deal."

The major potentials for injustice as a result of plea negotiations are: (1) innocent persons may plead guilty in fear of the consequences of a trial; (2) persons who plead guilty may be rewarded with a sentence unsuited to their correctional needs; and (3) the ends of justice may be defeated by one of the antagonists securing a greater "advantage" from the plea agreement than justified by the facts.

While plea negotiations result in conviction without trial, there is nothing improper in arriving at substantial justice which is agreeable to all parties to the litigation without the time and expense of a trial. Instead of a jury or judge determining what is justice in a specific case, the parties at interest and the judge arrive at the proper and final disposition.

The Advantage in Plea Bargaining

There is an initial pressure on prosecuting attorneys to conclude plea negotiations with a plea of guilty because this agency of criminal justice is universally understaffed. Just as the judiciary has a vested interest to reduce the number of accusations that move on to become court trials, so too has the prosecutor. In addition, as an elective official, prosecutors survive or perish in the community's evaluation of their professional competence. At the very least, successful plea negotiation will give a prosecutor a conviction ratio beginning at 90 percent. If an inept prosecutor, or one with a subpar staff, loses half the cases that go to trial, he can point with pride to a conviction ratio of about 95 percent. Plea negotiations in 90 percent of all cases has made a paper tiger out of many prosecutors who are failures as trial lawyers.

Because of the nature of the work and the frequency of contact with the criminal element of a community, there is also a potential for corruption in plea negotiation. There is the danger that the prosecutor will be offered monetary or political rewards for his cooperation—an advantage of sorts.

On the defense side, one of the basic advantages is the resolution of a pending case rapidly and without trial. In all jurisdictions the institutionalized legal services in public defender's offices are grossly overcrowded and there is a need for this shortcut. Privately retained counsel have more lucrative law work with clients other than those charged with crime. Most good trial attorneys have a heavy work load and must allocate their time to the best advantage of their clients and the successful operation of their practice. They, too, find plea negotiations an excellent shortcut.

The major advantage to the defense, however, is in planning a client's strategy of defense. Plea negotiation sessions are informative. A great deal can be learned of the prosecution's case when the defense counsel is skilled at these negotiations and the prosecuting attorney is less skilled or careless. In addition, the overview of a case may indicate to a skilled attorney that the defendant will be convicted as charged if the case goes to trial, and his best service to his client is to advise him to plead guilty in return for concessions from the prosecutor.

Just as in trial proceedings, the prosecutor and the defense counsel are in opposition. Plea negotiating is bargaining. In winning at the conclusion of a plea negotiating session, one of the opposing attorneys must gain some advantage. For this reason, neither antagonist is completely open and honest about the chances of success for his side if the case goes to trial. In fact, prosecuting attorneys assure defense counsel that their client does not have a chance if the case goes to trial; and defense counsel quite appropriately (and with equal regard for truth) responds with assurances that the state just does not have sufficient evidence to go to trial on the original accusation. It is difficult to say, in an individual case, who is the buyer and who is the seller in these plea negotiations; but it is safe to say that the prosecuting attorney is the merchant in the beginning stages of plea negotiations.

There is a well-founded suspicion around most courthouses in America that police and prosecuting attorneys select the most serious possible charge as the base for the original accusation against a suspect. From this place of beginning, without any plea negotiations, it is not unusual for the prosecuting attorney to reduce the charge to a lesser crime more suited to the evidence collected in the case *if he has to go to trial.* Likewise, an omnibus indictment may be filed in the first instance, alleging a series of crimes, but the defection of witnesses or the likely suppression of evidence may result in the consolidation of these charges into a single accusation of crime if the case has to go to trial. Prosecutors sometimes press the most serious possible charge or multiple charges at the time of an arrest because past experience has indicated the time period between apprehension and trial is frequently sufficient to flush out unknown witnesses and discover other evidence of guilt. When this evidence is not forthcoming, the prosecutor must reduce the initial charges to meet his evidentiary needs if he has to go to trial. Since the lack of the necessary evidence to support the most serious charge is known only to the prosecutor (usually the police are unsure), he is in an advantageous position to begin talking to defense counsel about a plea agreement.

When a case fails to develop the evidence necessary for a conviction if it goes to trial, the prosecutor is not only willing, but possibly eager, to amend the accusation to a lesser charge, to dismiss other pending cases, and to seek judicial approval of leniency in the sentencing just so long as the accused will plead guilty and the case will not have to go to trial.

Under these circumstances, a defendant acting as his own counsel is not prepared to cope with an experienced prosecutor. Many otherwise skilled defense attorneys are poor advocates for their clients when faced with a prosecutor who is skilled in the give and take of plea negotiations and who knows the real situation as to the evidence in the case.

A thing of value to the prosecutor which may be turned to the advantage of a defendant is cooperation beyond the plea of guilty. This means an agreement to help the police and prosecutor by becoming a state's witness, if warranted by the circumstances of the case, or serving as an informant about other crimes (the facts of which are known to the defendant). Such cooperation is useful when the prosecutor must seek the approval of the sentencing judge for an assurance that the defendant will receive a reduced sentence as part of the plea agreement. Of course, the prosecutor can seek leniency on the mere plea of guilty, but additional cooperation is helpful in some plea negotiations.

Guilty or innocent, there is tremendous pressure on an accused awaiting trial. Life in a county jail is a miserable experience. Release on bail is no more than a marking time period. There is a building up of pressure to get it over with. It is a situation which encourages a plea of guilty. To many accused persons any deal appears more attractive than the risk of a threatened trial.

To protect defendants who enter into plea negotiations and then reject the idea of pleading guilty, there is a confidentiality to this act. The fact that the defendant, or his counsel, and the prosecuting attorney engaged in plea discussions, or made a plea agreement which was later rejected by the defendant, should not be received in evidence against or in favor of the defendant in any subsequent criminal proceedings.

In review, the fact that the ultimate decision in plea negotiations must be the defendant's, may be a mechanism for injustice rather than justice because of the pressure of the pretrial situation. The advantage gained in a plea agreement may be a far greater penalty than that which would have been imposed by any sentence after trial.

Conviction Without Trial

A person who pleads guilty makes an incourt admission of every essential element involved in the crime charged. This is the equivalent of a verdict of guilty after a trial. There is no trial on a plea of guilty; the plea formalizes and settles the issue of guilt or innocence. A plea of guilty must constitute an intelligent and understanding waiver of three basic rights: (1) the right against self–incrimination; (2) the right to trial by jury; and (3) the right to be confronted by witnesses.

In all jurisdictions, there must be a court arraignment for pleading after a formal accusation has been filed by the prosecutor. If a defendant does not have retained or assigned counsel at this time, he is advised of his right to counsel, and informed that the court will appoint counsel if he is indigent and cannot retain his own attorney. If the defendant or his counsel requires more time to consider a plea, it is common practice to allow a continuance for a reasonable period. This is a time of great importance to an accused person.

In the event the defendant enters a plea of guilty, there may be a judicial examination of the defendant's action as to whether the facts support or corroborate the guilty plea. The defendant must fully understand the nature and consequence of a plea of guilty, and it must be determined whether the plea is made voluntarily.[2]

Voluntariness of Plea

An accused's plea of guilty may be accepted by the court only if "voluntarily and understandingly made": the plea reflects the considered choice of the accused, free of any factor or inducement which has unfairly unfluenced or overcome his will. A guilty plea that is induced by coercion or promises, or which is otherwise unfairly obtained or given through ignorance, fear, or inadvertence, is involuntary and inconsistent with due process of law. Due process requires that before a guilty plea is accepted the court must determine that the defendant has a clear understanding of the charge, and is aware of possible defenses to it and circumstances in mitigation thereof, and that his admission of guilt is without reservation. A judge is not relieved of his duty to ascertain that a guilty plea was understandingly and knowingly made merely because the defendant is represented by counsel.[3]

The court's role in determining voluntariness is not so much to

2. Paul B. Weston and Kenneth M. Wells, *Criminal Evidence for Police* (Englewood Cliffs, N.J.: Prentice–Hall, 1971), pp. 197–99.
3. U.S. ex rel Elksnis v. Gilligan, 256 F. Supp. 244 (1966).

inquire as to whether the defendant made a wise decision in pleading guilty—although this is not out of order—but to make certain that the defendant is telling the truth when he states the decision was voluntary. Therefore, the assigned judge must inquire into the full circumstances under which the defendant made the decision to plead guilty. This is for the purpose of ascertaining whether the decision was voluntarily made, whether the defendant understands all the implications of his action, and that the defendant was not pressured into his plea and does not really understand what he is doing.

In times past, plea negotiation was as widespread as it is now, but there was a greater tendency to handle the details of the plea negotiations with some secrecy, and with a ritualized fiction for the court record. The court ritual required that for the public record, the defendant verbalize a denial that any promises were made to him in return for his plea of guilty, and that it was—in fact—voluntary. In truth, there had been tripartite discussions participated in by the prosecutor, the defense counsel, and the sentencing judge, and as a result an agreement had been reached to allow the defendant to plead to a lesser charge or to exchange a reduced sentence for a plea of guilty. No plea of guilty would have been made unless the defendant's attorney assured him that the prosecutor would amend the accusation, the judge would pronounce a reduced sentence, or both.

It is difficult to understand why many members of the judiciary tolerated this threat to the integrity of the entire process of justice. This ritual for the public record of court procedures never contributed in any fashion to the public image of the courts. So many persons involved in courts and court proceedings knew that as a standard operating procedure in plea negotiations, promises had been made to the defendant. They also knew that judges were fully aware of the methodology of these negotiations.

There is little wonder then, that the court's procedure for determining the voluntariness of a plea of guilty has always been clouded by the fact that the defendant would be forced to lie when queried in court as to whether promises had been made to him to induce his plea of guilty.

Under such circumstances, it is not surprising that the judicial examination required in all guilty pleas failed to uncover instances in which innocent persons pled guilty to crimes in which they were not involved.

The Plea Agreement

The American Bar Association (ABA) has proposed standards for plea negotiation which are intended to formalize the plea agreement for the protection of the defendant and the public. The proposed standards are within the concept of open disclosure of the entire plea negotiations. They would allow the prosecuting attorney to enter into plea discussions and agreements when such action is in the interest of the public and the effective administration of justice. These negotiations should be made through the defendant's lawyer unless the defendant is acting as his own attorney by order and agreement of the court.

These standards for plea negotiations would establish three major areas of plea agreement:

1. Acceptance of a plea to another offense reasonably related to the defendant's criminal conduct (lesser offense).

2. The dismissal of other charges or accusations (pending).

3. The type of sentence (probation, prison, fine), and its length of term.[4]

To insure uniformity of plea agreements, these ABA standards admonish the prosecuting attorney to make equal opportunities available to similarly situated defendants in order to comply with the constitutional mandate of equal protection. There is also the equally desirable criminal justice objective of demonstrating to defendants that they have been fairly treated by agents of justice responsible for their defense, their prosecution, their judgement, and their sentence.

To make certain that the ultimate decision as to the plea agreement is made by the defendant, these standards further suggest the following safeguard:

> Defense counsel should conclude a plea agreement only with the consent of the defendant, and should insure that the decision whether to enter a plea of guilty or *nolo contendre** is ultimately made by the defendant. To aid the defendant in reaching a decision, defense counsel—after appropriate investigation—should advise the defendant of the alternatives available and of considerations deemed important by him in reaching a decision.[5]

There is hope that these standards will provide the guidelines that will bring a new uniformity and openess to de facto procedures previously identified with secret deals and courtroom ritual in which the defendant was forced to state a basic untruth.

4. American Bar Association Committee on Minimum Standards for Pleas of Guilty, *Standards Relating to Pleas of Guilty* (New York: Institute of Judicial Administration, 1970), pp. 6–12.
*No contest.
5. *Standards—Pleas of Guilty*, pp. 69–70.

Judicial Participation in Plea Negotiations

There has always been a belief that active participation by a sentencing judge in plea negotiations threatens judicial integrity. Among the major reasons for such a belief are the following:

1. Judicial participation in plea negotiations can create the impression in the mind of the defendant that he would not receive a fair trial before this judge (after rejecting offers of a bargain plea).

2. Judicial participation may suggest to some defendants a risk in not going along with the disposition apparently desired by the judge, and this may create a pressure so great that the defendant will be induced to plead guilty even if innocent.

3. Judicial participation in these discussions make it difficult for the judge to objectively determine the voluntariness of the plea when it is offered.

4. Judicial participation to the extent of promising a certain sentence is inconsistent with the theory behind the use of presentence investigation reports, and the need of the sentence to serve as a general program of rehabilitation for offenders.[6]

The 1966 case of *U.S. ex rel Elksnis* v. *Gilligan*[7] is a good example of how any fundamental fairness of judicial procedures is jeopardized by a judge's active participation in plea negotiations. Almars Elksnis was arrested for the killing of his wife. He claimed his wife had attacked him first with a hammer and knife. The cause of death was stabbing wounds inflicted by the four-inch knife the defendant claimed he had wrested from his wife when attacked. He was promptly indicted for murder, pled not guilty, and retained counsel. After several conferences between defense counsel and the prosecuting attorney, the defendant and his counsel conferred with the assigned trial judge in his chambers about a change of plea (to guilty) and a sentence of no more than ten years. Considering all the circumstances of this case known to the judge at this time, the defendant and his counsel were assured that if the defendant would plead guilty to manslaughter (a lesser charge than murder), the sentence would be to a term in state prison not to exceed ten years.

Soon after this conference in the judicial chambers the defendant withdrew his plea of not guilty and pleaded guilty to manslaughter in the first degree. Sentence was deferred, and the prosecuting attorney filed an information charging the defendant as a second felony offend-

6. *Standards—Pleas of Guilty*, p. 73.
7. 256 F. Supp. 244 (1966).

er (that he had been previously convicted of assault, second degree). Defense counsel, based upon an official transcript which indicated the conviction was for assault in the third degree (a misdemeanor) challenged the accuracy of the information, whereupon the matter was put over. At a subsequent hearing the prosecution again charged that the defendant was a multiple offender, but this time presented a certified copy of the prior conviction. The judge then found as a matter of law that the prior conviction was a felony, and after an off the record "discussion between counsel and the Court" and a plea of mercy on behalf of the defendant, imposed a sentence of from 17 to 35 years—contrary to his promise that the maximum term would be ten years.

The circumstances in this case attendant upon the entry of the plea of guilty hardly supports a claim that it was understandingly and knowingly made. The defendant's answers in response to the questions by the court and the prosecutor immediately prior to the entry of the guilty plea do not clearly establish that he acknowledged guilt without reservation. Quite to the contrary, they reveal a challenge to the charge —an attempt to assert a plea of self defense or insanity—and yet without further inquiry by the court, the plea of guilty was summarily accepted. The transcript of the hearing record reveals the following dialogue between the defendant, the judge, and the prosecutor:

Prosecuting Attorney:

The defendant became involved in an argument with his so–called common law wife. As a result of which I believe he spilled some hot water on her and she became annoyed. Thereafter the argument grew worse and I understand there was some question relative to a hammer being used by the wife, which, of course, as your Honor knows, would be a matter of proof—and thereafter he tried to defend himself he was cut and became enraged, apparently, after which he disarmed her and thereafter stabbed her with a knife several times, after which, of course, the woman died.

The Court(to defendant):

Q: Did you use a knife in that fashion—you did stab her?

A: Not that I know that I stab her.

Q: But you were in a fight with her?

A: Yes, I remember I was in some kind of a fight; I know I was cut myself.

Q: You were the only one there?

A: I think so.

Q: Don't you know?

A: I don't know for sure, but I think so.

Q: You used the knife, didn't you?

A: Not to my knowledge.

Prosecuting Attorney:

Q: Now, Mr. Elksnis, you were engaged in an argument with your wife, is that right? You remember that? You had a fight with your wife?

A: I remember that, yes.

Q: And do you remember that she came at you with a hammer?

A: Yes, I was hit by the hammer.

Q: Was that hammer in your wife's hands?

A: Yes.

Q: After you were hit by the hammer did you then try to protect yourself?

A: Yes, I did.

Q: And then there was a knife produced?

A: Yes, she cut me in my hand.

Q: After she cut you with the knife, did you do something with the knife?

A: I was trying to get the knife.

Q: We want you to be certain about that. Did you try to get the knife away from your wife?

A: Yes, I was dodging that knife; I recall that, and I recall I twisted her arm.

Q: And you got the knife?

A: I think I did.

Q: And thereafter did you remember that you moved it toward your wife or made a thrust at your wife?

A: I don't know; something exploded in my head and it was black all around, a complete black.

Q: Was there anybody else with you?

A: Not when the argument started.

Q: Mr. Elksnis, are you stating to the Court that you did not do this?

A: No, I mean it is not in my mind or in my knowledge that I did.

Q: Is it your belief that you did do it?

A: I believe later, after the evidence was shown—there was blood on my clothes and it could not have been anybody else and I have come to the conclusion it must have been me.

The Court
We will accept the plea.

The New York Appellate Court reversed the judicial action of accepting this plea of guilty and the sentence imposed, and they ordered a trial on the merits of the case. Their conclusion was that the defendant had not pled guilty because he was, in fact guilty, but because he was compromising his claimed defenses in exchange for the sentence he then believed would be imposed upon him as previously agreed. The forthwith acceptance of the guilty plea without a searching inquiry as to the merits of the alleged self–defense plea and the defendant's claim that "something exploded in my head," stamp the plea as one not understandingly and knowingly made and this ground, too, requires that it be declared void.

In its majority opinion in this case, the New York Appellate Court judges summed up the importance of the judiciary remaining aloof from actual plea bargaining in these words:

> Petitioner first considered surrendering his right to trial and his defenses when his counsel informed him of the proposed reduction in the charge from murder to manslaughter, and that if he pleaded thereto the judge was agreeable to a sentence not to exceed ten years. As against the proffered sentence his lawyer stressed a possible term of from forty years to life in the event of conviction on the second degree murder charge. Then followed the chambers conference at which the judge made the express promise to the defendant. That it induced the plea cannot be gainsaid. To deny the compelling force of the promise is to deny the reality of experience.

> The unequal positions of the judge and the accused, one with the power to commit to prison and the other deeply concerned to avoid prison, at once raise a question of fundamental fairness. When a judge becomes a participant in plea bargaining he brings to bear the full force and majesty of his office. His awesome power to impose a substantially longer or even maximum sentence in excess of that proposed is present whether referred to or not. A defendant needs no reminder that if he rejects the proposal, stands upon his right to trial and is convicted, he faces a significantly longer sentence. One facing a prison term, whether of longer or shorter duration, is easily influenced to accept what appears the more preferable choice. Intentionally or otherwise, and no matter how well motivated the judge may be, the accused is subjected to a subtle but powerful influence. A guilty plea predicated upon a judge's promise of a definite sentence by its vary nature does not qualify as a free and voluntary act. The plea is so interlaced with the promise that the one cannot be separated from the other; remove the promise and the basis for the plea falls.

> A judge's prime responsibility is to maintain the integrity of the judicial system; to see that due process of law, equal protection of the laws and the basic safeguards of a fair trial are upheld. The judge stands as the symbol of even–handed justice, and none can seriously question that if this central figure in the administration of justice promises an accused that upon a plea of guilty a fixed sentence will follow, his commitment has an all–pervasive and compelling influence in inducing the accused to yield

his right to trial. A plea entered upon a bargain agreement between a judge and an accused cannot be squared with due process requirements of the Fourteenth Amendment.

This case points up the hazards of judicial participation in negotiating pleas of guilty, and indicates that when plea negotiations do involve a sentencing judge all participants should be instructed by him that his final action will depend upon all the facts being as represented to him by the various participants. It will certainly protect judicial integrity if it is fully understood by all concerned, and particularly by the defendant, that if the facts are subsequently found to be different from those represented to him for his agreement, then the judge may reject the entire plea agreement. He may allow the defendant to withdraw his plea and then bring the case to trial. In spite of this prior bargaining to a plea of guilty, there will be no prejudice at trial or at a sentencing session in the event of a verdict of guilty.

The Doctrine of Fundamental Fairness and Plea Negotiations

One of the major myths of the American legal system is that there is little or no injustice. While the major thrust has been to guard against the conviction of innocent people, there is also a belief that the legal system should operate in such a manner as to provide all persons accused of crime with a fundamental fairness, from the time of arrest until the final disposition of the charges.

The negotiated plea of guilty has always been a threat to this fundamental fairness because of the prosecuting attorney's power to make the decision as to which crimes to charge, and how many to be brought to trial. His power extends to his capability in securing the sentencing judge's cooperation in setting a sentence; and the vulnerability of a defendant once he enters a plea of guilty.

A classic case in this area of guilty pleas as they relate to fundamental fairness is *Boykin* v. *Alabama*.[8] Boykin was arrested and indicted for a two–week crime spree in Mobile, Alabama, consisting of a series of armed robberies of grocery stores, in two of which shots were fired. In one robbery, a shot was discharged into the ceiling without personal injury; but in the second shooting, a bullet hit the floor and then struck a customer in the leg. Before trial, the court of arraignment determined that the defendant was indigent and appointed counsel to represent him. Three days later, in a court appearance to plead to five indictments charging robbery—a capital offense in Alabama—the defendant pled guilty to all five crimes. The judge did not question the defendant, and the defendant did not address the court.

8. 395 U.S. 238 (1968).

In accordance with Alabama law, a penalty trial was held, with the prosecution presenting its case largely through eyewitness testimony. While defense counsel went through the motions of cross–examination, it was very brief, and the defense presented no character evidence and the defendant did not take the stand in his own behalf.

The judge's instructions to this penalty jury stressed that the defendant had pleaded guilty to five cases of robbery, each carrying a penalty provision of from ten years in the penitentiary (minimum) to death by electrocution (maximum). The jury deliberated and returned with a sentence of death on each of the five indictments. The Alabama Supreme Court reviewed the sentences and affirmed them.

In a review by the U.S. Supreme Court on the question of the voluntariness of Boykin's plea of guilty to five capital crimes, the court held that acceptance of Boykin's guilty plea under the circumstances of this case constituted reversible error because the record did not disclose that Boykin voluntarily and understandingly entered his plea of guilty. The following extracts from the majority opinion in this case review the doctrine of fundamental fairness in relation to pleas of guilty:

> A plea of guilty is more than a confession which admits that the accused did various acts; it is itself a conviction; nothing remains but to give judgment and determine punishment. Admissibility of a confession must be based on a "reliable determination on the voluntariness issue which satisfies the constitutional rights of the defendant." *Jackson* v. *Denno*, 378 U.S. 368. The requirement that the prosecution spread on the record the prerequisites of a valid waiver is no constitutional innovation. In *Carnley* v. *Cochran*, 369 U.S. 506, we dealt with a problem of waiver of the right to counsel, a Sixth Amendment right. We held: "Presuming waiver from a silent record is impermissible. The record must show, or there must be an allegation and evidence which show, that an accused was offered counsel but intelligently and understandingly rejected the offer. Anything less is not waiver."

> We think that the same standard must be applied to determining whether a guilty plea is voluntarily made. For, as we have said, a plea of guilty is more than an admission of conduct; it is a conviction. Ignorance, incomprehension, coercion, terror, inducements, subtle or blatant threats might be a perfect cover–up of unconstitutionality. The question of an effective waiver of a federal constitutional right in a proceeding is of course governed by federal standards.

> Several federal constitutional rights are involved in a waiver that takes place when a plea of guilty is entered in a state criminal trial. *First,* is the privilege against compulsory self–incrimination guaranteed by the Fifth Amendment and applicable to the States by reason of the Fourteenth. *Second,* is the right to trial by jury. *Third,* is the right to confront one's accusers. We cannot presume a waiver of these three important federal rights from a silent record.

What is at stake for an accused facing death or imprisonment demands the utmost solicitude of which courts are capable in canvassing the matter with the accused to make sure he has a full understanding of what the plea connotes and of its consequences.

When the process of plea negotiation becomes a visible, open, and public part of the administration of justice, it is more likely that fundamental fairness will be commonplace in the courts of America in which guilty pleas are entered by persons accused of crime. Secrecy, mysterious circumstances surrounding plea agreements, and the subversion of judicial integrity as it concerns promises to defendants, are at odds with the concepts of equal treatment, fundamental fairness, and the belief that defendants should only plead guilty when they know the nature of the charges and the consequences of this plea—and are, in fact, guilty as charged.

Selected References

Books

American Bar Association Committee on Minimum Standards for Pleas of Guilty. *Standards Relating to Pleas of Guilty.* New York: Institute of Judicial Administration, 1970.

Newman, Donald J. *Conviction.* Boston: Little, Brown & Co., 1969.

President's Commission on Law Enforcement and Administration of Justice. *The Challenge of Crime in a Free Society.* Washington, D.C.: U.S. Government Printing Office, 1967.

Radin, Edward D. *The Innocents.* New York: William Morrow and Co., 1964.

Cases

U.S. *ex rel* Elksnis v. Gilligan, 256 F. Supp. 244 (1966).

Boykin v. Alabama, 395 U.S. 238 (1968).

There need never be another Sam Sheppard
if enough people understand why...what...
and how it happened.   F. Lee Bailey

Chapter XI

Crime and Publicity

Justice cannot survive behind walls of silence. Justice requires a charge fairly made and fairly tried in a public tribunal free of prejudice, passion, excitement, and tyrannical power. These two basic concepts clash in our scheme of justice in the field of criminal proceedings.

Standards for the release of crime news, originating in court decisions or the action of authoritative organizations interested in criminal justice, will establish reasonable rules for news reporting of crime and criminals. News gatherers for the press, radio, and TV, however, are in a competitive business. The right of an accused person to a fair trial without prejudiced jurors is jeopardized in accordance with the newsworthiness of the case. Sensational crimes will test any standards for limiting news, and may require court action on an individual basis.

Secret Trial

The belief that justice for a person accused of a public offense is mutually exclusive from a secret trial (walls of silence) arose in the 1948 case of *In re Oliver*.[1] In this case a Michigan judge was conducting, in accordance with Michigan law, a secret one–man grand jury investigation of crime. A witness (Oliver) was held in contempt of court for alleged false and evasive testimony and sentenced to 60 days in jail. The proceedings were secret. The case was appealed to the U.S.

1. In re Oliver, 333 U.S. 257 (1947).

Supreme Court, and their majority opinion contained these words on the hazards of secret tribunals:

> Here we are concerned, not with petitioner's rights as a witness in a secret grand jury session, but with his rights as a defendant in a contempt proceeding. The powers of the judge–grand jury* who tried and convicted him (Oliver) in secret and sentenced him to jail on a charge of false and evasive swearing must likewise be measured, not by the limitations applicable to grand jury proceedings, but by the constitutional standards applicable to court proceedings in which an accused may be sentenced to fine or imprisonment or both.

Thus our first question is this: Can an accused be tried and convicted for contempt of court in grand jury secrecy?

First. Counsel have not cited and we have been unable to find a single instance of a criminal trial conducted in camera** in any federal, state, or municipal court during the history of this county. Nor have we found any record of even one such secret criminal trial in England since abolition of the Court of Star Chamber[2] in 1641, and whether that court ever convicted people secretly is in dispute. Summary trials for alleged misconduct called contempt of court have not been regarded as an exception to this universal rule against secret trials, unless some other Michigan one–man grand jury case may represent such an exception.

This nation's accepted practice of guaranteeing a public trial to an accused has its roots in our English common law heritage. The exact date of its origin is obscure, but it likely evolved long before the settlement of our land as an accompaniment of the ancient institution of jury trial. In this country the guarantee to an accused of the right to a public trial first appeared in a state constitution in 1776.[3] Following the ratification in 1791 of the Federal Constitution's Sixth Amendment, which commands that "In all criminal prosecutions, the accused shall enjoy the right to a speedy and public trial . . ." most of the original states and those subsequently admitted to the Union adopted similar constitutional provisions. Today almost without exception every state by constitution, statute, or judicial decision, requires that all criminal trials be open to the public.

The traditional Anglo–American distrust for secret trials has been variously ascribed to the notorious use of this practice by the Spanish

---

*A one–man grand jury comprised of a circuit court judge; unusual, but in accordance with Michigan law.

**In chambers; in private; when spectators (public) excluded.

2. Some authorities have said that trials in the Star Chamber were public, but that witnesses against the accused were examined privately with no opportunity for him to discredit them. Apparently all authorities agree that the accused himself was grilled in secret, often tortured, in an effort to obtain a confession and that the most objectionable of the Star Chamber's practices was its asserted prerogative to disregard the common law rules of criminal procedure when the occasion demanded.

3. Pennsylvania; North Carolina (criminal convictions only by jury verdict in open court).

Inquisition, to the excesses of the English Court of Star Chamber, and to the French monarchy's abuse of the *letter de cachet.** All of these institutions obviously symbolized a menace to liberty. In the hands of despotic groups each of them had become an instrument for the suppression of political and religious heresies in ruthless disregard of the right of an accused to a fair trial.

Whatever other benefits the guarantee to an accused that his trial be conducted in public may confer upon our society,[4] the guarantee has always been recognized as a safeguard against any attempt to employ our courts as instruments of persecution. The knowledge that every criminal trial is subject to contemporaneous review in the forum of public opinion is an effective restraint on possible abuse of judicial power. One need not wholly agree with a statement made on the subject by Jeremy Bentham over 120 years ago to appreciate the fear of secret trials felt by him, his predecessors and contemporaries. Bentham said: "... suppose the proceedings to be completely secret, and the court, on the occasion, to consist of no more than a single judge,—that judge will be at once indolent and arbitrary: how corrupt soever his inclination may be, it will find no check, at any rate no tolerably efficient check, to oppose it. Without publicity, all other checks are of small account. Recordation, appeal, whatever other institutions might present themselves in the character of checks, would be found to operate rather as cloaks than checks; as cloaks in reality, as checks only in appearance."

In giving content to the constitutional and statutory commands that an accused be given a public trial, the state and federal courts have differed over what groups of spectators, if any, could properly be excluded from a criminal trial. But, unless in Michigan and in one-man grand jury contempt cases, no court in this country has ever before held, so far as we can find, that an accused can be tried, convicted, and sent to jail, when everybody else is denied entrance to the court, except the judge and his attaches. And without exception all courts have held that an accused is at the very best entitled to have his friends, relatives and counsel present, no matter with what offense he may be charged.

The Court's holding in *Oliver* was that the secrecy of the trial for criminal contempt violated the due process clause of the Fourteenth Amendment: 1. The facts of the case did not justify a secret trial of an offense punishable by fine or imprisonment. 2. An accused is entitled to a public trial, at least to having counsel, relatives and friends present, no matter what the offense. 3. As a minimum, due process requires that an accused be given: a. reasonable notice of the charge against him. b. the right to examine witnesses against him. c. the right to testify in his own behalf, d. the right to be represented by counsel.

*An order of the king that one of his subjects be forthwith imprisoned or exiled without a trial or an opportunity to defend himself.

4. Public trials come to the attention of key witnesses unknown to the parties. These witnesses may then voluntarily come forward and give important testimony.

Fair Trial Without Prejudice

The standard of criminal justice in America; that an accusation be fairly made and the accused fairly tried in a public tribunal free of prejudice or other disabling factors is a constitutional right applicable to state agents by the due process clause of the Fourteenth Amendment. The U.S. Supreme Court, in *Chambers* v. *Florida*[5] summed up the dimensions of this right in the majority opinion, and the following extract from this opinion not only explains the rationale for unprejudiced trials, but also terms this right one of the "blessings of liberty":

> The Fourteenth Amendment—just as that in the Fifth—has led few to doubt that it was intended to guarantee procedural standards adequate and appropriate, then and thereafter, to protect, at all times, people charged with or suspected of crime by those holding positions of power and authority.

> Tyrannical governments had immemorially utilized dictatorial criminal procedure and punishment to make scapegoats of the weak, or of helpless political, religious, or racial minorities and those who differed, who would not conform and who resisted tyranny. The instruments of such governments were, in the main, two. Conduct, innocent when engaged in, was subsequently made by fiat criminally punishable without legislation. And a liberty loving people won the principle that criminal punishments could not be inflicted save for that which proper legislative action had already by "the law of the land" forbidden when done. But even more was needed. From the popular hatred and abhorrence of illegal confinement, torture and extortion of confessions of violations of the "law of the land" evolved the fundamental idea that no man's life, liberty or property be forfeited as criminal punishment for violation of that law until there had been a charge fairly made and fairly tried in a public tribunal free of prejudice, passion, excitement, and tyrannical power.

> Thus, as assurance against ancient evils, our country, in order to preserve "the blessings of liberty," wrote into its basic law the requirement, among others, that the forfeiture of the lives, liberties or property of people accused of crime can only follow if procedural safeguards of due process have been obeyed.

> The determination to preserve an accused's right to procedural due process sprang in large part from knowledge of the historical truth that the rights and liberties of people accused of crime could not be safely entrusted to secret inquisitorial processes. The testimony of centuries, in governments of varying kinds over populations of different races and beliefs, stood as proof that physical and mental torture and coercion had brought about the tragically unjust sacrifices of some who were the noblest and most useful of their generations.

A free press bulwarks all of a citizen's freedoms under the constitution, among them the right to a fair trial. Freedom of the press was so

5. 309 U.S. 227 (1939).

highly regarded by the framers of our constitution that it was included in the first amendment to the constitution. The legislative intent was that the liberty of the press should be as broad as was consistent with an orderly society. In probing all areas of government, however, there has emerged a well–founded belief that a free press would insure that criminal accusations and trials be open to public scrutiny. The possibility of public disclosure of any miscarriage of justice would prevent police, prosecutors, or the judiciary from any acts of oppression or other injustice.

On the other side of the coin is publicity, which by its nature and quantity, can be a threat to the integrity of the trial itself. Such publicity makes it impossible for an accused to receive a fair trial because of the prejudice generated by the news media among local residents likely to be jurors, witnesses, or other participants in the trial.

The Case of Sam Sheppard

The case of Dr. Sam Sheppard in Cleveland, Ohio, in 1954, is a classic example of the ability of the press to create a situation in which a fair trial is unlikely or impossible.[6] Dr. Sam Sheppard was accused, tried, and convicted of the murder of his wife. The facts are these: Sheppard's pregnant wife was beaten to death with an unknown instrument in her upstairs bedroom in their home in a suburb of Cleveland, Ohio, on July 4, 1954.

Immediately after discovery Sam Sheppard gave the following story: Sheppard and his wife had entertained friends that night. When the friends left, his wife went to bed and Sheppard dozed off on the couch in the living room. The next thing he remembers is hearing his wife cry out. He ran upstairs to the bedroom and saw a form standing next to his wife's bed. He fought with this person, but was struck and knocked unconscious. When he became conscious again, he looked at his wife, checked her pulse and decided she was dead. He ran down stairs and pursued a figure (who was leaving the house) to the beach, where another struggle took place, and Sheppard was again struck and knocked unconscious. He awoke on the beach, hurried home, went upstairs again to his wife and checked her pulse. He found no pulse, went to the telephone, and called a friend (the local mayor who lived nearby), who came over immediately.

Sam Sheppard became the prime suspect in the case. Police arrested Sheppard, and he was formally accused of murder and brought to trial in the city of Cleveland, county of Cuyahoga, state of Ohio.

This was a case that could not be dropped or delayed. A young and

---

6. Paul Holmes, *The Sheppard Murder Case* (New York; David McKay Co., 1961), pp. 303–06.

expectant mother had been brutally bludgeoned and had died in her bed. There was public pressure on police, coroner, and prosecutor to produce the killer. It was a case, however, in which the police–prosecutor team could only gather a limited amount of evidence against Dr. Sheppard. However, when the investigation of the case failed to disclose any other person as the murderer, or even as another suspect, the prosecutor's decision was to go ahead with the trial despite the less–than–conclusive evidence.

Up to this point the news media had a field day in reporting their theories of the crime, interviews with so-called experts in homicide, and police views and reports relating to the investigation and to Dr. Sheppard as the major suspect—all of it prejudicial to Sheppard. Some of the headlines and editorial headings were:

Doctor Sheppard Balks at Lie Test

Somebody is Getting Away with Murder

Why Isn't Sam Sheppard in Jail?

Quit Stalling—Bring In Sheppard

The trial itself was unbelievable. Twenty–five days before the trial the names and addresses of 75 selected prospective jurors were published in the papers. As a result, all of them received phone calls concerning the impending trial from friends as well as anonymous callers. In a courtroom 26 feet by 48 feet, 20 local newspaper representatives were assigned front row seats; and behind them television, radio, and out–of–town newsmen were assigned the next four rows of benches. Special telephone and broadcasting equipment was set up in the courthouse for the news media. All the participants were photographed, including the jurors and witnesses, and the testimony of each witness was printed verbatim in the newspapers on each day of the trial, together with all the court rulings and attorneys' motions. These extensive daily summaries were headed by, or contained, editorial comment that repeatedly expressed certainty of Dr. Sheppard's guilt and the expected verdict of guilty.

The publicity totaled such proportions that one reporter commented: "The question of Dr. Sheppard's guilt or innocence still is before the courts. Those who have examined the trial records carefully are divided as to the propriety of the verdict. But almost everyone who watched the performance of the Cleveland press agrees that a fair hearing for the defendant, in that area, would be a modern miracle."[7]

7. John M. Harrison, "The Press vs. the Courts," *Saturday Review*, 15 October 1955, pp. 9–10, 35.

Sheppard v. *Maxwell*—Court Rule Making

To assure the public full information about government and its affairs, to protect an accused's right to a public trial, and to prevent the suppression of other individual rights, the American press is free. Only when the historic right to a fair trial is endangered is there a question about whether there must be some limitation on the press to protect an accused from prejudicial publicity which inflames public opinion against him and creates a preverdict judgment of guilty as charged.

Basic limitations were established in the U.S. Supreme Court's review of Dr. Sam Sheppard's conviction in Ohio for the murder of his wife. The case, *Sheppard* vs. *Maxwell*[8] was decided in 1965, and the Court's holding was:

1.   The massive, pervasive, and prejudicial publicity attending petitioner's prosecution prevented him from receiving a fair trial consistent with the due process clause of the Fourteenth Amendment.

    a. Though freedom of discussion should be given the widest range compatible with the fair and orderly administration of justice, it must not be allowed to divert a trial from its purpose of adjudicating controversies according to legal procedures based on evidence received only in open court.

    b. Identifiable prejudice to the accused need not be shown if, as in *Estes* v. *Texas*, 381 U.S. 532, and even more so in this case, the totality of the circumstances raises the probability of prejudice.

    c. The trial court failed to invoke procedures which would have guaranteed petitioner a fair trial, such as adopting stricter rules for use of the courtroom by newsmen as petitioner's counsel requested, limiting their number, and more closely supervising their courtroom conduct. The court should also have insulated the witnesses; controlled the release of leads, information, and gossip to the press by police officers, witnesses, and counsel; proscribed extrajudicial statements by any lawyer, witness, party, or court official divulging prejudicial matters; and requested the appropriate city and county officials to regulate release of information by their employees.

2.   The case is remanded to the District Court with instructions to release petitioner from custody unless he is tried again within a reasonable time.

The Court's majority opinion in the Sheppard case reveals its review of the prejudicial publicity, its belief in the accountability of the trial judge, and its response to the question as to limitation on a free press in its crime reporting. The following extracts sum up the Court's views:

8. 384 U.S. 333 (1965)

Sheppard stood indicted for the murder of his wife; the State was demanding the death penalty. For months the virulent publicity about Sheppard and the murder had made the case notorious. Charges and countercharges were aired in the news media besides those for which Sheppard was called to trial. In addition, only three months before trial, Sheppard was examined for more than five hours without counsel during a three-day inquest which ended in a public brawl. The inquest was televised live from a high school gymnasium seating hundreds of people.

While we cannot say that Sheppard was denied due process by the judge's refusal to take precautions against the influence of pretrial publicity alone, the court's later rulings must be considered against the setting in which the trial was held. In light of this background, we believe that the arrangements made by the judge with the news media caused Sheppard to be deprived of that judicial serenity and calm to which he was entitled. Bearing in mind the massive pretrial publicity, the judge should have adopted stricter rules governing the use of the courtroom by newsmen, as Sheppard's counsel requested.

First, the number of reporters in the courtroom itself could have been limited at the first sign that their presence would disrupt the trial. They certainly should not have been placed inside the bar. Furthermore, the judge should have more closely regulated the conduct of newsmen in the courtroom.

Secondly, the court should have insulated the witnesses. All of the newspapers and radio stations apparently interviewed prospective witnesses at will, and in many instances disclosed their testimony. A typical example was the publication of numerous statements by Susan Hayes, before her appearance in court, regarding her love affair with Sheppard. Although the witnesses were barred from the courtroom during the trial the full verbatim testimony was available to them in the press. This completely nullified the judge's imposition of the rule.

Thirdly, the court should have made some effort to control the release of leads, information, and gossip to the press by police officers, witnesses, and the counsel for both sides. Much of the information thus disclosed was inaccurate, leading to groundless rumors and confusion.

More specifically, the trial court might well have proscribed extrajudicial statements by any lawyer, party, witness, or court official which divulged prejudicial matters, such as the refusal of Sheppard to submit to interrogation or take any lie detector tests; any statement made by Sheppard to officials; the identity of prospective witnesses or their probable testimony; any belief in guilt or innocence; or like statements concerning the merits of the case.

Being advised of the great public interest in the case, the mass coverage of the press, and the potential prejudicial impact of publicity, the court could also have requested the appropriate city and county officials to promulgate a regulation with respect to dissemination of information about the case by their employees.

In addition, reporters who wrote or broadcast prejudicial stories, could have been warned as to the impropriety of publishing material not introduced in the proceedings. The judge was put on notice of such events by defense counsel's complaint about the WHK broadcast on the second day of trial.

In this manner, Sheppard's right to a trial free from outside interference would have been given added protection without corresponding curtailment of the news media. Had the judge, the other officers of the court, and the police placed the interest of justice first, the news media would have soon learned to be content with the task of reporting the case as it unfolded in the courtroom—not pieced together from extrajudicial statements.

From the cases coming here we note that unfair and prejudicial news comment on pending trials has become increasingly prevalent. One process requires that the accused receive a trial by an impartial jury free from outside influences. Given the pervasiveness of modern communications and the difficulty of effacing prejudicial publicity from the minds of the jurors, the trial courts must take strong measures to ensure that the balance is never weighed against the accused.

Of course, there is nothing that proscribes the press from reporting events that transpire in the courtroom. But where there is a reasonable likelihood that prejudicial news prior to trial will prevent a fair trial, the judge should continue the case until the threat abates, or transfer it to another county not so permeated with publicity. In addition, sequestration of the jury was something the judge should have raised *sua sponte** with counsel.

If publicity during the proceedings threatens the fairness of the trial, a new trial should be ordered. But we must remember that reversals are but palliatives; the cure lies in those remedial measures that will prevent the prejudice at its inception. The courts must take such steps by rule and regulation that will protect their processes from prejudicial outside interferences. Neither prosecutors, counsel for defense, the accused, witnesses, court staff nor enforcement officers coming under the jurisdiction of the court should be permitted to frustrate its function. Collaboration between counsel and the press as to information affecting the fairness of a criminal trial is not only subject to regulation, but is highly censurable and worthy of disciplinary measures.

Since the state trial judge did not fulfill his duty to protect Sheppard from the inherently prejudicial publicity which saturated the community and to control disruptive influences in the courtroom, we must reverse the denial of the habeas petition. The case is remanded to the District Court with instructions to issue the writ and order that Sheppard be released from custody unless the State puts him to its charges again within a reasonable time.

F. Lee Bailey, Dr. Sheppard's counsel in the above proceedings and in the ensuing trial that exonerated Sheppard, commented that public opinion can be a real source of strength to the proper administration

*Upon his own responsibility; of his own motion.

of justice only when it is not misinformed or deliberately misled, saying: "There need never be another Sam Sheppard if enough people come to know and understand this one, and understand what happened to him, how it happened, and why it was all so unnecessary."[9]

Standards for the Release of Crime News

The accomodation of the First Amendment guarantee of a free press with the Sixth Amendment right to a speedy and public trial before an impartial jury must be solved without interfering with the press' invaluable function in discovering and disclosing public corruption and injustice. The solution to the problem of the publicity that surrounds crime must also be responsible to the possible adverse impact of news coverage on: (1) the investigation of the crime, (2) the opinions of potential or actual jurors; (3) the conduct of police, prosecuting attorney, defense counsel, and trial judge; and (4) the integrity and stature of the adjudicating process and our legal system. This accomodation between the First and Sixth Amendments will require the adoption of limitations, both as to content and timing, on the release of information by members of the bar and by law enforcement agents about the apprehension and trial of criminal defendants. Appropriate remedies will have to be made available whenever there is evidence to show that a fair trial has been jeopardized by adverse publicity to the accused.[10]

There are excesses in publicity about crime and criminals which can be removed without real damage to the freedom of the press, or the right of the public to know; and which will increase the probability of a fair trial for the accused. Two problems are identified, and three areas are isolated as potential sources for solutions:

    1. *Problems*

        a. What matters reported endanger the fairness of the criminal process?

        b. How can such matters be reduced or eliminated from reporting without abridging freedom of speech and press and open trials?

    2. *Solutions*

        a. The conduct of attorney.

9. Dr. Sam Sheppard, *Endure and Conquer* (Cleveland: The World Publishing Co., 1966), pp. *vii–x* (Foreword by F. Lee Bailey).

10. Paul C. Reardon and Clifton Daniel, *Fair Trial and Free Press* (Washington, D.C.: American Enterprise Institute for Public Policy Research, 1968), pp. 1–27.

b. The conduct of law enforcement officers and judicial employees.

c. The conduct of judicial proceedings.

Identification of the basic problem, the persons whose conduct will be significant in its resolvement, and guidelines for the release of information by such persons have been superimposed on the time clock of a criminal proceeding by a committee of the American Bar Association.[11] These standards do not directly offer any control over the press, but rather suggest procedures that will control the source of news in regard to crime and its publicity. The control of the source of crime news is suggested by these standards as follows:

At the time of arrest—Law enforcement agents and officials should release no more information than the identity of the person arrested, the circumstances of the arrest, the crime charged, and the identity of the victim. Officials should not give out results of investigative examinations or tests; the existence or content of a "confession"; the information that an accused has refused to make a statement; or the accused's prior criminal record, if any. Officials should not state personal opinions about the guilt of the accused or about the credibility of witnesses or any other matter which might jeopardize a fair trial. In addition, as a general rule, no information should be released that is highly prejudicial, unless public disclosure serves a significant law enforcement function.[12]

Prior to trial—Law enforcement personnel, prosecutor, and defense counsel may release information concerning the commission of the crime and its general scope, but may not release data which identifies the suspects prior to arrest, except for the purpose of assisting in discovery and apprehension of suspects, or in the furtherance of the investigation. The results of scientific or other tests should not be released, nor should those involved in the investigation express opinions which may prevent a fair trial. The court may either close the pretrial hearing or order that certain evidence presented not be disseminated by the news media if good cause is shown that such evidence produced at the hearing may be inadmissible at the trial, and thus its dissemination would or could jeopardize a fair trial.[13]

During the trial—It is ethically improper for a lawyer of either side to make out of court statements about the trial, the issues, the parties, or witnesses except to quote from the public record of the trial. The court may order

11. American Bar Association Advisory Committee on Fair Trial and Free Press, *Standards Relating to Fair Trial and Free Press* (New York: Institute of Judicial Administration, 1966), pp. 7–14.

12. *Standards—Fair Trial and Free Press*, pp. 98–109.

13. Ibid., pp. 80–90.

others (parties, witnesses, and court personnel) not to make extrajudicial statements regarding the case or their part in the case. Where the court feels it proper he may exclude all except the parties and their attorneys in matters of law or fact which are taken up outside the presence of the jury, and should grant a change of venue if he believes, because of news coverage, the defendant cannot obtain a fair trial in his jurisdiction.[14]

Rules of the court have long been familiar to lawyers and police officers. Such rules are necessary for the orderly procedure vital to the operation of the courts. They can be extended to cover the enforcement of reasonable regulations limiting publicity, in accord with the "standards" cited above. This does not mean that law enforcement agencies, prosecutors' offices, and institutionalized legal services for the defense (public defender, legal aid groups), should not adopt similar regulations for their employees. The recommended rules of the court would support such action by local agencies and provide a statewide application. Certainly, such action is within the role of any court to assure fair trials.[15]

In prior years, newspapermen have been skeptical about any codes or standards because restricting the release of news is prior censorship. Since every newsman employed by any of the communications media is a participant in a competitive business of getting the news, there is likely to be some prying and probing to get data not released by criminal justice agents or agencies.

In Minot F. Jelke's first trial on charges of compulsory prostitution the press was excluded from the courtroom on the orders of the trial judge. The judicial rationale was concerned with public morals: the probable content of the testimony of the call girl prostitutes scheduled to appear as witnesses in this case. The reality of news reporting, however, failed to shield public morals, and all of the colorful testimony of the prostitutes was not kept secret. Newsmen used second–hand sources of information because of the judge's edict. In addition, Jelke's conviction was reversed on appeal because the press was barred from the courtroom. In the opinion that ordered a new trial for Jelke, the New York Appellate Court stated:

> "Due regard for the defendant's rights to a public trial demanded, at the very least, that he not be deprived of the possible benefits of attendance by the press."[16]

News media will publish data when sensational crimes occur, wheth-

---

14. Ibid., pp. 90–97.

15. Council of Judges of the National Council on Crime and Delinquency, *Model Rules of Court on Police Action from Arrest to Arraignment* (New York: National Council on Crime and Delinquency, 1969), pp. 27–28.

16. Jelke v. New York, 308 N.Y. 85 (1954).

er it is obtained from secret sources, leaks in the criminal justice establishment, witnesses, or other persons concerned with the circumstances of the crime or suspects. However, the staff of an increasing number of newspapers, weekly news magazines, and radio and TV news bureaus are aware that the abuse of the freedom of the press jeopardizes the right to a fair trial and they have displayed a willingness to accept internal controls. Hopefully, it will be in alignment with the standards for releasing data on crime and suspects by agents of criminal justice.

Have You Formed or Expressed an Opinion?

The theory of trial by jury is that a body of citizens will be more likely to discover the truth on the issue of guilt or innocence than a single person—a judge or magistrate. In the early years of jury trials, local citizens who knew the circumstances of the crime or the facts of life about the defendant were sought for jury. Later, it was found that more equitable verdicts were returned by jurors without any knowledge of the crime or the defendant. In modern jurisprudence, the panel of citizens called for jury duty must be representative of local citizenry and no group of citizens can be systematically excluded because of race, color, creed, sex, or national origin. Individual prospective jurors are then examined in a *voir dire* session to make certain they are not bigoted or prejudiced, and can arrive at a verdict as a result of the evidence presented during the trial. What is being sought in this *voir dire* examination is a completely objective and impartial juror.

Publicity cannot be discounted as an influence on jury verdicts because on voir dire, in response to questions from the attorney or judge, jurors reply that they either haven't formed opinions, will not form opinions, or will not read about the case. While the court will instruct jurors to decide the case only on the evidence adduced in court and not to read news articles about the case, such instructions often go unheeded.

Too many cases have been recorded showing the influence of publicity on juries to consider verbal admonition by the trial judge an adequate safeguard. For instance:

1. Out of 430 prospective jurors, 268 were excused for cause because they had fixed opinions as to guilt. Ninety percent admitted to some opinion.[17]

2. After extensive publicity accusing the defendants, every member of the trial jury admitted to a prior opinion of guilt.[18]

17. State v. Kociolek (1955) 20 N.J. 92
18. People v. Lessard (1962) 58 Cal. 2d 447

3. Of 68 prospective jurors questioned, eight were seated on *voir dire*, and four of these individuals said they had an opinion of guilt they could not set aside.[19]

4. After the defense counsel used all of the defense's peremptory challenges, there were four prospective jurors who admitted to an opinion based on what they had read, and who stated they would not want one of their loved ones tried by a jury with their attitudes.[20]

5. All of the prospective jurors said that they had heard or read of the case in which pretrial reporting included extensive details of the crime and the defendant's confession.[21]

6. Despite the court's instructions to the jury to decide the case only on the evidence adduced at the trial, there was mention in the jury deliberations of the indictment of the defendant on another crime of violence which was not a part of the evidence in the present case.[22]

7. A juror had read an inaccurate news report of the trial, discussed it with other jurors, and based his opinion of guilt upon it.[23]

8. Several jurors had read about confessions of the defendant in an unrelated case (the confessions were later discredited), and discussed them during their deliberations.[24]

When excessive publicity endangers a fair trial the standard remedy is a motion for a change of venue to a locality where publicity and citizen involvement is not a factor. However, there must be a show of threat, then a motion for change of venue will be granted when it is determined that because of the dissemination of potentially prejudicial material, there is a *reasonable likelihood* a fair trial cannot be held. A show of actual prejudice is not required. An alternate method is a request for a continuance to delay the actual trial and jury selection, until the impact of the excessive publicity has diminished. However, time and again, a defense counsel is forced to rely on the voir dire examination and his ability to challenge for cause, or his limited peremptory challenges to secure objective jurors.

When there is a likelihood that jurors will be ineligible because of exposure to adverse publicity to the defendant, the questioning (voir

19. People v. Whitmore (1965) 257 N.Y.S. 2d 787
20. Irwin v. Dowd (1961) 366 U.S. 717
21. Juelich v. U.S. (1954) 214 F2d 950
22. Hagan v. State (1962 Texas) 372 SW2d 946
23. People v. Duncan (1960) 350 P2d 103
24. People v. Odom (1963 Mo.) 369 SW2d 173

dire) must probe what the prospective juror has read and heard about the case and how his exposure has affected his attitude towards the trial and the defendant. A prospective juror who states he is unable to overcome his prejudgment or preconceptions is subject to challenge for cause. One who remembers a great deal of the content of the prejudicial news which is significant on the issue of guilt or innocence (confession; incriminating evidence), and may be inadmissible in evidence during the trial, is also subject to challenge for cause, despite claims of an impartial attitude. Other prospective jurors exposed to such publicity must be examined to determine whether the exposure— or their recall of the news content—creates a substantial risk that the juror's judgment has been prejudiced.[25]

An early case, *People* v. *Brown*,[26] sets out the kind of questioning which is proper to determine bias or prejudice from pretrial publicity.

During the examination of prospective jurors, M.P. Troxler was questioned as to his qualifications. He stated that he had heard some talk of the case, had read accounts of the affair in the local newspapers, thought he had read the evidence taken before the coroner, and had formed an opinion in reference to guilt or innocence of the defendant. He was then asked by defendant's counsel:

Q: Was that opinion favorable or unfavorable to the defendant?

(Objection by prosecutor; sustained by court.)

Q: What is your opinion *now* from what you read as to the guilt or innocence of the defendant?

(Objection by prosecutor; sustained by court.)

Q: What impression did the reading of these articles make on your mind?

(Objection by prosecutor; sustained by court.)

Q: Could you enter upon the trial of this case with the presumption that the defendant is innocent until he was proved guilty? Or would you enter upon the trial presuming that defendant is guilty, and desiring to see him vindicated by the testimony of the witnesses here?

A: I don't think I could.

Q: That is, you don't think you could enter upon the trial of the case with the belief that the defendant is innocent?

A: No sir.

25. Alfred Friendly and Ronald L. Goldfarb, *Crime and Publicity—The Impact of News on the Administration of Justice* (New York: Twentieth Century Fund, 1967), pp. 95–106
26. 72 Cal. 390 (1887)

Q: Do you think you could give the defendant a fair and impartial trial?

A: I think I could, notwithstanding I have an opinion from what I have heard and read. It would take good evidence to remove that opinion.

Q: In other words, you would be of opinion that defendant is guilty until he had proved himself innocent; isn't that the exact state of your mind?

(Objection by prosecutor; sustained by court.)

While the trial court refused to rule that this prospective juror was prejudiced (he was challenged for actual bias), and allowed him to remain on the jury, the California Appellate Court approved the questions of defense counsel and ruled that the juror should have been excused for bias when challenged.

The court's opinion in the *Brown* case sums up the important question of publicity as a threat to trial by jury in these words:

> The precise question before the court was as to the existence of a state of mind on the part of the juror which would or might prevent him from acting with entire impartiality, and without prejudice to the rights of defendant. It was evident the juror had a fixed opinion as to the guilt of defendant, which he said would require good evidence to remove. The purpose of the attempted examination was to ascertain so far as possible the extent of this opinion, its character, and whether it resulted to any extent from prejudice against defendant or his case. We think the examination was proper, and that the court erred in sustaining the objections of the prosecuting attorney.

Lack of impartiality and objectivity on the part of jurors may originate in circumstances other than excessive publicity, but publicity adverse to the defendant has been identified as one of the most common causes of bias and prejudice. To ruin any opportunity for a fair trial, entertaining a fixed opinion that the defendant is guilty is not necessary; all that is required is a preconception or suspicion of guilt.

It is to prevent such suspicions from developing in the minds of prospective jurors (and others who may be significant to the outcome of a trial, such as witnesses and criminal justice personnel) that reasonable standards are necessary to limit the freedom of the press to prevent its abuse and the destruction of the right to a fair trial.

Sensational Crimes—The Corona Case

The major problems surrounding crime and publicity occur when a crime is sensational; one with great news value. It may be because of the newsworthiness of the participants (the Lindberg kidnapping case in New Jersey), an unusualness or new dimension of monstrosity (the Sharon Tate case in Los Angeles), sex and murder (the Wylie–Hoffert case in New York City), or mass murder. A case of mass murder was, literally, unearthed when law enforcement agents in Yuba City, California, dug up the remains of 25 murder victims from orchards north of the city.

These were grisly murders; the farm labor victims had been hacked with a sharp–edged weapon. The total number of victims made this a record crime (newsworthy in itself), outranking the 16–victim mass murder in Texas by Charles Whitman (the "tower sniper" at the University of Texas); young psychopath Howard Unrah's shooting attack in New Jersey in which he killed 13 people in a few moments; and the eight nurses murdered by Richard Speck in Chicago.

To make this Yuba City case even more newsworthy, it appeared that the times of death spanned no more than a two–month period before the discovery of the victims, indicating a systematic execution modus operandi. The victims were all transients, homeless men and "winos" from the skid rows of Yuba City and neighboring Marysville; without friends or relatives who would miss them when they were murdered and who would normally report their absence to police.

Reporters, photographers, and television crews swarmed into Yuba City: this might be the crime of the century. The sheriff and his deputies were restrained during the initial period, as were the prosecutor and the local judge who issued the search warrant when the first suspect developed. No one knows the mechanics of the breaking down of this restraint on the part of public officials, or the results of such restraint on newsmen already under tremendous pressures from employers and professional competition. What did happen between the discovery of the crime and the time the prime suspect was indicted and formally accused of murder is a fine example of how the search for news (in sensational crime cases) and its publication can rob an accused of his opportunity for a fair trial.

What happened in the reporting of this case of mass murder is indicative of how judges and law enforcement officials can err in their judgment and release data prejudicial to the accused. Men and women of the news media will find imaginative ways of reporting such gaffes, and when no further information is released, they will obtain some news from secret sources and present it as the truth.

Chronologically, this is a sampling of the reporting of the details of these murders and the interpretations concerning the guilt of the accused in the local press.*

On May 30, 1971, a front page story headlined the arrest of the only

---

*The *Sacramento Bee.* This is a daily paper with a mass circulation audience in Northern California, and it has wide circulation in Yuba City (45 miles from Sacramento) and in Sutter County.

major suspect in this case: MASS MURDER AND THE SUSPECT. The story briefly reviewed the fact that Juan Corona was a Mexican–born labor contractor, 37, and the father of four children. Then, it went on to the main content of the story: a detailing of data released by the local judge who had ordered the suspect's home searched on the authority of a search warrant. The following extract of Sutter County Sheriff Roy Whiteaker's application for a search warrant was quoted in its entirety:

> The nature of the wounds and their savagery, the disposition of the bodies of the murder victims, and the sheer number of victims indicates that the perpetrator of these offenses is at least seriously mentally ill and probably a homicidal maniac.

One of the following paragraphs quoted the same source and stated that a police official had talked to a man (unnamed) who knew the Corona brothers (Juan's brother lived nearby) and their families. This man had informed the police officials that Juan Corona was known to have fits of temper that were so bad that the family had to take ropes and tie him down until he became quiet again. The article concluded with this statement from an unidentified source: "Corona had often indicated to friends that he had no use for white, transient farm laborers, particularly winos, who only had one desire and that was to earn enough for another bottle."

Also on May 30, 1971, but in a story on an interior page, alongside the carryover of the page–one story, there was an alleged report of contact with Juan Corona's mother in Mexico, headed: "SUSPECT'S MOTHER STUNNED." Two nearby stories also related to this crime. One was headed: "MASS MURDERS TALLY—YUBA CITY MULTIPLE SLAYINGS WILL BECOME CLASSIC IN ANNALS OF GRISLY CRIMES." It began with the Jack–the–Ripper case in London and progressed through seven or eight mass murder cases to the Boston Strangler's chain of murder. The other was headed: "WHY JUDGE RELEASED DOCUMENTS," and was a self–serving documentary detailing the judge's explanation for releasing 65 pages of police reports and investigative documents filed with him by the Sutter County sheriff for the purpose of justifying his application for a search warrant.

On May 31, 1971, the following headlined articles appeared on a single page:

Empty Skid Row, Killings Clean Out Area Where Men Loitered

Sutter Mass Killer Slew Many of Skid Row Mission's Flock

Lax Labor License Law Failed To Uncover Corona's Mental History

An earlier report had disclosed an interview with the foreman of the ranch on which most of the victims were found. In this interview, the foreman was quoted as saying that Corona was mentally ill. In a follow-up story, it was disclosed that many years ago (1956) Juan Corona had been committed for a few months to a nearby state hospital treating mental illness. Diagnosis, it was alleged, classified Juan's problem as schizophrenia.

On June 4, 1971, an article on the front page headlined: SUTTER COUNTY MURDER LIST OF VICTIMS IS REVEALED. Although the article conceded that the district attorney refused to confirm or deny the story, or even discuss such a list, it proceeded to detail the circumstances of this list and its contents in the following way:

> Sutter County officials are investigating what they believe is an itemized "mass murder list" found on May 26th in the home of the accused murderer, Juan Corona. The list contains thirty-four names, five of the names are the same as those of murder victims in the Yuba City case.

Then the article stated:

> It was first speculated that the men on the list owed Corona money or were men who might have contacted him for prospective farm labor jobs, but officials are completely convinced the list is a compilation of victims in the case, the dates the men disappeared, and in some cases times and sites of burial.

The list was then printed, apparently verbatim. After the list, the article then states without identifying its source of information, that one victim was shot, the bullet was recovered during the autopsy, and that cartridges of the same size were found in Corona's van (labor bus).

On June 8, 1971 the front–page lead article headlined BLOOD IS FOUND ON WEAPONS FROM THE HOME OF ACCUSED SUT-TER MASS SLAYER CORONA. The story noted: "Reliable sources confirmed that human blood has been found on several weapons recovered during a predawn search on May 26 of the Juan Corona home." These same reliable sources were also given as the source of a following paragraph which stated that two Bank of America deposit receipts bearing Juan Corona's name were found when one of the bodies was unearthed earlier. The discovery of the receipts was related to previous disclosures from another unidentified source that two grocery receipts had been found buried six inches above the thigh of one of the victims. The story noted that both the sheriff and the district attorney refused to acknowledge any of the disclosures, but the article used this comment in a fashion that suggested this silence was strongly supportive of the merits of the story and its disclosures.

On June 7, 1971, the widely read news weekly, *Time,* allocated DEATH IN THE ORCHARDS almost a full page of copy. These are extracts from this story:

1.   Police arrested a Mexican–born farm–labor contractor named Juan Corona, 37, married and the father of four daughters, but they were by no means sure that they had come to the end of the trail of bodies. They evidently discovered some of the corpses by checking out X

marks on a crude map found in Corona's Bible. "I don't know where it's going to stop," said Sutter County Sheriff Roy Whiteaker. "We'll keep digging until we quit finding bodies."

2.   Sheriff Whiteaker said of Corona, "We are sure that he committed the murders."

3.   Although Corona had no criminal record in Sutter County, in 1956 he spent three months in DeWitt State Hospital, a nearby mental institution, after being committed by his brother, Natividad; two doctors tentatively diagnosed his illness as schizophrenia. He was released as cured.

The news reporting in this case was reflected in the news broadcasts of radio and television stations that blanket the Sutter County area. From the foregoing samples it can be readily noted that the murdered victims were tied in with the suspect, Juan Corona, by the disclosures about a murder list, bloodied weapons, X–marks on a map, and bank receipts; and the monstrosity of the case related to the alleged temper and mental illness of Corona. Collaterally, the silence of public officials was utilized to suggest they also knew about these items of evidence, but could not in good conscience make any public admissions. Strangely, the silence of the public officials in this case appeared to give news reporters a license to print unvalidated material or speculative reports. The use of *reliable sources* is so vague that there is little or no chance of checking the source to make certain that the news is valid and not mere speculation.

In sensational crimes the conflict between free press and fair trial is unresolved. It is only the ordinary crime, the routine crime, the unimaginative crime that will benefit from the efforts thus far made to limit criminal trials to courtrooms: trials in which a jury comprised of impartial jurors has not formed opinions, nor been bombarded with the extrajudicial evidence of the news media. However, it isn't this latter type of criminal case which is threatened by an unfair trial. It has little newsworthy appeal and the publicity, if any, has always been buried in back pages and small print. The well–intentioned committees, commissions, and associations which suggest solutions for the problem of fair trial vs. free press have not as yet found the answer for the sensational criminal case which is so newsworthy that it makes headlines no matter where it happens. The Lindbergh kidnapping, the murder of Mrs. Sheppard, the Kennedy assassinations, and the Sharon Tate case are the types of stories which will be told in great detail, despite the likelihood that such publicity will ruin the accused's right to a fair trial.

Selected References

Books

American Bar Association Advisory Committee on Fair Trial and Free Press. *Standards Relating to Fair Trial and Free Press.* New York: Institute of Judicial Administration, 1966.
Holmes, Paul. *The Sheppard Case.* New York: David McKay Co., 1961.
Dr. Sam Sheppard. *Endure and Conquer.* Cleveland: World Publishing Co., 1966.

Periodicals

Harrison, John M. "The Press vs. the Courts." *Saturday Review,* October 15, 1955, pp. 9–10, 35.

Cases

Sheppard v. Maxwell, 384 U.S. 333 (1965).

Chapter XII

Justice for Juveniles

Children who engage in acts which would be criminal if committed by adults, or who are likely to become or are in danger of becoming delinquent, present a different problem for the community than the problem of adult criminal behavior. Sanction law specifies actions against persons or property which are criminal by statute, and assigns a range of appropriate penalties without regard to the age of the offender.

However, in our legal system the age of the offender is a factor in determining criminal responsibility. Children under seven years of age are free of criminal liability for an act which would be criminal if committed by an adult; children over the age of seven but under the age of 16 to 18 (varies in different states) are considered juvenile delinquents rather than criminals. Some states have special youthful offender laws to lessen criminal responsibility for persons up to 21 years of age. In the lawmaker's actions, such legal provisions reflect the community belief in the immaturity of children and youths, and the fact that society has always viewed our youngsters as its resource for future growth and development.

The protective nature of such laws, however, are only justified when supported by measures which will provide for the rehabilitation of delinquent juveniles without injustice to them or their parents. Since public officials are held accountable in a democratic society, they must justify their decisions and the decision making apparatus.

The separate legal system which evolved in America to protect its resources of children and youth was informal and private so that the

223

judge might act as the benevolent parent. The proceeding was not subject to the glare of publicity which could follow the child through the rest of his life. The major thrust of the law was to protect the juvenile from the stigma of criminal conviction for his offenses. It is presumed that these acts are committed at a time when the juvenile lacks the mature judgment to understand the possible consequences on the remainder of his life.

Systematic inquiry has disclosed that, through evolution, juvenile courts now are conducted under a system of extensive screening done by police officers and probation personnel, identifying young people who are delinquent and referring them to court for a hearing. This screening is often discriminatory and decisions crucial to the young person are made on improper criteria, such as the juvenile's attitude and parental accessibility. Often, in the screening process, juveniles are asked to place their trust and confidence in their interviewers, and their inculpatory statements are used against them.

The doctrine under which special courts for juveniles were established was the doctrine of *parens patriae.** The court's role as a substitute parent, however, was sometimes very authoritative, with the presiding judge assuming an administrative rather than a judicial role. The proceedings often switched from the adversary process guaranteed to all adult accused persons in the American legal system, to a semi–inquisitorial system which jeopardized the basic rights of juvenile offenders.

Juvenile Delinquency

The breadth of the court's jurisdiction is usually justified by its advocates as the means of placing before the court the child in need of its services. The principal difficulty with this position is that it has created a court of law with almost limitless power over children. The definitions are broad enough to label nearly every child a delinquent at some point in his life. The builtin danger of the nonspecific definitions of delinquency in many states is that it permits, if it does not compel, the court to apply subjective standards of morality and child care: whether the juvenile's conduct qualifies as delinquent depends in great measure on the judge's own code of human behavior.

In New York City, the children's court in each county (there are five) is given exclusive original jurisdiction within the county to hear and determine all cases or proceedings concerning children under the age of 16 who are, or who are alleged to be delinquent. The Domestic Relations Court Act of the City of New York defines as a juvenile

*In substitution for parent.

delinquent any child over seven and under 16 years of age who:

1. violates any law of the United States or of this state or any ordinance of the City of New York, or who commits an act which if committed by an adult would be a crime (child of 15 years may be tried as an adult in criminal courts if the act he committed is punishable by death or life imprisonment);

2. is incorrigible, ungovernable or habitually disobedient and beyond the control of his parents, guardian, custodian or other lawful authority;

3. is habitually truant;

4. without just cause and without the consent of his parent, guardian or other custodian, deserts his home or place of abode;

5. engages in any occupation which is in violation of law;

6. begs or who solicits alms or money in public places;

7. associates with immoral or vicious persons;

8. frequents any place the maintenance of which is in violation of law;

9. so deports himself as wilfully to injure or endanger the morals or health of himself or others.

Whether a juvenile is guilty of serious delinquency depends on:

1. Whether the alleged offense was committed in an aggressive, violent, premeditated or wilful manner.

2. Whether the alleged offense was against persons or against property, greater weight being given to offenses against persons especially if personal injury resulted.

The Screening Process—Parents and Schools

Many children are referred to juvenile court not because of any delinquent behavior, but because they do not get along with one or both parents. These are the incorrigibles, the youngsters beyond control of their parents, or minors in need of supervision. These parents use the juvenile court concept and its original jurisdiction over children in a weird combination of parental discipline and the sloughing off of responsibility for the conduct of their child. A juvenile who is not getting on with his parents should not need the informal probation supervision of a consent decree, nor should he be threatened with future referral to juvenile court if he doesn't respond to parental control, or institutional care as a result of a juvenile court hearing.

Justice might be better served if the youngster's parents found a relative or friend to provide a substitute home for the child while they attended counseling sessions to gain the necessary know–how to resolve the problem, without stigmatizing their child as incorrigible.

Any examination of the records of a juvenile court will indicate that delinquent young people often have records of truancy. However, the court records are silent on whether truancy is a threshold to delinquency, or whether the label of truant is a jet assist to the life style of a juvenile delinquent. A child does not have to qualify as a chronic truant to warrant some kind of special in–school action which will discover the reason or reasons for the absences. In some jurisdictions, there is inquiry by responsible teachers and conferences with the parents, and possibly a referral to the school counseling unit, but in many areas there is just a report to the pupil personnel office. When little more than the recording of absences and notifying the parents fails to have the necessary magical qualities, the truancy is reported to the probation department for adjustment. In some cases, action by the probation department must overcome a long history of poor marks and suspension from a neighborhood school because the truancy problem was not vigorously resolved by concerned school personnel. When the youngster presents a problem on probation, the record of truancy and bad marks in school is cited in the petition to the juvenile court almost as a self–fulfilling prophecy of delinquency.[1]

Parents and teachers are better equipped to work with children than are the more distant probation officers or staffs of juvenile institutions. Incorrigibles and troublemakers often yield to an early solution of their problems, and the child or youth is not lost to his home or school. Concerned parents, teachers, and school counseling personnel can serve as diagnosticians and therapists when they make a sincere effort accompanied by some expertise. Interception of these youthful problem children before they really become delinquents, is a better quality of justice than labeling them as wards of the juvenile court and giving them a record that may be part of a criminal history when they become adults.

The Screening Process—Police Encounters with Juveniles

Close to half of all the juveniles who are taken into custody originate with the police screening process. This is a process in which police do not acknowledge the juvenile's right to privacy, silence, or representation by counsel, and which may result in an official record for the juvenile and possibly some interference with his liberty.

1. David L. Bazelon, "Beyond Control of the Juvenile Court," *Juvenile Court Journal*, 21, no. 2, (Summer 1970): 2–6.

The police role in serving young people is essentially a negative one. Rarely are police encounters with juveniles used for any purpose except to admonish or take into custody. The protective laws planned to allow police to help juveniles become restrictive to them and evoke resentment toward the police. Attempting to prevent or even control juvenile delinquency, has led to a polarization between youth and the police. Reports that police discriminate against juveniles and harass them are fairly numerous. In urban areas, there is the "battle of the corner," and in rural areas there is the "battle of the highway," setting police beat officers and traffic patrolmen against young people in a deadly serious combat in which both parties see a challenge in the behavior of the other.

The stated police function in relation to children and youths is protective rather than repressive. But the states' laws defining delinquency provide so many conditions which may be the basis of police action, that young people fail to understand the wide range of police response possible during these encounters.

As a part of general law enforcement, police note young people who gather on street corners or in premises (such as pool halls and drive-ins) with a local reputation for disorders and criminal activities. Police frequently admonish, warn, or take into custody some of these youngsters when they violate curfew or other laws. They also conduct field interrogations when the behavior of juveniles strongly suggests criminal behavior. Such police tactics are without blemish when not misused. A sincere interest in juveniles no doubt motivates most police officers to engage in such encounters when no overt, actual criminal, or delinquent behavior is observed by the officer. However, many youngsters believe this is harassment unless they are caught "doing something."[2]

The officials of many police departments ask their officers on patrol to take action against juveniles in violation of local laws against loitering. This is within the concept of aggressive patrol, serving to prevent or deter crime and possibly discover conduct requiring appropriate police action. Officers are directed to apply the law only for a specific violation and not to use it as a status violation, and to enforce it without regard to location or persons involved (impartial as to neighborhood or juvenile). The recommended method of handling this type of enforcement is:

1. On first contact, where there is no problem between the juvenile and the officer, the juvenile should be sent home after a field interview (FI) card is prepared.

---

2. President's Commission on Law Enforcement and Administration of Justice, *Task Force Report: The Police* (Washington, D.C.: U.S. Government Printing Office, 1967), pp. 179–86.

2. On second contact, where there is no juvenile–officer problem, cite juvenile for the violation to probation department.

3. On subsequent contacts, or where a problem develops between the officer and the juvenile, remove the juvenile to the police office or station, notify parents to pick up the youth and cite juvenile, or deliver into custody of juvenile hall if parents cannot be located.

The violation itself generally plays an insignificant role in the police action. While a number of these juveniles are seen as serious delinquents deserving arrest, many others are perceived as good boys. Thus, in police–juvenile encounters the assessment of character—the distinction between serious delinquents, good boys, misguided youths, and so on—and the dispositions which follow from these assessments are based on the juvenile's personal characteristics and not the offense or suspicious conduct. In exercising this discretion policemen are strongly guided by the demeanor of the juvenile. This practice ultimately means that certain youths are treated more severly than other juveniles for comparable conduct.

To a substantial extent, this discretion of police officers is simply an extension of the juvenile court philosophy: in making legal decisions regarding juveniles, more weight should be given to the juvenile's character and life–situation than to his actual offending behavior. However, police officers during these encounters do not have the data about juveniles available to juvenile court judges. Therefore, they must use fairly simple cues. Juveniles who are contrite about their conduct, respectful to officers, and fearful of the authority that might be employed against them, are viewed as basically law–abiding and amenable to informal or formal reprimand to guarantee their future conformity. In contrast, juveniles who are argumentative or who appear nonchalant during their encounters are likely to be viewed as would–be tough guys or punks who fully deserve the most severe sanction: arrest.[3]

There is a rationale to police response to insolence and noncooperation by juveniles during these encounters. It is a belief in the importance of fostering a positive and cooperative attitude toward police, and it is their professional opinion that a negative attitude is indicative of delinquent tendencies. While police admit that a youth's attitude in an encounter with police is often significant to the outcome, they believe the police response is more than an emotional reaction.[4]

Unfortunately, the basic injustice of such police encounters is that

3. Irving P. Liavin and Scott Briar, "Police Encounters with Juveniles," *American Journal of Sociology* 70 (September 1964): 206–14.

4. David R. Barrett et al, "Juvenile Delinquents: The Police, State Courts, and Individualized Justice," *Harvard Law Review* 79, no. 4, (February 1966): 775–810.

there is too great a range for police action. Often the dynamics of the encounter rather than the juvenile's offense or misconduct becomes the probable cause for determining which juvenile is to be officially branded as delinquent, and brought to the attention of the juvenile probation office or the juvenile court. Certainly, it is not comparable to the probable cause for arresting and accusing an adult of a similar criminal act.

The accessibility of a juvenile's family is often a factor in the screening of juveniles by police. It is not infrequent that two boys will be picked up for some infraction such as joy–riding. (This is auto theft under the criminal law.) Both boys are taken to the police station for the routine reports and calls are made to their parents. One boy's parents can not be located, he is detained overnight in the local juvenile hall; the other boy's father answers the telephone and responds promptly by coming to the police station and picking up his son. He is not detained; the police have no reason to do so. However, one boy's record will always show "detained," while the other boy's record will indicate "released." It may not work out unfairly in Future screening; it depends on the police officer (or others) who review these prior records in the future.

The Screening Process—Probation

The police are the major source of referrals to the probation unit. Most of the referrals are by citation, with the summons directing the juvenile to appear at the probation office on a specified time and day, usually within a few days from the day of issuance of the citation. In some cases, the referrals concern juveniles detained by police at the local juvenile hall. Others may originate with parents or school officials. In any event parents are notified of the situation and requested to appear with their child.

The discretionary powers of a probation officer, and the dynamics of his encounters with juveniles, are unlike the police officer in the police–juvenile encounter. The police officer can almost create delinquency and the necessity for referral by categorizing the behavior of the juvenile as such in his police report of the event. But the practitioner in probation has usually been trained in the nonlegalistic and nonpunitive approach of casework, and the rehabilitative objectives of his probation agency. In the actual screening of juveniles and the articulation of instructions given during training suggestions, there are instances in which the application of referral standards may depend on the availability of resources rather than the immediate needs of the juvenile or the nature of his problem.

The basic choice of a probation officer at an initial interview is between various nonjudicial alternatives and the filing of a petition seeking judicial action. The initial probation interview is an informal meeting with the minor and his parents, at which the alternative dispositions to filing a petition are discussed:

1. *Dismissal*—this action is justified when the preinterview investigation, and the facts disclosed in discussing the case with the juvenile and his parents, indicates to the probation officer that the case is unfounded, or the evidence is untrustworthy or insufficient and does not warrant or sustain the charges.

2. *Referred to Resident Jurisdiction*—this referral is appropriate when the juvenile resides elsewhere and the problem does not justify action where the act of misconduct occurred.

3. *Referral to Other Local Agencies*—this is proper action when the investigation and discussion indicates another local agency is better equipped to handle the juvenile and his problem (usual referrals are to the welfare or mental health agencies).

4. *Counseling and Dismissal*—this action goes beyond outright dismissal, but not beyond a simple counseling session in which all concerned discuss the problem and plan possible solutions.

5. *Informal (consent) Supervision*—this is the most serious nonjudicial alternative. It involves the provision of probation supervision to the juvenile with the consent of the parents (parent or guardian), and is only justified when it is apparent that the juvenile requires professional assistance in solving his problem. When initiated, the case is then processed through the probation agency to determine the supervision and counseling services that will be necessary, and the juvenile becomes part of the informal supervision caseload of the probation agency.

In making a decision as to alternatives for a judicial processing of a juvenile, probation officers often attempt to isolate and identify the most important single factor. Was it the current offense, the prior record of delinquency, or the attitude of the juvenile and his parents? (At this initial probation interview the intensive social–history case study needed to file a petition for juvenile judicial appearance has not been made.) The decision may be a combination of all three factors. Injustice can occur when the offense alone (except at felony levels) justifies referral to juvenile court. The previous history data of an offender at this stage of the screening process is generally no more than brief references, and usually fails to indicate if the current offense is part of a general pattern of delinquency—really the only justifiable grounds for considering past misdeeds when making this decision.

Attitude is subject to appraisal at any time. One juvenile may accept an opening statement by the probation officer about the purpose of the interview (whether to refer to court or not), while another may strongly resent this screening. As the interview progresses, there are many moments when some juveniles will strongly disagree with the way it is progressing; others submit silently without protest. Often there is a language barrier, or a communications gap, when the interviewer uses college level conversational style or professional terminology with poorly educated juveniles and their parents. It is certainly a miscarriage of justice to allow derogatory judgment of attitude to become a major influence in the action taken.[5]

Among the factors that may operate against an innocent juvenile are: (1) dispositional decisions in these initial interviews are often made from improper criteria because more relevant data is not visible and easily ascertainable at this stage of the screening process; (2) the juvenile court referral is used as a threat to enforce the authority of the interviewer; and (3) an interview is usually terminated if the juvenile persistently denies his guilt when there is some evidence of his involvement.

Questioning of Juveniles

The theme of protecting a child from a life of crime or imminent hazard to his health or morals carries over into the area of questioning juveniles as to their conduct. Police are intent on the extent of a youth's involvement in crime or other misbehavior, and probation personnel and the juvenile court judge seek the true facts of a situation in order to take appropriate official action. In defense of this questioning, and the failure to warn the juvenile of his right to silence in accord with the privilege against self–incrimination, these agents of criminal justice have always claimed that when a juvenile is taken into custody or given a citation to appear at an official hearing, it is not an arrest. All the processing of juveniles are civil rather than criminal actions, and this includes the juvenile court hearings. Further, it is argued that the entire structure of agents and agencies involved in juvenile justice is investigative, diagnostic, and prescriptive, rather than merely accusatorial and adjudicative.

There are also some expressed opinions in the literature of child saving that confession is good for children and youths. This is within the concept of the protective laws spelling out delinquency and aligned with the therapy of the juvenile court process. It is a means of developing the necessary attitude of trust and confidence toward the agents of juvenile justice who have the basic responsibility for handling juve-

---

5. James T. Carey et al, *The Handling of Juveniles from Offense to Disposition* (Washington, D.C.: U.S. Dept. of Health, Education and Welfare, 1967), vols. 1 and 2, passim; vol. 3, pp. 13–14, 24–25, 48–49, 57–58.

nile offenders. On the other hand, there is an emerging belief that the individualized treatment of juveniles does not warrant compelling a child or youth to answer questions, without warning, parental guidance, or legal counsel. Bitterness and hostility are the likely products of confessions secured by persons in a parens patriae relationship, and these attitudes are subsequently used against the juvenile. These reactions certainly handicap any rehabilitation program.

The original humanitarian philosophy of the juvenile justice process was centered around a wholly informal and flexible procedure of gentle and friendly probing by officials in juvenile justice agencies to uncover the roots of the child's difficulties and to make informed decisions on how to best meet his problems. Informality in both procedure and disposition thus became a basic characteristic of handling juveniles. On the other hand, for police officers or any official of juvenile justice to use the social service approach to secure inculpatory statements from juveniles is certainly open to critical appraisal.

In a recent case before the District of Columbia Juvenile Court the presiding judge rejected the proffer of oral statements made to police by four juveniles who had been taken into custody for alleged involvement in an assault and attempted robbery.[6] The court explicitly stated that it did not rest its decision on a showing that the statements were involuntary, but because they were untrustworthy:

> Simply stated, the Court's decision in this case rests upon the considered opinion—after nearly four busy years on the Juvenile Court bench during which the testimony of thousands of such juveniles has been heard—that the statements of adolescents under 18 years of age who are arrested and charged with violations of law are frequently untrustworthy and often distort the truth.

However, an in–depth examination of an earlier case provides an overview of this problem of questioning and taking statements from juveniles about their guilt in acts which would be crimes if committed by adults. The case is based on a trial held in an Ohio court. The facts and circumstances of the case are: The robbery of a store resulted in the fatal shooting of its owner. The police and prosecutor's theory, supported by some evidence, was that a boy aged 15, and two others, aged 16 and 17, committed the crime. Five days after the crime— around midnight—a 15–year–old boy named Haley was arrested at his home and taken to police headquarters. Beginning shortly after midnight, Haley was questioned by the police for about five hours without friend or counsel present. Around 5 A.M.—after being shown alleged confessions of his 16 and 17–year–old crime partners—the Haley boy confessed. A confession was typed in question and answer form by the

6. *In the Matter of Four Youths* no. 28–776-J, 28–778-J, 28–783-J, 28–859-J, Juvenile Court of the District of Columbia, April 7, 1961.

police beginning with a statement that the youth was therein being informed of his constitutional rights, and that the law gave him the right to make a statement or not as he saw fit, with the understanding that it may be used at a trial in court either for or against him or anyone else involved in the crime. Haley completed the statement. He was put in jail about 6:00 A.M. or 6:30 A.M. on Saturday, shortly after the confession was signed, and taken before a magistrate and formally charged with a crime on the following Monday.

At his trial for murder in criminal court, over defense objections, Haley's confession was adjudged sufficiently voluntary to admit into evidence for the jury to weigh its voluntariness. The judicial instructions directed the jury to disregard the confession if they did not believe that Haley had made the confession voluntarily. Haley was convicted and sentenced.

The Haley conviction was reversed by the U.S. Supreme Court[7] because of Haley's age; the early morning hours of the questioning and its length; the absence of friend, parent, or legal counsel; and the assumption by police that a warning as to constitutional rights just before making and signing a confession, was sufficient for a 15–year–old boy (without counsel) to be equipped with the freedom of choice necessary to a valid waiver of his right to keep silent. In fact, the court termed the questioning of Haley under these circumstances an inquisitorial session which mocked the Fourteenth Amendment's guarantee of due process of law to man or child:

> What transpired would make us pause for careful inquiry if a mature man were involved. And when, as here, a mere child—an easy victim of the law—is before us, special care in scrutinizing the record must be used. Age 15 is a tender and difficult age for a boy of any race. He cannot be judged by the more exacting standards of maturity. That which would leave a man cold and unimpressed can overawe and overwhelm a lad in his early teens. This is the period of great instability which the crisis of adolescence produces. A 15–year–old lad, questioned through the dead of night by relays of police, is a ready victim of the inquisition. Mature men possibly might stand the ordeal from midnight to 5 A.M. But we cannot believe that a lad of tender years is a match for the police in such a contest. He needs counsel and support if he is not to become the victim first of fear, then of panic.

> The constitutional privilege against self–incrimination is applicable in the case of juveniles as it is with respect to adults. We appreciate that special problems may arise with respect to waiver of the privilege by or on behalf of children, and that there may well be some differences in technique—but not in principle—depending upon the age of the child and the presence and competence of parents. The participation of counsel will, of course, assist the police, juvenile courts and appellate tribunals in

7. Haley v. Ohio, 332 U.S. 596 (1947).

administering the privilege. If counsel was not present for some permissible reason when an admission was obtained, the greatest care must be taken to assure that that the admission was voluntary, in the sense not only that it was not coerced or suggested, but also that it was not the product of ignorance of rights or of adolescent fantasy, fright or despair.

We do not think the methods used in obtaining this confession can be squared with that due process of law which the Fourteenth Amendment commands.

The Juvenile Court

When all other dispositional alternatives have been exhausted in the screening process, a juvenile presenting major problems to police, probation agencies, his school, or parents is referred to juvenile court. The court reviews the allegations of delinquency, incorrigibility, truancy, or other misbehavior, and decides whether the youth is involved in the alleged misconduct and makes a disposition of the case responsive to the juvenile and his problem.

Each juvenile appearing in a juvenile court is processed as a case; a person with some unique qualities and characteristics in a problem situation. Judicial assessment requires more than a guilt or innocence decision, but rather a decision based on the multitude of facts collected and presented to the court as part of the petition (complaint) on which the juvenile is arraigned. From factual data such as a brief life history and details of the current offense, the judicial role is to assess the juvenile and the problem and decide if the youngster is in need of the array of services available to the court, from admonishment through probation and allowing the child to remain at home, to institutional care and treatment.

Police, probation officers, and the staff of local schools (usually guidance and counseling personnel) are the referring persons who petition the juvenile court to review the case of a young person. These professionally educated workers do not refer children and youth to this court until, in their opinion, the juvenile has a problem which cannot be resolved by other and lesser remedial action. Therefore, any delay, refusal to act, or action contrary to the desires of these referring persons are regarded as judicial action jeopardizing the legitimate expectations of the referring person, and the police agency, probation department, or school—as the case may be. Reaction to any judicial failure to live up to these expectations will range from frustration to antagonism, but one thing is certain, and this is that referring persons expect the juvenile court to act in line with their expectations or those of their organization. In fact, these individuals and their agencies impose these demands almost as if they were the customers or clients of the court, and the court's primary purpose was to serve them rather than the juvenile with a problem.[8]

One of the major problems of the juvenile courts is to weigh the life history data and current situation of a juvenile and make a decision as to the juvenile's correctional needs. Judges of these courts have the stated recommendation of the referring person and agency, and the basic implication in the referral itself: urgent, this juvenile needs shock therapy, forceful and energetic handling, and disposition. However, justice for juveniles may require rejection of prescriptive recommendations, and, instead, an in–depth inquiry, and a judicial decision on the merits of the case.

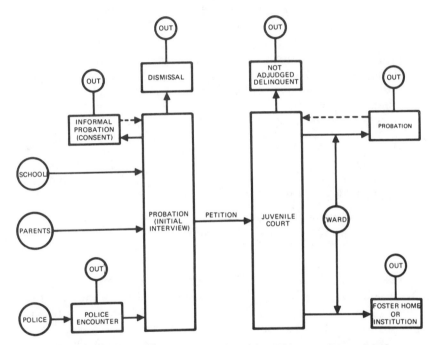

The screening process for juveniles reported by police, school, or parents as incorrigible or delinquent. Juveniles may be screened *out* of this process during the police encounter or initial probation interview; when adjudged *not* to be incorrigible or delinquent; or (when made a ward of the court), after a period of probation, in a foster home, or a juvenile-care institution.

When these judicial decisions emanate from the original philosophy

8. The President's Commission on Law Enforcement and Administration of Justice, *Task Force Report: Juvenile Delinquency and Crime—Report on Juvenile Justice and Consultant's Papers* (Washington, D.C.: U.S. Government Printing Office, 1967), Appendix C, Robert Vinter, "The Juvenile Court as an Institution," pp. 84–90.

of the juvenile court, a humanitarian compassion for offending children and youths, then juveniles, their parents, and the community can rest assured of the rehabilitation objectives of the judicial decision. However, when the screening process, the expectations of referring persons and their agencies, and other nonrehabilitative factors are allowed to influence these judicial decisions there is a great potential for injustice.

That these influences impinge on, and possibly ruin, the role of juvenile court judge to effectively serve in any *parens partriae* capacity is suggested by a 1967 recommendation of the authoritative President's Commission on Law Enforcement and Administration of Justice. The following segment of a series of proposals aimed at restructuring juvenile justice contains this recommendation:

> The cases that fall within the narrowed jurisdiction of the court and filter through the screen of prejudicial, informal disposition modes would largely involve offenders for whom more vigorous measures seem necessary. Court adjudication and disposition of those offenders should no longer be viewed solely as a diagnosis and prescription for cure, but should be frankly recognized as an authoritative court judgment expressing society's claim to protection. While rehabilitative efforts should be vigorously pursued in deference to the youthfulness of the offenders and in keeping with the general commitment to individualized treatment of all offenders, the incapacitative, deterrent, and condemnatory purposes of the judgment should not be disguised.

This recommendation concluded by terming a hearing in juvenile court an adjudicatory hearing, and suggested it be conducted in accordance with the principles of due process and fundamental fairness. It is doubtful, however, that this viewpoint is supportive of justice for juveniles, when the modern concept of adult corrections rejects penalties as a factor in reducing crime (deterrence); believes imprisonment alone (incapacitation) achieves little more than an annual crop of repeating offenders; and aligns any labeling of offenders (condemnation) with archaic concepts of revenge and punishment.

The U.S. Supreme Court in *Kent* v. *United States*[9] noted that all states had juvenile court systems rooted in social welfare philosophy rather than in *corpus juris*.* They are theoretically engaged in determining the needs of the juvenile and the community rather than adjudicating criminal conduct, and more concerned with the objectives of guidance and rehabilitation (for the child and the protection of the community) than the fixing of criminal responsibility, guilt, and penalty. In its majority opinion, the Court expressed concern for the gulf between theory and performance in juvenile court hearings, saying:

9. 383 U.S. 541 (1966)
*The body of the law.

While there can be no doubt of the original laudable purpose of juvenile courts, studies and critiques in recent years raise serious questions as to whether actual performance measures well enough against theoretical purpose to make tolerable the immunity of the process from the reach of constitutional guaranties applicable to adults. There is much evidence that some juvenile courts lack the personnel, facilities and techniques to perform adequately as representatives of the State in a *parens patriae* capacity, at least with respect to children charged with law violation. There is evidence, in fact, that there may be grounds for concern that the child receives the worst of both worlds: that he gets neither the protections accorded to adults nor the solicitous care and regenerative treatment postulated for children.

Legal Change in Juvenile Court

The danger of injustice in the philosophy of the juvenile court and police and probation screening practices is inherent in any situation in which well–intentioned persons are placed in positions of authority and allowed various sanctions to enforce their decisions. Justice Louis D. Brandeis pointed this out in his opinion in *Olmstead* v. *United States* [10] when he warned:

> Experience should teach us to be most on our guard to protect liberty when government purposes are beneficient. Men born to freedom are naturally alert to repel invasion of their liberty by evil minded rulers. The greatest dangers to liberty lurk in insidious encroachment by men of zeal, well meaning, but without understanding.

Almost a half century later, the decision of *In re Gault* [11] reflected the wisdom of Justice Brandeis. Gerald Gault was a 15–year–old boy. He was arrested (along with another boy) in June 1964, because of a verbal complaint by a neighbor who complained of a lewd and indecent phone call. No notice was given to the parents, or message left at their home. No steps were taken to advise them of the arrest of their son. The parents only learned of the arrest through other neighbors after inquiry.

A deputy probation officer filed a petition against young Gault which only said: "Minor is under the age of eighteen years, and in need of the protection of this honorable court, and that said minor is a delinquent minor." At the hearing on a later date the complaining witness (victim) was not present to testify as to what was said or to make any voice identification of which of the boys (if either) said the obscene words. There was a conflict of memory as to what young Gault

10. 277 U.S. 438 (1928)
11. 387 U.S. 1 (1967)

said at the hearing. There was no transcript, recording, or other record made of the proceedings. The judge, at the conclusion of the hearing committed Gerald Gault to the State Industrial School for the period of his minority (until 21 years) unless sooner discharged by due process of law. No appeal was permitted by Arizona law.

The juvenile court judge stated at a subsequent habeas corpus proceeding that he committed Gerald under the law that states: "A delinquent child is one who has violated a law of the state or an ordinace or regulation of a political subdivision thereof," and that the law that Gerald was found to have violated was: "A person who, in the presence or hearing of any child uses vulgar, abusive, or obscene language is guilty of a misdemeanor." The penalty for this violation which would apply to an adult was a fine of $5 to $50, or imprisonment for not more than two months.

Contrary to the due process clause of the Fourteenth Amendment, Gerald Gault was denied in these proceedings the notice of charges, right to counsel, right to confrontation by witnesses (and cross–examination), and the privilege against self–incrimination. The United States Supreme Court reviewed the philosophy of juvenile justice and its operation in this case, and they found it wanting, saying: "Neither the Fourteenth Amendment nor the Bill of Rights is for adults alone." In the majority opinion of the Court in this case, the Court examined the entire problem of juvenile justice:

> The juvenile court movement began in this country at the end of the last century. From the juvenile court statute adopted in Illinois in 1899 the system has spread to every state in the Union, the District of Columbia, and Puerto Rico. The early reformers were appalled by adult procedures and penalties, and by the fact that children could be given long prison sentences and mixed in jails with hardened criminals. They were profoundly convinced that society's duty to the child could not be confined by the concept of justice alone. They believed that society's role was not to ascertain whether the child was "guilty" or "innocent" but "what is he, how has he come to be what he is, and what had best be done in his interest and in the interest of the state to save him from a downward career." The child—essentially good as they saw it—was to be made "to feel that he is the object of (the State's) care and solicitude," not that he is under arrest or on trial. The rules of criminal procedure were therefore altogether inapplicable. The apparent rigidities, technicalities, and harshness which they observed in both substantive and procedural criminal law were therefore to be discarded. The idea of crime and punishment was to be abandoned.

From the point of view of the juvenile caught in the web of juvenile benevolence, the most confusing, disturbing, and disillusioning part of the process was the many–sided role of the probation officer. The first contact was paternal, helpful, and understanding and the juvenile was asked or instructed to trust and confide in this official. The next contact was in a court, and the probation officer was acting out his role as prosecutor, that is, persuading the judge that the child was a delinquent. The third contact after the juvenile was declared delinquent would be, "trust me again, and let me rehabilitate you." A confusion of roles incomprehensible to a child's mind. It is small wonder, that many juveniles have a distorted and critical opinion of the American system of justice.

The decision in the case of Gerald Gault opened the way to a change in processing juvenile offenders. It allowed that juveniles are people and that the basic liberties must apply to them also. The court felt that the new direction must be somewhere between treatment as an adult, and the denial of all constitutional rights. Perhaps there is a middle ground which will allow the juvenile his constitutional liberties before the determination of guilt or innocence, and yet be concerned for the fact that he is a child and should not be held as fully accountable for his acts as a mature adult: that he should not be placed in an environment which will encourage and teach him criminal attitudes he did not already have.

The Court's directions in *Gault* were:

1. When proceedings may result in incarceration in an institution of confinement, "it would be extraordinary if our Constitution did not require the procedural regularity and exercise of care implied in the phrase 'due process.' "

2. Due process requires, in such proceedings, that adequate written notice be afforded the child and his parents or guardian. Such notice must inform them "of the specific issues that they must meet" and must be given "at the earliest practicable time, and in any event sufficiently in advance of the hearing to permit preparation."

3. In such proceedings the child and his parents must be advised of their right to be represented by counsel and, if they are unable to afford counsel, that counsel will be appointed to represent the child.

4. The constitutional privilege against self–incrimination is applicable in such proceedings: "an admission by the juvenile may not be used against him in the absence of clear and unequivocal evidence that the admission was made with knowledge that he was not obliged to speak and would not be penalized for remaining silent."

5. Absent a valid confession, a juvenile in such proceedings must be afforded the rights of confrontation and sworn testimony of witnesses available for cross–examination.

Parents, school officials in the area of guidance and counseling, police, and probation officers are the sources referring children and youths to juvenile court. In such referral, unhappily, there is a tagging or labeling process and the child or youth becomes, in the eyes of many people, a delinquent.

There is a screening process throughout the handling of juveniles, from the initial referral to the disposition of the case through probation procedures or court assessment of the juvenile and his problems. However, examination of the encounters between juveniles and police officers, the differential referral of probation officers, and the gap between theory and performance in juvenile courts have developed reasonable grounds to believe that justice for juveniles may be rank injustice.

The protective laws which relieved the young of criminal responsibility were enacted by lawmakers to protect juveniles from the stigma and consequences of being arrested, tried, convicted, and sentenced as an adult criminal. But such laws should not be utilized to deprive the young of the rights of adults or to diminish in any fashion the critical importance of any action by the juvenile court or its referral sources which labels a boy or girl as delinquent.

Selected References

Books

Carey, James T. et al, *The Handling of Juveniles From Offense to Disposition.* Washington, D.C.: U.S. Government Printing Office, 1967.

President's Commission on Law Enforcement and Administration of Justice. *Task Force Report: The Police,* and *Task Force Report: Juvenile Delinquency and Crime—Report on Juvenile Justice and Consultant's Papers.* Washington, D.C.: U.S. Government printing Office, 1967.

Periodicals

Barrett, David R. et al. "Juvenile Delinquents: The Police, State Courts, and Individualized Justice." *Harvard Law Review* 79, no. 4 (February 1966): 775–810.

Bazelon, David L. "Beyond Control of the Juvenile ·Court." *Juvenile Court Journal* 21, no. 2, (Summer 1970): 2–6.

Liavin, Irving P., and Briar, Scott. "Police Encounters with Juveniles." *American Journal of Sociology* 70 (September 1964): 206–14.

Cases

In re Gault, 387 U.S. 1 (1967).

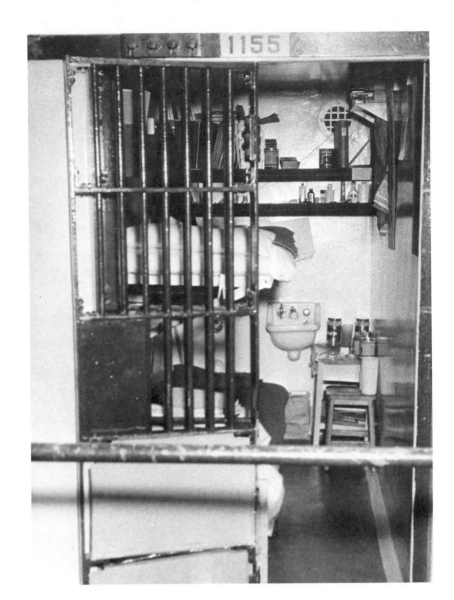

Chapter XIII

Organized Crime

Organized crime is a reality that is almost beyond belief. Long underground as part of the pattern of crime and delinquency in America, and a prime mover in the country's urban graft and politics, this criminal syndicate was not officially recognized until 1951. It was not named with certainty until 1962, not defined until 1968, and not combatted adequately until recent years when nationwide surveillance of the top executives of this national crime mob led to exposure and prosecution at levels not previously attained.

The 1950-51 United States Senate Crime Investigating Committee, commonly referred to by the name of its chairman, the late Senator Estes Kefauver, uncovered an elusive and furtive organization of criminals and established the existence of a national conspiracy of crime: of local mobs associated into a national crime syndicate known as the *Mafia*.[1]

The Cosa Nostra

In 1962, an insider, a knowledgable member of the criminal syndicate broke the syndicate's code of silence and disclosed to another U. S. Senate committee the name and the game of organized crime. Joseph Valachi, in the largest intelligence breakthrough in the history of crime and its investigation, said the name was not the Mafia, but *Cosa*

1. Estes Kefauver, *Crime in America* (Garden City, N. Y.: Doubleday and Company, 1951), pp. 2–340.

244 LAW ENFORCEMENT AND CRIMINAL JUSTICE

Nostra. The Mafia term was a label used by outsiders; the Cosa Nostra was a term used by its members.

Joseph Valachi revealed that Cosa Nostra was divided into major territorial and functional (criminal activities) segments known as *families.* The ruler of each of these major segments was a *capo* or boss, and next in command was a *soto capo* or underboss; while the *troops, soldiers* or *buttons* at the level of criminal operations were supervised by several *caporegime* or lieutenants.[2]

The game was still crime on a national scale under the executive leadership and operational secrecy of a membership that was more clan than club, more ""Murder, Inc." than big business, and more a confederation of criminals than the often arrested and imprisoned losers of the underworld. Cosa Nostra was crime on a scale never previously visualized. It was big and powerful, flouted law enforcement, corrupted police and public officials, and serviced a multiplying complex of criminal operations and rackets (honest businesses run dishonestly, or almost-legal enterprises). It was a national crime syndicate, with international ties and foreign resources, conducting daily illegal activities over a period of no less than half a century in an environment of relative safety; immune to arrest and successful prosecution.

Organized Crime and Its Activities

The Congress officially defined organized crime and its membership in 1968 as follows:

> "Organized Crime" means the unlawful activities of the members of highly organized, disciplined association engaged in supplying illegal goods and services, including but not limited to, gambling, prostitution, loansharking, narcotics, labor racketeering, and other unlawful activities of members of such organizations. "Organized Crime Offender" means a person who, with intent that conduct constituting a series of crimes be performed, plans, counsels, promotes, finances, organizes, manages, advises, supervises, directs, or conducts a conspiratorial relationship, composed of five or more conspirators, involving a structured division of labor, and having as its objective the engaging in or causing of the performance of such conduct as a part of a continuing course of activity. A person shall not be considered an organized crime offender within the meaning of this definition unless conduct constituting more than one crime as part of a continuing course of activity is engaged in or caused by one or more of the conspirators to effect the objective in the relationship.[3]

2. Peter Maas, *The Valachi Papers* (New York: G. P. Putman's Sons, 1968), pp. 35–47.
3. Omnibus Crime Control and Safe Streets Act of 1968.

The national crime syndicate caters to public demands for illegal goods and services, forbidden in various overreaches of sanction law, and they participate in any illegal activity which offers a high return on their investment of time, money, and know–how. Its major operations include gambling, loan sharking (shylocking), narcotics, labor racketeering, the infiltration of legitimate business, and such lesser areas as prostitution, stealing, and merchandising stolen property.

Gambling provides a basic source of daily revenue to all of the "families" of organized crime. In ghetto areas, the income source is the numbers game, or policy racket. It is a nickles-dimes-and-dollars game that cuts the normal odds of any lottery to insure that players cannot win any significant percentage of the day's action. In all except the most rural areas, there are card and dice games, and gambling on horse races or sporting events. Horse race and sports betting is another major income source, with the bookmakers hedging against any severe daily losses by spreading their customer's wagers among fellow members of the crime syndicate.[4]

Loan sharking or shylocking is usury. It has been described time and again as a wondrous money machine by leading members of the crime syndicate. Usury is a profession akin to prostitution in that it goes back many years and has always returned a good income to its practitioners. Loan sharking predates World War II and probably originated during the depression years after the 1929 stock market crisis led to financial problems for a multitude of people. There are reasonable grounds to believe that the membership of the crime syndicate has found loan sharking to be an effective way of investing their money and watching it multiply. The boss loans a substantial amount of money to one or more of his lieutenants, who in turn use one or more of their button men or soldiers to supervise on–the–street lenders. The average rate of interest paid by borrowers for short–term loans is 260 percent annually. The terms are inflexible; weekly interest payments must be made, penalties are exacted for delays, and the principle is due on demand. Murder and severe beatings, one the outgrowth of the other in many instances, awaits borrowers unwilling or unable to meet these terms.[5]

The illicit traffic in narcotics has long been a source of income to the national crime syndicate. Less respectable than gambling or loan sharking, the narcotic trade is conducted in secret so as not to boggle the minds of some of the syndicate's allies in public office. It is difficult to buy immunity for a trade as heinous as narcotics selling. Today, the

---

4. Frederick Egan, The *Plainclothesman—Handbook of Vice and Gambling Operations* (New York: Arco Press, 1958).

5. "Loan-sharking: The Untouched Domain of Organized Crime," *Columbia Journal of Law and Social Problems,* 5 No. 1, pp. 91–136.

different families in Cosa Nostra insulate their membership as much as possible from arrest by the use of "share-croppers"—pushers who do the retail selling and take the greatest risk of arrest. The syndicate has an underground transportation system for bringing heroin and other hard drugs into the United States. The business of importing and wholesaling illegal narcotics is lucrative. It is a buy low and sell high business of enormous profits which would be impossible except for the relationships of trust, and the strong internal security among syndicate members.[6]

Labor racketeering began in the 1930s, when Prohibition was about to be repealed. It was a new way of making money from an illegitimate enterprise or a legitimate one that was operated illegitimately. It was the earliest years of labor racketeering that spawned the syndicate's first troops specializing in murder: the local mob in Brooklyn's Brownsville section led by Abe (Kid Twist) Reles and later named "Murder, Inc."[7] Labor rackets range from extortion to looting welfare and pension funds. There's a fee for labor peace as the syndicate members control many unions or union locals, and there are millions in the welfare and pension funds. Side benefits are the salaries paid to the syndicate's personnel who function as union organizers, business agents, and union officials. Sweetheart contracts, conspiracies between management and dishonest labor officials, pay union members low wages while dishonest officials obtain illegal lump sum payments.[8]

Business infiltration is marked by the use of venture capital from the huge profits of gambling, or foreclosure on a loan shark's usurious loan. The syndicate moves in its trusted personnel to control the operations of a business, and introduces its standard illegitimate operating procedure. These activities range from no-cost sweetheart contracts with syndicate unions, through fraud in bankruptcy proceedings, to the looting of money collected as tax revenues, and the skimming of cash income to avoid the payment of taxes. The syndicate favors restaurants, bars, taverns, and vending machine merchandising because the cash intake of these businesses has little relation to the actual costs of operation, and cash can easily be skimmed off the top. They have also prospered in the field of legal gambling enterprises in Nevada (a licensed business operation).[9]

In any review of the organization and activity of organized crime the

6. Paul B. Weston et al, *Narcotics, U.S.A.* (New York, Greenberg—Publisher, 1952), pp. 129–40. *See also* Alvin Moscow, *Merchants of Heroin* (New York: Dial Press, 1968), pp. 169–180.

7. Burton B. Turkus and Sid Feder, *Murder, Inc., the Story of the Syndicate* (New York: Farrar, Straus & Giroux, 1951), pp 74–106.

8. President's Commission on Law Enforcement and Administration of Justice, *Task Force Report: Organized Crime* (Washington, D. C.: U. S. Government Printing Office, 1967), p. 5.

9. Wallace Turner, *Gambler's Money—The New Force in American Life* (Boston: Houghton Mifflin Co., 1965), pp. 27–30.

most frightening aspect is the apparent ability of the syndicate to corrupt persons in public life, particularly agents of criminal justice. It may be that corruption begins in a meeting of the minds that nothing is really *wrong* with gambling; after all, it has been legalized in Nevada. However, beneath the cloak of syndicate gambling, are the associated ventures of loan sharking, narcotics, labor racketeering, and murder— as the syndicate kills and maims to enforce its operational rules. Because of basic contracts made between public officials and syndicate gambling operators, the connection is developed for immunity in other illegal operations. It is primarily for this reason that the private government of organized crime must be recognized as a force threatening democratic government and its concepts of law and justice. It must be combatted at both local and national levels with a new vigor and new directions which will expose its vast operations and curtail its criminal activities, because "if we do not on a national scale attack organized criminals with weapons and techniques as effective as their own, they will destroy us."[10]

The hierarchy of organized crime allows for this vital business of nullification of law enforcement by recognizing a position in each "family" of a counselor or *corruptor,* "whose role is to bribe and negotiate with public officials. In some families, corruptees of some rank and esteem handle relations with the top elected officials and judiciary who can be reached through friendship or previous contracts on syndicate business. Others, at lesser organization levels, are assigned to deal with police at the local levels.[11]

The mechanics of corruption, favors, pressures, and bribes was exposed in a New York case in which a public official was corrupted by a syndicate labor official. Bribes were passed to secure city contracts for controlling firms, and even the city's largest public utility was compromised. A former political czar of New York City, Carmine DeSapio, was sent to jail as a corruptor.[12]

The FBI Newark Transcripts

In New Jersey, almost an entire city was under indictment at one time. Mayor Hugh Addonizio and almost a dozen other city officials were indicted by a federal grand jury for tax evasion and extortion along with Anthony (Tony Boy) Boiardo, a reputed Cosa Nostra mem-

10. Daniel P. Moynihan, "The Private Government of Crime," *Reporter,* 6 July 1961, pp. 14–20.

11. Donald R. Cressey, *The Theft of a Nation—The Structure and Operations of Organized Crime in America* (New York, Harper and Row, 1969), pp. 248–89.

12. Walter Goodman, *A Percentage of the Take* (New York: Farrar, Straus and Giroux, 1971), pp 60–68, 150–189.

ber. In a related federal indictment Simone (Sam the Plumber) DeCavalcante, a reputed capo of the Cosa Nostra, was charged with operating an interstate numbers game. A great deal of the evidence was obtained through electronic eavesdropping of DeCavalcante's office. Authorized by federal statutes, the eavesdropping was monitored by FBI agents. It covered the period 1961 to 1965 and the contents were made public at DeCavalcante's trial.

The following extracts from these transcripts of recorded conversations[13] are a manual on the Cosa Nostra, offering a stark insight into the operations of the crime syndicate.

Tape No. 1

The first extract from these transcipts is the record of a conversation between DeCavalcante, Sam the Plumber, and John and Joe, both subordinates to Sam the Plumber in the organization:

Sam: John, have you got something to say?

John: Yes, Sam. I came to you yesterday, because I felt that as caporegime, I'm not getting the respect that I should get from Joe *(last name not clear)*.

Sam: And you told me yesterday you had something to say, right? And I didn't give you a chance to open your mouth, right? Whatever is to be said is said face to face—then I decide.

John: That's the proper way.

Sam: So what has happened that you don't think you're getting the right respect? Now let me tell you one thing, John, tell only from the time that I am in the administration. We don't want to take any old things. Okay, go ahead.

(John explained that in everything he sees Joe about, whether one of his soldiers or himself, he is always fighting uphill. Never does he give cooperation and it's always necessary that John take the issue to Sam.)

John: I came to Joe once for Jacoby's son. After all, I'm responsible for Jacoby. I had a battle, or else I got no satisfaction. Same with my father. I got tired of going to Joe because it always ended up here. I came to you because my father wanted a job. *(John said he had explored all possibilities of this without creating friction. The job was to last four weeks. When John talked to the foreman, he learned that after the four weeks his father was through. John pointed out that there were nonmembers* who were being retained.)* Sam, I had the idea that our people came first. I think we came

---

13. United States v. DeCavalcante, Vastola and Annunziata, U.S . District Court, New Jersey (Index number: Criminal 111-68).

*Apparently of the "family."

in and asked for the job before anybody else outside of our people. I don't get the cooperation or the respect from Joe. I have to answer to my father and I have to answer to Mr. Jacoby.

Joe: Did he have the job?

Sam: Jacoby's son?

Joe: Jacoby's son.

John: That's not the point, Joe. Let me finish. Now, if I'm gonna have this all the time, Sam—first, I feel offended as an *amica nos** that I can't go to my friend and get a favor for one of our soldiers. Second, even as a caporegime, I can't do nothing. I want to know why. When I went to Joe about my father, I know there was four positions open. He told me no, there was only one opening and it was promised.

Sam: *(Critical of John for not being more forceful as a* caporegime, *he then turns on Joe and lays down the ground rules that there will be no heated arguments and everything will be resolved amicably.)*

Joe: *(He said he never had a chance to act on any requests because John always went immediately "to the Supreme Court," meaning Sam.)*

When your father came into the picture that job was already given out, and Sam knows that—but he got the job anyway didn't he? Another thing, when there was a general layoff, your father and the Super cooked something up that he got the job. What does your father think, that all the jobs are his? *(Joe became slightly belligerent and Sam pounced on him. Joe related that he had had refusals to work from workmen who were put under the foremanship of John's father. The conversation persisted in this manner and it appeared to be a simple personality clash between John and Joe and some others of the union. They mentioned a worker Anthony, who is not amico nos. Suddenly, with a remark by John, Joe questioned his authority as* caporegime *Sam exploded! In no uncertain terms he told Joe that he should never be so foolish as to make a remark like that again. Long periods of silence followed. Then Sam tried to resume the discussion, noting that he had recently performed tasks for the commission at great personal danger, all for the good of the organization. Without discipline, the organization would fail.)*

Sam: Joe, you owe John an apology. Right?

Joe: Okay, I apologize.

Sam: Joe, do you mean that? Shake hands. I won't permit it this way. Joe, I'd give my life for our people. This cannot exist as long as I am alive. What are you guys, deaf ? Joe, John, get up! Both of you get up!

*Friend (of ours), member.

Now I want this all forgotten. I don't ever want to hear this story repeated John.

John: I'd be ashamed to repeat it. It'll never happen anymore.

Tape No. 2

This tape reports a conversation between Sam (the Plumber) DeCavalcante, Anthony (Tony Boy) Boiardo, and Angelo (Ray) DeCarlo—indicted in another federal indictment shortly after Boiardo's and DeCavalcante's indictment. It is a conversation that begins with a murder and then rambles on about syndicate business and members:

Tony Boy: When are you leaving, Ray?

Ray: Next week.

Tony Boy: Where?

Ray: Grand Bahamas. We'll play golf every day for 10 days. We catch the plane in Fort Lauderdale. It's only 20 minutes.

. . .

Ray: What the hell happened? How did Vic walk in there like that? Did you tell him to walk in to Spina?

Tony Boy: We set it up, Ray.

Ray: Did he make a statement that he did this more or less?

Tony Boy: Because the girl took the whole rap.

Ray: Well, yeah, according to Albano (medical examiner), she's the one that did. . . .

Tony Boy: He didn't hit him in the head.

Ray: But he's going to be an accessory. He'll wind up with a bit.

Tony Boy: Oh yeah.

Ray: Who squealed on him? How did they know he was there?

Tony Boy: They had him nailed, fingerprints and all. Then Carmine *(Battaglia)* went around screaming about it.

Ray: Well, if we get a good judge, he'll get a small bit. What was he doing up in that joint* and who was this broad? She had a junkie rap and everything.

Tony Boy: He met this broad and she used to go out with this. . . .

*A gambling place operated by one of the "family."

Ray: Who?

Tony Boy: The guy that got killed.

Ray: Oh, she must have wanted to go in that joint.

Tony Boy: Yeah, she did. But she stood up just as good as he did.

Ray: I hear it is the truth.

Tony Boy: It is. This guy started making up to her and she pushed him. The FBI went to see Byrne *(Brendon Byrne, Essex Co. Prosecutor)* and asked him about this Pisauro—how come he gave himself up. Byrne told them, "This Pisauro is Tony Boy's man."

(At this point an individual referred to by DeCarlo as Sam entered the room).

Sam: Tony, 30 or 35 years ago if a — — — was even seen talking to a cop they looked to hit him the next day. They figured he must be doing business with the cop.

Ray: Today if you don't meet them and pay them you can't operate.

Tony Boy: The only guy I handle is Dick. Gino and them guys handle the rest of the law. About seven or eight years (ago) I used to handle them all.

Sam: Did you ever see the way Ham operated on 14th Street?

Ray: For $5,000 Ham and Tony *(Bananas)* thought they bought a license.

Sam: This was before the $5,000.

Ray: They walk into precincts and everything. You can't have a man and be seen with him. He's no good to you then.

Sam: And how long do you think it will take the federal men to find out?

Ray: The federal men, they know everything that's happening.

Tony Boy: You know Hughie got hold of me. He said, "Look, tell Ray that the FBI knows about Irving Berlin." I'll tell you how much the FBI knows. This kid Vic *(Pisauro)* that turned himself in. The prosecutor *(Byrne)* told the FBI that he's one of my boys and that I made him give himself up to the director.

Ray: So they asked the prosecutor, "How come he turned himself into the director?"

Sam: I'm not surprised. The FBI. . . .

Tony Boy: No, I'm not surprised. I'm trying to let you know how the word got to me what the prosecutor told them. How well informed they are.

Ray: They know who we're with and who we ain't with, who the mobs are, and everything else.

Sam: Well, did Louie tell you that when he was in Washington they had the boss, Profaci. They had a chart, like a map of the United States and they had me listed as Profaci's lieutenant in Trenton. They had my name on there.

Tony Boy: Ray, they got you way up on the list.

Ray: As long as they can't prove nothing I don't care. *(The conversation drifted to a discussion of the recent killing of Cadillac Charlie in Youngstown Ohio. All were critical of the method used, and of the fact that his 4–year–old son was also killed. Ray DeCarlo stated that as a result, the word has been passed that no hand grenades will be used in the future. DeCarlo further suggested that the best way to dispose of someone is to give the individual a fatal shot of dope and put him behind the wheel of his automobile where he will be found.)*

Ray: That's what they should have done with Willie *(Moretti).**

Tony Boy: Oh yeah.

Ray: You got five guys there, you talk to the guy. Tell him this is the lie detector stuff. You tell him, "You say you didn't say this."

Tony Boy: How many guys you going to con?

Ray: Well if you don't con him, then tell him. Now like you got four or five guys in the room. You know they're going to kill you. They say, "Tony Boy wants to shoot you in the head and leave you in the street or would you rather take this, we put you behind your wheel, we don't have to embarrass your family or nothing." That's what they should have done to Willie.

Tony Boy: How about the time we hit the Little Jew? . . .

Ray: As little as they are, they struggle.

Tony Boy: The Boot hit him with a hammer. The guy goes down and he comes up. So I got a crowbar this big, Ray. Eight shots in the head. What do you think he finally did to me. He spit at me and said, "you — — — —."

Ray: They're fighting for their life.

Sam: Ray, you told me years ago about the guy where you said, "Let me hit you clean."

*Formerly a boss of one of New Jersey's families who was shot and killed in a gangland assassination.

Ray: That's right. So the guy went for it. There was me, Zip and Johnny. So we took the guy out in the woods, and I said, "Now, listen." Zip had the . . . on him. I said, "Leave him alone, Zip." I said, "Look"—Itchie was the kid's name. I said, "You gotta go, why not let me hit you right in the heart and you won't feel a thing." He said, "I'm innocent, Ray, but if you've go to do it. . . ." So I hit him in the heart, and it went right through him.

Sam: The guy we were supposed to. . .*(inaudible)* They were spitting all over me you know.

Ray: Oh well, I would have left them on the street.

Sam: They didn't want them on the street. They didn't want the rest of the mob to know that permission. . . .

Ray: But I mean a guy like Willie *(Moretti)*. "We like you and all but you gotta go. You know it's an order. You gave enough orders."

Tony Boy: It would have been better.

Ray: Sure, that man never should have been disgraced like that.

Sam: It leaves a bad taste. We're out to protect people. When they made you they say, "————*(Italian phrase)*." Do you know what————*(same phrase)* means? Don't, not to abuse you. To protect people from being abused. When they made me, they made me in Italian. They spoke all in Italian.

Tony Boy: My father said you must be made 25 to 30 years ago.

Sam: No, 20 years. About the same time as you, Ray.

Ray: Around 1945.

Sam: No you wasn't, it was '45.

Ray: Wait a minute, my father died in '44.

Sam: When we had the game* in Princeton you was already made.

Ray: I was supposed to be made in Philadelphia.

Tony Boy: (to Ray) You were made with the blade, weren't you?

Sam: No he was made before the blade. Two or three years before the blade.

Ray: Me and Sy was made at the same time in Carmine's house.

Sam: He was made. . . .

*Apparently a dice or card game.

Tony Boy: Was the Boot made before you, Ray?

Ray: Yeah, he was made about six months or a year before me.

Sam: That's right.

Tony Boy: Where the hell is Joe Rogers?

Ray: I heard he was over in the Dominican Republic.

Sam: You know what wrecked him? That Cuban deal.

Ray: He would have been one of the richest mob guys around if Batista hadn't lost.

Sam: You hear a lot of stories. Him and I was never too close just until lately. I hear he wasn't too good with a buck either.

Ray: I don't know about that.

Sam: But you know a guy who never went for a cent was Settimo, my cousin.

Ray: Oh, he never went for anything. You know how he made his money? Some kids came to us with a lot of stamps. They wanted one–eighth of a cent for each of them. We had the crap game in South Plainfield and couldn't handle them. So they went to Settimo. He made about $50,000 profit.

Sam: He made money with Carl with the counterfeit.

Tony Boy: Carl who?

Sam: Gambino. They made a million dollars with counterfeit.

Tape No. 3

In this conversation Ray DeCarlo is explaining to a friend, identified only as Sammy, how profitable loan sharking was as a business.

Ray: The best racket in the world is the shylock racket.

Sammy: Oh yeah?

Ray: We're getting away from all gambling. This guy that just left has got $60,000.

Sammy: Who is that guy?

Ray: Milton. . . .We get $200 for every $10,000 per week. That's $1,-200 a week. At the end of a year you got your money back and he still owes $60,000.

Sammy: For a guy to go into that he must be in trouble.

Ray: Yeah, but Milton does business with those big factories. He's got good customers to deal with. He's been doing it for two years.

Sammy: You mean he makes more money on top of what you make?

Ray: No. We lend out $60,000 and he lends out $60,000 of his own. Me and Sy have got $60,000 with him. He has $120,000 out.

Sammy: Oh, I see. He doesn't use it himself. He lends it out.

Ray: Yeah. He lends it out. Now we got another guy down at the shore shylocking. We got about $13,000 out with him, which is $300 a week.

Sammy: How did you make out with that pocketbook guy?

Ray: That————, he's paying me $150 a week. He'll have to pay me for the next 15 years. If he pays me for three or four years, I'll have my money back. He's still in business, that's what counts.

Tape No. 4

This is the record of another short conversation, and one as equally informative as the previous dialogue on loan sharking. The subject this time is politics and how the "family" rewards its friends. It is between Ray DeCarlo and a friend only identified as Jack, a brother–in–law of a local judge, probably in the city court system of Newark.

Jack: My brother–in–law, the judge got hold of me. He said I should get hold of you: Jack talk to Ray, and Ray would get hold of Skinny* and Skinny could make him the county judge in Essex County.

Ray: Skinny could make who?

Jack: The judge, my brother–in–law.

Ray: How could Skinny do that?

Jack: That's what I told him.

Ray: Oh.

Jack: Yeah.

Ray: Oh yeah, maybe he can. . . .

Jack: This guy don't want to do no favors.

Ray: No, he don't do no favors. You don't want favors, you want to pay him.

Jack: He's obligated now. He knows it's going to come from Ray, why

---

*Apparently a local political figure.

shouldn't he do a favor? Why shouldn't he do things? And he said you gotta work fast. He told me, for in two weeks they're going to make this new county judge.

Ray: We sit down with the guy, and tell him you want to do what's right. We don't want you to deal with eight million guys. You deal with one guy. He'll deal with you, that's all. If Tony Boy gets a man in trouble you want to do some business, pay him, straighten it out. Say, "What the hell?" We don't want to put a guy in there who won't take money. We want to pay for whatever favors we get even if we get you the job. The jobs are made to make money with. Not just to sit there. If you want the reputation of being a judge, you better get it for yourself. Just tell him there ain't a judge on them benches who ain't put in there through somebody. Somebody can always do business with them, or they don't get the jobs.

Action Program—Supression of Organized Crime

A program for effective control of organized crime should have five main thrusts:

1. An "Organized Crime Unit."
2. Training.
3. Intelligence.
4. Research and strategy development.
5. Development of legislation.

It is obvious from the foregoing taped conversations that organized crime differs fundamentally from other crime by reason of its organization and espirit de corps. This organization and its method of operations is also different in its social disruption, its social impact, and its economics—both in terms of profits to organized crime and losses to the general economy.

In view of the potential of organized crime, it is not at all unreasonable to undertake long–term commitments to the support of a special squad of police and other experts (attorneys and accountants). This group would receive special training in the conduct of comprehensive investigations, the essential elements of crimes common to the national syndicate, the evidence necessary in these cases, and the common defense strategy of organized crime, particularly their corruption of friends in positions of authority.

The collection of intelligence is nothing more than securing a data base for proceeding against a well–organized criminal group. Without it, there is little likelihood that any police group will understand the assortment of relationships in organized crime. Federal agents have made excellent use of informants, undercover agents, and court–approved electronic eavesdropping. These are standard methods of intelligence gathering, but the syndicate's membership is alert and skilled in counterintelligence gathering and spoiling sources of information.

Innovative research and the development of attack strategy should be aimed at specialized investigative techniques, such as: the detection of revenue violations; the general financial investigation of conspiracy and corruption; the discovery of the availability of illegal goods and services at local levels; and specialized prosecutorial techniques. The legislation unit would study existing legislation that permits wiretapping, electronic surveillance, or other interception techniques; the constitutional compatibility of adequate monitoring; the legislation necessary to grant immunity and to provide for contempt convictions, if witnesses refuse to talk despite immunity; the legislation for special grand juries and for blue ribbon trial juries; and other legislation which may be necessary to combat organized crime.

The high cost of organized crime is not always measurable. People lose money gambling, pay high interest on loans, buy narcotics (sometimes die of an overdose), and union members and businessmen are victimized. But the more critical cost to the people of a community can be measured in terms of fear and loss of confidence in the government's ability to protect it from murder and corruption: the imposition of a second government upon the community.

Selected References

Books

Cressey, Donald R. *The Theft of a Nation—The Structure and Operations of Organized Crime in America.* New York: Harper & Row, 1969.

Egan, Frederick. *The Plainclothesman—Handbook of Vice and Gambling Operations.* New York: Arco Press, 1958.

Goodman, Walter. *A Percentage of the Take.* New York: Farrar, Strauss and Giroux, 1971.

Maas, Peter. *The Valachi Papers.* New York: G. P. Putnam and Sons, 1968.

President's Commission on Law Enforcement and Administration of Justice. *Task Force Report: Organized Crime.* Washington, D. C.: U.S. Government Printing Office, 1967.

Periodicals

Moynihan, Daniel R. "The Private Government of Crime." *Reporter,* 25, no. 1 (July 6, 1961): 14–20.

–––. Loan–sharking: The Untouched Domain of Organized Crime." *Columbia Journal of Law and Social Problems* Vol. 5, No. 1., pp. 91–136.

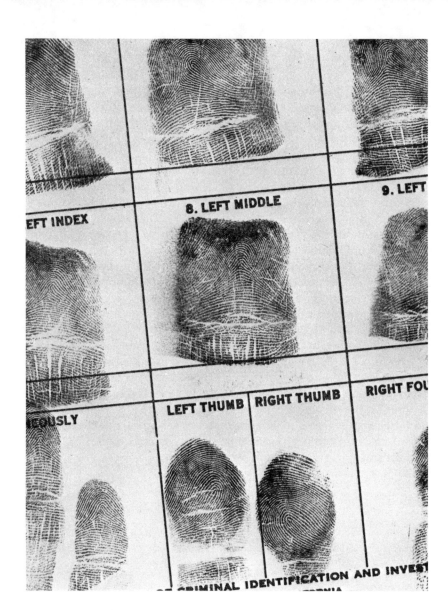

8. LEFT MIDDLE

9. LEFT

EFT INDEX

LEFT THUMB | RIGHT THUMB | RIGHT FO

OUSLY

CRIMINAL IDENTIFICATION AND INVES

Chapter XIV

Crime and Punishment—Corrections and Rehabilitation

Crime deterrence and prevention has always relied upon legislative penalties in various criminal or penal codes (imprisonment, fines, probation), or the morality of members of the community, and neither of these two forms of social control has ever been as successful as desired or expected. There is some evidence that a new awareness of the ineffectiveness of these traditional measures is leading to the funding of social justice programs to fight poverty, discrimination, and some of the other inequities in American communities which, to some degree, foster delinquency and crime. However, to date, the only supplement has been the reform role of corrections in the criminal justice system. In organizing for this role, local and state governments provide field agencies (probation; parole) and institutions (prisons; jails) for care and rehabilitative treatment of offenders, with the aim of changing their criminal behavior to noncriminal behavior.

After a crime as an event, there is a major thrust to apprehend the offender. When an investigation does focus on a suspect, the case against the accused moves rapidly to the point at which the prosecutor must make his decision whether to charge. When the decision is to charge, the prosecutor pushes for trial, or a plea negotiation session. Sentencing is equally prompt after a trial or plea of guilty. Then, when the convicted person has been sent away, the process hesitates and slows to a stop.

Up to this point, the major thrust of the criminal justice process is to investigate the crime as an event and to make a determination as to the guilt or innocence of the accused. Now, beyond the trial and its verdict, the police, prosecutor, and defense counsel are through. As for the trial judge, his only remaining duty is the sentencing session. After a verdict of guilty, the defendant becomes a convicted person, and after sentencing he is a prisoner to be committed to the care and custody of a corrections agency, as provided by law. His contacts are now with agents of the probation agency, or the staff of the institution in which he will serve his sentence. Outside of an abstract interest in justice, these agents are not concerned with the question of guilt or innocence. Institutionally, they assume guilt and work from this base toward the rehabilitation and eventual return of the offender to the community.

The sentence of a convicted offender reflects the judgment of the trial judge within limits prescribed by law. First offenders may be given probation without any term of imprisonment. However, the crime for which the accused was convicted may forbid the granting of probation and require the sentencing judge to impose a mandatory minimum sentence, set an extremely high maximum term, or forbid parole until a minimum number of years has been served in prison.

Imprisonment is the most common sentence for serious crimes in American courts. It was developed by humanitarians in the eighteenth century as an alternative to capital punishment, floggings, and other physical punishments. Summary physical punishment, as a direct reaction to the guilt of an offender, was a carryover from the precourt years in which the family or friends of a victim sought vengeance or revenge. Imprisonment was and is punitive; deprivation of liberty is painful. At the time of the transition from physical forms of punishment to imprisonment as a major tool of sentencing judges, a long term of years in confinement was believed to be a deterrent to the repetition of criminal acts upon release. It was a guarantee to the community that the law–abiding citizens would not be molested in any way by the offender while incapacitated in prison. Additionally, the example of imprisonment was seen as a deterrent to others to avoid criminal acts.

Over the years, however, a suspicion among nineteenth–century criminologists that imprisonment was ineffective in changing the behavior patterns of convicted offenders, became a twentieth–century belief among experts in law and its penalties. Mere restraint does not achieve the purposes for which a sentencing judge commits a convicted person to prison. Institutions for the custodial care of sentenced offenders tend to isolate them from the community, cutting them off from interaction with family, friends, and community services which provide the supportive influences necessary for any person to achieve minimum levels of social and material success. Prisons, with their procriminal subculture, do not prepare inmates for a law–abiding life upon their release. The cultural impact of a prison community for any extended period of time accustoms inmates to criminal lives.

The switch from suspicion to belief in the failure of prisons to correct convicted criminals may also be a switch from the old rule, "Let the punishment fit the crime," to a new creed of, "Let the treatment fit the needs of the individual offender." In this reform, the main focus of the postconviction period is not the deterrence of crime or the protection of the community by storing offenders in prisons, but rather a focus upon the individual offender for the purpose of rehabilitation. The community will be safer with this reform, by changing the behavior patterns of offenders so that they do not return to crime upon release from prison.[1]

Corrections in the United States have a federal, state, county, and, sometimes, municipal level. In this probation–prison–parole complex a substantial number of persons are returnees, recidivists who have committed one or more crimes after release on a prior committment. Of course, these backsliding individuals may have committed the new offense or offenses due to the causative factors which lead to crimes, despite supervision on probation or parole, or treatment during a term of imprisonment. Unfortunately, some of the most meaningful work done by agents and agencies in this field of corrections is negated by the complex influences acting upon the released inmate as soon as he returns to the free world and tries to rejoin the community.

The Ethics of Punishment

Revenge as punishment belongs to the early years of community approved sadism. Sanction law rejects the concept of retribution in assigning penalties for criminal acts.

The gibbet at the crossroads, and the exhibition of severed heads in public places were techniques of terror associated with the doctrine that if whipping, severe flogging, and exposure in the pillory did not prevent crime, then capital punishment was justified. In the beginning of sanction law, this was a trial–and–error period. It was soon discovered, however, that severe punishment alone was a failure. In eighteenth–century England, as the number of crimes for which the sentence could be death grew, the total number of crimes increased.

When Cesare Beccaria and Jeremy Bentham first probed crime and the rationale of punishment, they asked as to the efficacy of the death penalty: Is it really useful or necessary for the safety and good order of society? In Beccaria's view, the role of a legislator in assigning penalties to a crime was to set a punishment which would counteract

1. President's Commission on Law Enforcement and Administration of Justice, *The Challenge of Crime in a Free Society* (Washington, D.C.: U.S. Government Printing Office, 1967), pp. 159–65.

the motives that led to such crime. Bentham, had a mathematical concept of motives for crime and believed that an ascending schedule of punishment could serve as a deterrent to crime. This is the classical view that man is a calculating animal with free will, and not a person influenced by constitutional factors related to heredity; by compulsive drives, or unconscious motivations; or by the influences of environment and stress. In Beccaria's and Bentham's utilitarian concept, the principal end of a criminal punishment was to prevent like offenses.

Both of these early utilitarians also stressed the need for humanitarianism in setting penalties and passing sentences: punishment should be no greater in amount than the minimum necessary to deter men from the commission of crime. The amount of punishment should not be governed by the moral transgression of the offender or the intensity of public indignation over the crime, but rather by the social need to prevent such crimes. The utilitarian concepts of Beccaria and Bentham also extend the concept of humanitarianism to offenders who commit crimes due to extenuating circumstances. For instance, punishment would be less severe when the circumstances of a crime indicated extreme provocation, economic need, or reaction to sudden stress.[2]

In this classical view of crime and punishment, the main purpose of penalties set by legislators in sanction law is not in the punishment of convicted persons, but rather in the operation of the threat of punishment as a deterrent to crime by the far larger number of potential criminals. The eighteenth–century sentencing judge was assigned the role of putting its penalty into operation. Lawmakers and the judiciary served as agents of criminal justice in attempting to achieve the community objective of preventing crime.

The American viewpoint of punishment evolved from the penalties provided for various crimes in the English common law, the moralistic code of the Puritans who settled New England, and the administration of justice during the westward march of frontier settlements. Case law allowed the colonists to relate a specific crime to a range of punitive actions, and the Puritan mind provided a ready answer to any question as to the purpose of punishment: the spiritual welfare of the citizen and the good of the community. From these beginnings, punishments for crime in the United States were shaped by the close relationship between the rudimentary courts of justice and local citizens in frontier mining, lumber, and cow towns. Trials were frequently informal affairs attended by crowds of onlookers seeking satisfactory outcomes. The concept of criminal punishment in America may be summed up as originating in an accumulation of judicial decisions, the Puritan combi-

2. Sir Walter Moberly, *The Ethics of Punishment* (Hamden, Conn.: Archon Books, 1968), pp. 43–59.

nation of ecclesiastical and secular authority, and the frontier citizen's demands for an observable and satisfactory justice.[3]

As part of the nineteenth–century evolution of punishment within the various criminal codes in the United States, the values of deterrence and incapacitation (public protection) were joined with corrections—restoring the offender to his basic role as a law–abiding citizen in the community. Lawmaking allowed for greater judicial discretion in granting probation and introduced the concept of the indeterminate sentence (and its correlated parole release). Such discretion not only allows the sentencing judge to set an appropriate sentence for the individual offender, but also permits him to forego or shorten imprisonment in favor of a correctional treatment program which will minimize the offender's dislocation from the community and enhance his opportunity to readjust to community life.

Utilizing an objective analysis of available data as a prelude to the sentencing episode, the judicial response bridges the gap between the apprehension–and–trial phases of criminal justice with the terminal phase of corrections. If the judiciary does not impose a sentence of imprisonment except as necessary for public protection against persistent or professional criminals or violence–prone persons (and works within the minimum and maximum terms of an indeterminate sentence), then they are working with the practitioners in probation, prison, and parole agencies for the rehabilitation of offenders.

In aligning the judiciary's interest in the offender as a person and the apparent intent to encourage rehabilitation in postconviction years, the practitioners in correctional agencies have developed a related correctional philosophy. This philosophy has five major aspects:

1. Convicted and sentenced offenders are social deviates requiring treatment.

2. The sentence imposed by the sentencing judge is the "criminal punishment" of sanction law.

3. It is the obligation of the correctional agency to administer its program to equip offenders to cope with life in the community upon release.

4. The treatment needs of individual offenders vary in accordance to what is "wrong" with them; the duration and circumstances of treatment for individual offenders have a corresponding variance.

5. There is an obligation by all correctional agencies to maintain

3. Louis B. Schwartz, "The American Penal System: Spirit and Technique," *Annals—Crime and the American Penal System* 339, (January 1962): 1–10.

control over offenders committed to their supervision, or care and custody.[4]

It should not be forgotten, however, that corrections has been and always will be handicapped by the basic assumption that crime can be reduced by increasing the severity of punishment.* A survey authorized by the California Assembly's Committee on Criminal Procedure studied penalties and deterrents. This study revealed that California's general public was almost unaware of the severity of criminal penalties, but the most delinquent group was quite aware of the severity of criminal penalties.** California's legislators had long assumed that more severe penalties would deter criminals and noncriminals from committing crimes, but it is apparent that a policy of severe penalties did not deter these offenders and would be unlikely to deter an unknowing member of the general public. The research team on this project concluded: "We can find no evidence that crime can be reduced by increasing the time served."[5]

In a followup study, a total of 7,925 California parolees were interviewed to determine whether time served in prison related to postrelease success on parole. The findings of these researchers were that recidivism rates for offenders who had served comparatively long terms of imprisonment (compared to others in the same offense category in the sample population) were higher than those who served short terms; and, in constructing mathematical models composed of significant characteristics to predict postrelease success, it was found that time served was *not* useful in predicting postrelease success.[6]

In regard to the philosophy of criminal punishment in America, it appears safe to assume that there has been a trend away from the classicist viewpoint: that fear of criminal punishment as a penalty for criminal acts is an effective deterrent. There is more acceptance of the concept that the sentencing of offenders should be oriented to their rehabilitation and not tied to any residual aspects of punishment. On the other hand, one must concede that many individuals have mixed emotions and attitudes on criminal penalties. For instance, a mailed questionnaire about crime and punishment surveyed 313 state and federal supreme court judges and revealed these mixed feelings among the 119 respondents. The question was: "Our treatment of

4. John P. Conrad, *Crime and Its Correction—An International Survey of Attitudes and Practices* (Berkeley and Los Angeles, University of California Press, 1967), pp. 11–14.

*Defined as increasing the amount of time served in prison.

**Inmates in California's youth centers and prisons answered 6.3 questions correctly out of a total of 11 queries; the general public's average was only 2.6.

5. California Assembly Office of Research, *Crime and Penalties in California* (Sacramento, Calif.: California Legislature, 1968), pp. 1–17.

6. California Assembly Select Committee on the Administration of Justice, *Parole Board Reform in California: Order Out of Chaos* (Sacramento, Calif.: Assembly of the State of California, 1970), pp. 20–22.

criminals is too harsh; we should try to cure not to punish them." The judges were asked to indicate whether, on the whole, they *agreed strongly, agreed, neither agreed nor disagreed, disagreed,* or *strongly disagreed* with this statement. The statistically significant responses on this scale were:

Agree Strongly	Agree	Neither Agree or Disagree (Neutral)	Disagree	Strongly Disagree
5	20	22	48	24

There is certainly grounds for concern in an analysis of these responses: (1) the average judicial respondent in this survey was torn between being neutral and disagreeing with the statement about cure being preferable to punishment in our treatment of criminals; (2) only 20 judges could agree that at this time there was too much of the punishment factor in our present treatment of criminals, while 48 disagreed with this belief; and (3) only five responses strongly agreed to favor cure, but 24 responses strongly disagreed that punishment was too harsh.[7] The foregoing analysis indicates that among the judiciary there will be some sentencing judges who will seek alternatives to imprisonment, while many others will place deterrence and incapacitation ahead of rehabilitation and impose imprisonment.

In little more than a century criminal punishment (penalties based on sanction law), has changed from the crude philosophy of simple deterrence to a philosophy of correctional rehabilitation of offenders. There is still some recognition that the sanctions of criminal law serve as deterrents to many potential offenders. However, sentencing is more and more a judicial referral to the practioners in corrections with the hope that professional care and treatment will lead to personal and legal rehabilitation.

Capital Punishment

The penalty of death by execution for a criminal act such as murder or kidnapping has long been a subject of controversy. In theory, its severity has been termed a deterrent to similar acts by others; its certainty pointed to as an asset (there can be no reduction in the sentence by parole); and its basic financial economy has even been lauded. On the other hand, there is persuasive evidence that capital punishment does not deter: murder rates are not affected by punishing

7. Stuart S. Nagel, *The Legal Process from a Behavioral Perspective* (Homewood, Ill.: Dorsey Press, 1969), pp. 234–35.

people with death. The type of crimes for which death has been a penalty in the twentieth century are usually committed during an emotional episode—and murderous anger or rage leaves little room for intellectual consideration of the penalty. There is also significant evidence that the poor and members of minority groups are more likely to be given a death sentence, with less likelihood that it will be changed to life imprisonment prior to execution. While the pardoning authorities may strive to review the nature of the crime, the fairness of the trial, and the rehabilitation potential of the offender as a grounds for this executive clemency, the reality of these decisions will often be based on the public pressure in the case and the executive's personal and political response to it.[8] Lastly, there is an awful finality to capital punishment. Post–mortem evidence of innocence does no more than restore the reputation of the executed offender.

The moral argument which questions the right of the state to take human life as punishment for behavior labeled as criminal by lawmakers is reinforced by the cold–blooded politeness of the execution. The person who is about to be put to death is expected to collaborate in a nice, sensible manner, as if it were to be an experience no worse than minor surgery; and if the victim is a woman she must put on waterproof underwear just prior to the execution.[9]

When a person accused of murder is convicted, the judgment and sentence decision is a solitary one. Sometimes, the recommendation of a penalty jury is helpful, but in the final analysis the sentencing judge must make his decision alone. In selecting sentencing alternatives the judicial mind must weigh the various objectives of sentencing and the corrections system together with the needs or best interests of the offender and the community.

Some years ago, the authors encountered a precisely written judicial comment on the basic problem of the sentencing judge in deciding between the death penalty and life imprisonment. The case was murder, the two defendants were brothers, the trial was fair, and the verdict of guilty was warranted by multiple evidence of guilt.[10] This trial judge,* with the awesome responsibility of determining whether two young men should live or die for a murder they had committed decided on life imprisonment. He describes the matter of sentence and penalty in these words:

8. Richard Quinney, *The Social Reality of Crime* (Boston: Little, Brown and Co., 1970), pp. 184–90.

9. Arthur Koestler, "Reflections on Hanging," in *Perspectives on Correction*, edited by Donal E. J. MacNamara and Edward Sagarin (New York: Thomas Y. Crowell Co., 1971), pp. 239–77.

10. People v. Lokey, Superior Court, Sacramento, California (No.26156).

*Honorable Leonard R. Freedman, then judge of the California Superior Court, presently justice of the California District Court of Appeal. Third Appellate District.

I do want to state the reasons for my judgment... so that the two defendants may know the reasoning of the person who has held their lives in the balance....The choice becomes a personal and internal one. Internal choices are secretly made and then publicly announced. It is possible to reach a judgment based entirely on subjective considerations. It is possible through anger to reach a harsh judgment and it is possible through pity to reach a soft judgment. Either judgment would find its critics, and its supporters who would marshall facts and arguments to criticize or praise a sentence which, while not intrinsically wrong, was reached by an emotional and, hence, erroneous process.

Judges and lawyers who have been instilled since the beginning of their training with zeal for equal justice intuitively dislike and avoid arbitrary judgments. Now, if in the course of what our State Supreme Court has called the "grim business" of selecting life or death, the law offers us an arbitrary choice, we must reject it and reach out strenuously for such objective standards as are available. Realistically, we know that subjective and, hence to that extent arbitrary, elements will insinuate themselves into the process. We must reduce and contain them so far as possible. We cannot reach a decision by mechanically perfect means, but it must be a rational decision.

Penologists have discerned four objectives of punishment; first, retribution; second, to protect society by executing or confining the wrongdoer; third, to deter others from crime; and fourth, to correct and rehabilitate. Were retribution a primary factor and were Bobby and Galen Lokey to be judged mainly by the terrible consequences of their action, they should certainly pay the heaviest penalty known to the law. If we were to judge these defendants by the law of the talon, an eye for an eye, and a tooth for a tooth, then the court might impose the death penalty upon them as the expression of an outraged community, and the outrage of the community is perfectly justified. Enlightenment, however, tells us that retribution is no longer a desirable object of punishment. A judgement grounded to any extent on social vengeance would degrade our progressive notions of criminal jurisprudence.

What about the objective of protecting society against future crimes by these defendants? Certainly, their death will accomplish that aim, but will life imprisonment do any less?

Now, deterrence. Certainly deterrence must be a prime objective of the sentence. To say that the death of Bobby and Galen would prevent other youthful delinquents from running amuck is patent error. To say that life imprisonment would encourage repetition of their crime is idiotic. The hard fact is that there are no facts which would sustain a choice between life and death for the purpose of deterrence. Each type of punishment is equally effectual and equally ineffectual. Since under California law there is no preference between the death penalty and life imprisonment, the fact of deterrence does not militate in either direction.

Now, we reach the fourth objective of penology, rehabilitation. From a temporal standpoint, death is utterly without rehabilitative value. At this point the scales tip significantly in the direction of life imprisonment. The Court was at some pains to ascertain whether either of these young men is afflicted with personality disorders tending toward incurable sadism; they are not so afflicted. In short, these defendants are good prospects for rehabilitation.

Galen Lokey will commence his life term at the age of twenty. He will become eligible for parole while still a young man. There is a prospect that at some future day he will return to the world of freedom equipped with sufficient maturity, self–command, and, above all, with a set of goals, which will enable him to live decently, even happily.

Nor is rehabilitation irrelevant to the case of Bobby Lokey. It is ironic and terribly sad that this young man, hardly more than a boy, this young man of 23 should be sitting before me with relief pumping through his veins at the sour prospect of spending the rest of his life behind prison bars. The prison community, I would say to Bobby, is like the outside world in this respect, that it is populated by good, indifferent, and bad people. Bobby has had a talent for trouble since his childhood, and there are a lot of people in prison with a talent for trouble, and their talent manifests itself even in prison, and they are troublemakers there. But, in prison there are also decent people, there are opportunities for useful work, and, most important, for education. Decency and usefulness and knowledge are there and available to Bobby Lokey if he will reach out for them. At any rate, in his case, too, the rehabilitation factor calls for life imprisonment rather than death.

Sentencing Alternatives

The alternatives to a sentence committing an offender to prison, or a sentence of death, are: (1) fine, (2) probation, and (3) diminishment of the term of imprisonment by release on parole. There is a sentencing hierarchy in America, in which authority is divided among the lawmakers, the judiciary, and the correctional officials (parole boards). Sanction law includes the lawmakers' views as to an appropriate penalty, either by the grade of crime (minor infraction, misdemeanor, or felony), or by some statutory provision affecting sentencing. When the sentencing judge fixes imprisonment as the proper alternative for an offender, a short term (misdemeanants) can be for a fixed period, tied in with fine or probation, or both; but modern criminal justice practices usually require an indeterminate sentence when severe sentences (felons) are imposed. While the judiciary, often under statutory provisions, sets the minimum and maximum terms of these sentences, the corrections agency officials appointed to the parole board set the date for release on parole.

Lawmakers, in setting penalties in sanction law and in enacting provisions for mandatory sentencing procedures act in response to many influences ranging from research findings to public pressure and political advantage. The sentencing judge bases his action on statutory requirements and data known to him at the time of sentencing, either from the trial, the penalty trial (if appropriate), or the presentence report conducted by an investigating probation officer and delivered to him prior to the appearance of the convicted offender for sentencing. Oftentimes, data is supplied by the prosecutor or the defense counsel, or incorporated in their arguments related to the sentencing. He may also gain data, in some jurisdictions, from the innovative practice of 60– to 90–day commitments to a corrections agency for diagnosis and report. The parole officials base their decision on reports of the behavior and progress of the offender while in prison. These officials have not only the data available to the sentencing judge, but also have access to their own compiled postsentence data, which includes psychological test reports, unavailable to any judge at the time of sentencing.

Judicial thought in the United States is that probation and the indeterminate sentence offer new and stimulating flexibility in sentencing convicted offenders. Of course, sentencing judges are still bound to the guidelines of sanction law with its penalties graded according to the lawmakers view of the seriousness of the offense. However, in their role as penologists America's judiciary has developed sentencing practices which emphasize rehabilitation as an objective of sentencing, and the use of comprehensive personal data about the offender as a criteria for sentencing.

America's judiciary has not forgotten its obligation to the community in judgment–and–sentence decisions. The use of various alternatives to imprisonment indicates an awareness of the victim and the degree of violence in the offense. When the elements of physical force or coercion and the intent to injure or actual wounding are lacking, the severity of a sentence diminishes. A rank order usually is murder, felonious (aggravated) assault, armed robbery, narcotics violations, rape, fraud, burglary, larceny or theft, and auto theft.[11] The severity of a sentence reflects not only the judicial response to the offender as a potential threat to community safety but an evaluation of the offender as a habitual or professional criminal who is not a suitable candidate for alternatives such as probation or even early release by the parole board.

In some instances, the statutory factors force the imposition of a severe sentence. For instance, courts must impose: (1) increasingly severe prison terms on recidivists; (2) a fixed minimum term of imprisonment on certain offenders to postpone any early eligibility for parole; and—in some jurisdictions—(3) consecutive sentences on

11. Edward Green, *Judicial Attitudes in Sentencing* (New York: St. Martin's Press, 1961), pp. 1–41.

offenders convicted of two or more offenses at one trial. Repeating offenders, and those who use weapons in crime, enter homes at night, or sell addicting drugs are the usual targets of these mandatory and severe sentencing laws.[12]

Since the felony category of crime embraces a wide range of crimes against persons and property, many model and revised criminal codes have subdivided felonies by degree, from the most serious to the less serious. A proposed revision of the penal code in California recommended five categories of relative seriousness as sufficing for legislative penalty provisions: felonies of the first, second, third, fourth, and fifth degrees.[13] The sentencing guidelines were to be:

Conviction of	Minimum Sentence	Maximum Sentence
1. Felony—first degree	7 years	Life or death
2. Felony—second degree	2 years	25 years
3. Felony—third degree	18 months	15 years
4. Felony—fourth degree	1 year	7 years
5. Felony—fifth degree	6 months	3 years

Since California pioneered in the use of the indeterminate sentence, it is not surprising that in a revision of its penal code the state would retain this concept of twentieth–century corrections. However, the broadening of the range of the maximum term of imprisonment does modify the indeterminate sentence concept to allow participation by the sentencing judge. Sentences for the lesser range of years protects offenders from adverse decisions by parole boards which would continue them in prison to the limits of a maximum sentence, or close to such limits. This is in line with the belief that long imprisonment has no greater deterrent effect than short terms in prison. In the higher degrees rehabilitation is projected as a slow process, and a lengthy sentence also incapacitates a dreaded and dangerous person for the protection of the community.

A study of the real amount of time served by most offenders (90 percent) over a period of 17 years (1945–62) revealed a correction between the maximum time served in prison prior to first release on parole and the minimum and maximum range of the foregoing recommended sentences. The average time served in prison was found to be: 1. Murder, 8 years; 2. Rape (forcible) 6½ years; 3. Robbery first de-

12. The President's Commission on Law Enforcement and Administration of Justice, *Task Force Report: The Courts* (Washington, D.C.: U. S. Government Printing Office, 1967), pp. 14–18.

13. Joint Legislative Committee for the Revision of the Penal Code, *Penal Code Revision Project—Staff draft* (Project Office: 307 State Building, 217 West First Street, Los Angeles, California, 1971), pp. 18-20.

gree, 5½ years; 4. Robbery, second degree, 4 years; 5. Burglary, first degree, 5 years; 6. Burglary, second degree, 3 years.[14]

An interesting segment of this California report provided for an extended sentence of a case. Innovatively, the sentencing judge and the parole authorities had recourse to it by petition to the sentencing court whenever, during a felon's imprisonment, they believed an extension of the term of imprisonment was necessary.[15] The extended sentence was to be operative when a person was convicted of a second or third degree felony. The maximum term was to be set at 15 years, and the sentencing judge was to enter the reasons for his action on the record of the case. Criteria for a sentence to an extended term of imprisonment are:

(a) On petition of the Adult Parole Authority to the court in which a person was originally sentenced to imprisonment, the court shall extend his maximum term of imprisonment five additional years upon a finding beyond a reasonable doubt that there is a serious risk that, if released, he would at some future time kill or inflict serious bodily injury upon any person.

(b) The petition must be filed at least six months before expiration of the person's maximum term of imprisonment and the trial must be commenced within sixty days after the filing of the petition unless good cause for a continuance is shown.

(c) The person shall be entitled to a trial by jury, unless a jury is waived, and to all other rights to which a person on trial for a felony is entitled, except bail.

(d) If the court extends the person's maximum term of imprisonment, the court retains jurisdiction to grant petitions for additional extensions of the person's maximum term.

The extended term on the petition of the parole authorities (in California, the Adult Authority) was based on administrative necessity, and the petition to the court became part of the case record along with the court's response to it.

This is a modification of the objective of rehabilitation and a return to the sentencing goal of incapacitation. The idea, however, is that this offender has made little or no improvement toward rehabilitation goals, and has demonstrated such dangerousness that public protec-

14. Joint Legislative Committee for the Revision of the Penal Code, *Penal Code Revision Project—Tentative Draft No. 2* (Berkeley, Calif.: Revision of the Penal Code Project Office, School of Law, University of California, 1968), p. 19.

15. Joint Legislative Committee for the Revision of the Penal Code, *Penal Code Revision Project—Staff Draft*, pp. 27-28.

tion is not adequately assured by sentencing him to the term previously set for his felony. The parole releasing authorities are given the opportunity to hold him for a longer term than would otherwise be possible while they continue to seek a rehabilitation objective.

The rationale of any indeterminate sentence is that the period of controlled observation and supervision in the institutional setting affords an excellent opportunity to assess those attitudes and behavior of an individual that are relevant to the sentencing decision. While the sentencing judge has some data available to him at the moment of sentencing, the indeterminate sentence provides a secondary sentencing authority, the parole board, with up-to-the-minute data just before a decision is to be made on the prisoner's suitability for release on parole. This contemporary data includes all the clues about future behavior revealed by life in the prison community.

The sentencing alternatives range from fine and probation to imprisonment under an indeterminate sentence in which the actual release of offenders is based on more current and comprehensive data than available to the judiciary when sentencing. It is then apparent that rehabilitation is the major objective; incapacitation for public safety is operative only when warranted; deterrence is subordinated; and any thought of vengeance–punishment is discarded entirely.

Data Base

To achieve both specific and overall objectives, an organization requires facts, and a data storage and retrieval system which will link these facts together so that the interrelationships of data can be readily apparent when decisions must be made in the corrections process. A proper data base should provide sufficient information about a person to indicate whether probation is more desirable than prison; when a stay in prison can be cut short for release on parole; or the dimensions of a specific program of probation or parole supervision determined by the care and treatment program in prison. In short, the data base should serve as a guide to the solution most likely to effectively rehabilitate a specific offender.

The most adequate data base is a records system in the correctional process which will connect up all the available information on a first offender from police and court sources, and serve as a continuous inventory of the convicted offender from the time he is first placed under the control of a correctional agency. The basic background study of all offenders is the presentence report, and this is followed up with a classification report when the offender is sentenced to prison. In either case, the progress reports of correctional personnel while an offender is on probation, in prison, or on parole complete the data bank on each individual. When an offender is returned to a correctional agency upon conviction for a subsequent crime committed after his release from probation or prison, the data base continues to function in its continuous inventory of a specific person.

Case or Career Management

The continuous inventory concept of record keeping is aligned with case or career management, a new concept in corrections. Case management brings the full range of correctional care and treatment programs to each offender early in a criminal career. It is a means of developing a therapeutic program for each offender which will be oriented to solving specific individual problems as soon as possible. In addition, cases may be managed in groups when there is some relationship between criminal careers: correlated cases of crime partners such as wives, girl friends, or other family members; cases originating in a specific neighborhood; or cases involving other members identified with one or more subjects in the group (youth gangs; semicriminal groups such as the Hell's Angels, and the professional associations of organized crime).[16]

Case management based on factual data and innovative correctional practice holds great promise for achieving the objectives of rehabilitation as soon as possible in the career of an offender. In a report by the President's Commission on Law Enforcement and Administration of Justice, it was demonstrated that funds expended to nip a budding criminal career shortly after its known formal inception (first arrest and conviction) would be less costly to the community than allowing such careers to go unchecked until the repeating offender has returned to the criminal justice system time after time.[17]

Data Elements

The data base continuous inventory records system is made up of elements providing factual information about the offender, his current offense, his prior crimes, and data likely to be significant in his rehabilitation.

16. Institute for Defense Analyses, *Task Force Report: Science and Technology,* for the President's Commission on Law Enforcement and Administration of Justice (Washington, D. C.: U.S. Government Printing Office, 1967), pp. 64–65.
17. Ibid., pp. 65–66.

Personal Information—data to identify the offender to the administrations of the courts and correctional agencies, and to provide police and prosecutor with a prior arrest history in case of rearrest. It consists of pertinent information on the offender's:

1. Age and place of birth
2. Physical characteristics (including data on spouse, if any)
3. Occupation
4. Race (color)
5. Permanent home address
6. Residence (present)
7. Marital status
8. Children (sex, age, custody)
9. Parents (name, address, alive, deceased).

Current Offense Data—all known information as to the crime and its circumstances is placed in this portion of an offender's record. For instance, data about the following would aid in understanding the crime as an event:

1. Time and place of occurrence
2. Legal description of crime (common name, essential elements, grade of crime, and penalties)
3. Nature of offense and criminal agency used (directed against property or people; violence, unnecessary violence; entry into residence at night; weapon used)
4. Victim and crime situation (relationship between victim and offender; provocation or stress situation)
5. Progress of case (plea, plea negotiation, change of plea, insanity defense, trial, verdict).

Prior Criminal History—information on prior offenses, including data on crime partners should comprise this data element. It should be arranged to indicate that a thorough search of available sources of information has been made (FBI, state, local). Pertinent facts are usually:

1. Date and place of most recent felony arrest
   a. Name in which arrest was recorded; description of arrestee
   b. I.D. number given at time
   c. FBI number

    d. Charge (crime and final disposition)

    e. Circumstances of case

    f. Crime partner

    g. Connect–ups with other crimes

  2. Data on other prior arrests in chronological order.

Basic Rehabilitation Data—block of information containing data useful to understand the specific individual problems of an offender, and to evaluate him as a person. This data element should include the following:

1. Family background (parental deprivation or rejection of offender as child; social–economic level)

2. Neighborhood (stable or transient, low rent, minority group, high crime area)

3. Education (grades, level attained, attitude toward school and teachers)

4. Employment history (job titles, average term of employment, salaries)

5. Religion (formal, informal; offender's attitude to preferred religion, if any)

6. Patterns of personal relationships (school, job, neighborhood, family)

7. Patterns of relationship to authority figures (police, courts; job supervisor)

8. Patterns of aggressiveness (disputes at school or with parents, wife, neighbors, fellow employees)

9. Leisure time activities (hobbies, school, travel)

10. Strengths and weaknesses (broad summary, including any evidence of drug abuse or mental illness).

Classification Work–up—data element containing information secured from an offender during a period of quarantine in a correctional institution. Usually termed a professional work–up by practitioners in corrections, it is primarily a report of tests and measurements and diagnostic interviews. This area of information usually provides relevant data on:

1. Attainments, abilities, interests and attitudes (educational, mechanical, vocational and motivational)

2. Results of physchological examination

3. Personal and social inventory, bringing the evaluation up to date—a summary of the present situation against the known background data

4. Interpretation or overview of his problems

5. Recommendation for appropriate correctional program.

Progress Reports—compilation and analysis of raw data on the behavior and progress of the offender while under the care and control of a correctional agency. Among the useful items of information are:

1. Adjustment to supervision, violations of conditions of probation

2. Adjustment to imprisonment

3. Disciplinary record and interpretation

4. Participation in correctional programs (assigned and volunteer), and vocational planning

5. Attitudes toward current offense, correctional rehabilitation, and release in the community

6. Continuing family and personal relationships in "free world" and reality level of support for offender upon release (review of correspondence and visits)

7. Violations of conditions of parole

8. New crimes (in prison or while on probation or parole)

Probation

By definition, probation is a device providing an individual correctional program for an offender who is:

1. Unlikely to get in trouble again

2. Likely to rehabilitate himself without institutionalization (prison)

3. Willing to comply with the conditions of probation

4. Amenable to supervision

5. Appreciative of the sentencing judge's power to promptly recommit him if he fails to meet the conditions of probation.

Not all offenders are entitled to probation. It is a concept used mainly for first offenders or as a penalty for lesser offenses. Except in unusual cases, most state laws forbid probation for offenders convicted of serious felonies such as robbery, assault with a deadly weapon, armed forcible rape, or certain offenses such as selling drugs to juveniles.

Most misdemeanants are given a suspended sentence (or sentence is set and its execution suspended), and placed on an informal probation status without professional supervision. Any return to crime would result in the possibility that the suspended sentence would be activated immediately on arrest, or added to the sentence for the most recent crime.

Persons convicted of felonies, and some misdemeanants are placed on probation with supervision. The amount of supervision depends on the offender and his known problems. Progress reports prepared by a probation officer reveal whether he believes the offender is meeting the conditions of probation, adjusting adequately to the community, and not participating in any criminal behavior. Some conditions of probation set by the sentencing judge provide for imprisonment in the local jail (possibly over weekends), a fine, restitution, and—possibly— "keeping the peace." In any event, the role of the probation officer is to help the offender in his effort to meet the conditions of probation, and to supervise him while making sure he does so.

Criteria suggesting probation may relate to the crime, mitigating circumstances, the offender, and the existence of suitable resources in the community to assist in his rehabilitation. Criteria for probation includes:

1. The crime is a lesser offense, or resulted from misfortune rather than deliberate intent; the stress of provocation; overwhelming economic need; or did not cause or threaten serious injury to the victim.

2. The offender has been penalized by the humiliation of arrest and accusation; by a licensing agency (suspension; revocation); by substantial pretrial time in jail; by injury during the crime, pursuit or arrest; and by financial expenditures or losses (lawyer's fees, loss of salary).

3. The offender is willing to make restitution—when appropriate and warranted.

4. The offender is normally a good citizen, young, unsophisticated, with no past history of violence or disregard of the rights of others to their property; he is an offender with a criminal history of no more than minor and infrequent crimes, and no experience in jail, prison or youth corrections center (no previous failure while on probation); a person without bitterness because of past treatment by his family or agents of criminal justice; and an individual whose parents or spouse are law–abiding and willing or eager to help.

5. There is sufficient probation personnel available for the level of counseling and supervision to adequately control the

offender, and there are sufficient educational, vocational training, guidance, and job placement facilities available locally to develop a program for the offender's rehabilitation.

Of course, in the final analysis, the probation officer's recommendation for probation in his presentence report, and the sentencing judge's final decision as to probation, is going to rest on an evaluation of the offender's intelligence and attitudes. An offender will be recommended for probation, and released on this alternative to imprisonment, when he appears to understand all of the implications of his crime, indicates a sincere willingness to be law–abiding, and genuinely accepts the controls of the conditions of probation.

When probation is recommended (or is a possible sentencing alternative), probation officers often suggest conditions of probation. Such conditions would be aligned with the specific rehabilitation objectives and solutions for an offender. They are similar to the correctional program recommended by classification personnel when offenders are committed to prison. In this instance, however, the probation officer serves as the diagnostic technician to evaluate the problems of the offender and recommends a program of conditions helpful in the solution of the individual's problems.

When an offender is placed on probation it is usually for a term less than the maximum sentence set forth in the penalty for the crime for which he was committed. After a review of all the data in the case the supervisor of the probation agency determines the level of supervision required, notes any special conditions of probation in the sentencing judge's probation order, and assigns a probation officer to the offender. Supervision on probation is a combination of these relationships: (1) supervisor—supervised; (2) teacher—student; and (3) friend. Hopefully, the ideal situation will not deteriorate to either an overly supportive or grossly authoritative relationship.

Imprisonment

Execution and physical punishment (as a means of controlling criminal behavior) were replaced by imprisonment because it was sufficiently punitive to be accepted as a deterrent to such behavior, and because it protected the community by providing a closed, custodial place for convicted offenders. In the beginning, prisons were funded from the public treasury and thought of as places of incarceration, nothing more.

It was many years until even conditional acceptance of the concept that mere restraint did not reform or rehabilitate offenders. In 1878 the first city in the United States, Boston, allowed probation as an alternative to imprisonment in the sentencing of offenders. It was 1891 when the state of Massachusetts followed suit, and 1925 when the federal government enacted its law allowing probation for selected federal violators. Today, legislators and the general public only conditionally accept early release on parole as a successful alternative to long prison sentences. This acceptance is partly conditioned by the discovery in post–World War II years that early release of prisoners on parole is more economical than long imprisonment. Slow and grudging as it was, there is now firm recognition that prisons are places to keep people out of, or to release them from, as soon as possible.

The county jail is not a model of a prison. It is a way station for minor offenders serving short sentences. City jails are little more than drunk tanks in most areas. However, both city and county jails do house accused persons awaiting court action. At these local levels, jails are places in which little care, close custody, and no more is given to persons awaiting arraignment and trial or serving short sentences for minor violations or misdemeanors. Imprisonment in these institutions does not consider the goals of rehabilitation except for the impact of the time served. Very few of the thousands of local jails have any program of classification, education, vocational training, group counseling, or treatment.

It is at state levels, in a single prison or in a system of prisons, that these factors of classification, education, vocational training, group counseling, and treatment identify the new concept of imprisonment as providing a place and time for the care, custody, and treatment of offenders. Of course, the state prisons are closed and guarded; security –minded officials conduct roll calls and inspections; and there are lockups, off-limit areas, and a system of "ducats" to control prison traffic. Stealing, violence, coerced and volunteered homosexuality, and tyranny occurs in a closed society when the prison staff controls the lives of the inmates, or when violent and aggressive inmates assume control over their cell partners and fellow inmates. To overcome these handicaps, state prisons now provide facilities with various levels of security, and there are prison systems which house inmates in cottage colonies, forestry camps, and honor farms. There are institutions without guard towers, firearms, constant surveillance by roll calls, inspections, the restriction of lockups, or a ducat system to restrict the mobility of inmates. These are prisons in which the treatment programs for offenders join in making imprisonment less of a jungle experience in which survival justifies in–prison criminal behavior.

Classifying incoming inmates becomes a base for determining the needs of new or returning prisoners and matches them with the various in–prison programs available. Incoming prisoners are segregated for the period of time needed for a staff of professional counselors, psychologists, and psychiatrists to examine them, and to discuss and recommend various in–prison programs for their rehabilitation. Programs in education, vocational training, and group counseling are all part of the rehabilitation effort now sited in prisons. However, any effective treatment of inmates must join these programs of intellectual, occupational, and emotional self–improvement with an individual program for each inmate consisting of explicit tactics or procedures undertaken to change those conditions believed responsible for the inmate's criminal behavior. Treatment for any inmate implies a rationale that the criminal behavior of the individual is identified with particular causative factors, and the treatment program is designed to alter as many of these causative factors as possible.[18]

In the swing away from pure custody to custody and treatment, there has been greater employment of professional personnel capable of serving as correctional counselors or in–prison caseworkers. There are training programs which equip custodial staff personnel to help in innovative programs that are aligned with treatment objectives and the preparation of inmates for release on parole. This is a fortunate rearrangement of services available to inmates because it makes the prison a place to assess the prerelease needs of inmates. A new means is added to ongoing treatment programs that help inmates to get out of prison and to stay out of it.

There are also indications that modern correctional administrators accept the notion that collaboration between inmates and staff personnel can lead to better administration of a prison and to improved opportunities for achieving the goals of rehabilitation. When this new relationship is achieved, it may be a real breakthrough to the reintegration of offenders into the free community upon their release from prison. When rehabilitation becomes the joint responsibility of a prison's staff and its inmates, there is great hope that imprisonment will *not* continue as a means of building up a greater and greater number of repeating criminals.

Parole

Parole is the release of a prisoner before a sentence of imprisonment has been completed, on condition that the parolee agrees to obey specific rules of conduct and assists in developing a postrelease plan of employment and adjustment to the community. The purpose of parole has been stated as the protection of the public by: (1) releasing a prisoner when he has the best opportunity of achieving a noncriminal life, and (2) allowing for the return of the parolee to prison whenever he breaks the specified rules of conduct or commits a new crime. In addition, as further protection for the public prevailing correctional practices require: (1) use of the indeterminate sentence, to make certain all felons are not released without parole supervision; (2) supervision of parolees to include assistance, counseling, and some surveil-

18. Don C. Gibbons, *Changing the Lawbreaker* (Englewood Cliffs, N. J.: Prentice–Hall, 1965), p. 130.

ance; and (3) a policy that parolees are returned to prison after non-criminal conduct which threatens the parolee's chances of successfully completing his parole.[19]

The purposes of parole also include its role in the rehabilitation of the offender. While this is implied from the protection–of–society theme, it should be a stated purpose. One of the purposes of parole then, is to provide a sound correctional program after release, because all offenders (unless sentenced to death) do return to the open community. Imprisonment alone not only fails to reform but also operates to increase the risk of criminal acts following release.

Still another purpose of parole may be to save the state unnecessary expense. Since there is good evidence that primary reliance on closed, custodial institutions is self–defeating for any program of corrections keyed to the rehabilitation of offenders, there is now a further recognition of the fact that prison cost savings can be made by earlier parole releases. Emphasis on the public protection function of a prison assumes that many prisoners are dangerous persons. However, research findings do not support this assumption; rather they indicate only a small percentage of prison inmates can be considered dangerous. Therefore, incarceration (especially lengthy incarceration) for many offenders is a misuse of public funds.[20]

A rational parole system supportive of the tripartite aims of public protection, rehabilitation of the offender, and effective use of public funds, must be based on a determination of the optimum minimum time any prisoner should serve before release on parole. The controlling element in this determination cannot be public safety, although the public mood often affects parole board decisions. The only way to guarantee no danger to a community would be no release at all, and this is costly and inhuman. Nor can this determination be affected by the costs of institutional care and custody, although institutional population pressures have long been rumored to be a major factor in parole releases. The controlling factor in determining parole release should be the offender's potential for "making it" on parole and in future life. Parole should serve the offender, and by effectively doing so, also serve the community.

Criteria for release on parole swings between eligibility and ineligibility factors. The concept of a data base for each offender in corrections will provide basic data about an offender, his progress while in prison, and some idea of his readiness to return to the community. However, it must be supplemented by a prerelease program, an analysis by a correctional counselor or an institutional caseworker, and a

19. Daniel Glasner, *The Effectiveness of a Prison and Parole System* (Indianapolis: Bobbs–Merrill Co., 1964), pp. 28–29.
20. California Assembly Committee on Criminal Procedure, *Deterrent Effects of Criminal Sanctions* (Sacramento, Calif.: California Assembly, 1968), pp. 38–39.

parole board hearing that examines all the collected facts and interviews the offender. The decisional process in parole release is partly intuitive and partly a logical projection from known facts, just as the decision as to sentencing alternatives. However, the parole release decision makers are in possession of a better data base: the offender's continuous inventory which provides the parole officials not only with police and court data, but also with data about the offender while in prison. Additionally, they can interview the institutional counselor or caseworker and the offender, and seek their help in correlating known data to project future behavior patterns of the offender.

Criteria useful in making parole release decisions are:

1. The nature of the offender's response to correctional programs.

2. The offender's adjustment to life in the prison community.

3. The extent and kind of the offender's educational levels, and vocational preparation.

4. The kind of personal stability and responsibility exhibited by the offender.

5. The extent or degree of the offender's commitment to the criminal subculture and its values.

6. The offender's personal psychological characteristics, and how he perceives the world and his relationship to it.[21]

When a parole release date is not set and the inmate is held in the institution, the reasons for the parole board's decision should become a work–up recommending particular programs for the rejected inmate to give him enough points on the local parole readiness index to improve his chances of release. At the least, they should attempt to remedy the deficiencies militating against his release.

If a parole release program is to acquire the necessary integrity among its inmate clients, the parole officials must be selected on the basis of professional competence and must be allowed to function with no more administrative control than an evaluation of the merits of the program: its achievements against the program goals and costs. This will allow these decision makers to develop an understanding of the interaction between the inmate and his confinement. It will allow them to collect factual data on the effects of prison programs of self–improvement and preparation for release, noting failure or successes in paroles.

21. President's Commission on Law Enforcement and Administration of Justice, *The Challenge of Crime in a Free Society* (Washington, D.C.: U.S. Government Printing Office, 1967), pp. 179–80.

Individualization of Corrections and Rehabilitation

Nothing less than an individual approach to the problems of each offender on probation, in prison, or while released on parole, can possibly eradicate the causative factors and maladjustments responsible for the individual's criminal behavior patterns and lead to his rehabilitation and re-entry into the community. To have any hope of achieving broad objectives, each person convicted of a crime and passed on to a correctional agency must be considered a specific problem. For instance, John Doe is sentenced to three years on probation. The specific problem is rehabilitating John Doe. Doe must live and work in the community without committing a criminal act while on probation, and remain "clean" after being released from the conditions of probation. In turn, solving the specific problem of rehabilitating John Doe contributes to the overall goal of corrections: rehabilitation.

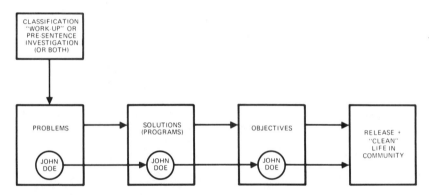

The corrections–rehabilitation function in criminal justice. The general problems, solutions (programs) and objectives are aligned with the individual offender (John Doe) through diagnosis at a time prior to sentencing or when admitted to the prison system. Individualization of treatment and care programs attempts to solve the problems of the individual offender and achieve the common objective of rehabilitation.

While imprisonment is only a prelude to parole release, both probation and parole are terminal programs in corrections. Probation is an after–care program in the postconviction period, and parole is an after–care program in the postprison period. Supervision of offenders in these terminal programs is not custodial. Probation and parole supervisors are not expected to control offenders assigned to their supervision, but they are expected to guide and assist them. Caseloads, except for some jurisdictions, are low enough to allow the contacts necessary for effective guidance and assistance.

This guidance and assistance in the after–care period is a means of educating the probationary offender or the parolee to develop resources within himself, so that when released from supervision he can adjust without support to life in the community.

To achieve overall objectives, the corrections function in criminal justice in America is concerned more with cure than punishment, more with care and treatment than custody, and more with postrelease success in the community than mere incapacitation.

Selected References

Books

Conrad, Joseph P., *Crime and Its Correction—An International Survey of Attitudes and Practices.* Berkeley and Los Angeles: University of California Press, 1967, pp. 11–14.

Gibbons, Don C. *Changing the Lawbreaker.* Englewood Cliffs, N.J.: Prentice-Hall, 1965.

Glasner, Daniel. *The Effectiveness of a Prison and Parole System.* Indianapolis, Ind: Bobbs–Merrill Co., 1964.

Institute for Defense Analyses. *Task Force Report: Science and Technology,* for the President's Commission on Law Enforcement and Administration of Justice. Washington, D.C.: U.S. Government Printing Office, 1967.

President's Commission on Law Enforcement and Administration of Justice. *The Challenge of Crime in a Free Society.* Washington, D.C.: U.S. Government Printing Office, 1967.

Moberly, Sir Walter. *The Ethics of Punishment.* Hamden, Conn.: Archon Books, 1968.

Nagel, Stuart S. *The Legal Process from a Behavioral Perspective.* Homewood, Ill.: Dorsey Press, 1969.

Periodicals

Schwartz, Louis B. "The American Penal System: Spirit and Technique." *Annals—Crime and the American Penal System* 339 (January 1962): 1–10.

PRISONER'S CRIMINAL RECORD
D D 24 (Rev 6-59)

POLICE DEPARTMENT
CITY OF NEW YORK

BUREAU OF
CRIMINAL IDENTIFICATION

NAME Arthur Flegenheimer-deceased   B # 50149

    Arthur Schultz

ALIAS Charles Harmon, Arthur Funsler, George Schultz,   E #_____
    (Aka "Dutch Schultz")

This certifies that the finger impressions of the above named person have been   D.C.I. #_____
compared and the following is a true copy of the records of this bureau.

     F.B.I. #_____

Date of Arrest	NAME	Borough or City	CHARGE	Arresting Officer	Date, Disposition, Judge and Court
11-22-19	Arthur Flegenheimer	NYC	Unl Entry	Knowles, 42 Pct.	12-16-19, Penty, Jdg. Mulqueen, Genl SessCt
X6-14-21	Charles Harmon	NYC	Gr. Larc.	Krause, 40 Pct.	8-30-21, Discharged, Jdg. Mulqueen, GenlSess
X2-24-24	Arthur Flegenheimer	Bronx	Fel Asslt	Schneider, Tr. "C"	2-25-24, Discharged, Jdg. Douras, 6th Ct.
X3-9-26	Arthur Funsler	NYC	Dis Con	Moore	2-17-26, Discharged, Jdg. Flood, 7th Ct.
X2-9-28	George Schultz	Bronx	Homicide	McGinty 14 Sq.	2-16-28, Discharged, Jdg. Corrigan, Hom.CT.
12-23-28	George Schultz	Bronx	Dis Con	Mara, 19Pct.	12-24-28, SentSusp, Jdg Glatzmeyer, 6 Ct.
X8-7-29	George Schultz	Bronx	Asslt & Robbery	Mara,42 Sq	8-8-29, Discharged, Jdg. Delargi, 6 Ct.
X10-4-29	George Schultz	Bronx	Robbery	Theis, 42Sq	10-6-29, Discharged, Jdg. McKinniry, 6 Ct.
5-20-30	George Schultz	NYC	FelAsslt	Salter, 28 Sq.	5-21-30, Discharged, Jdg. McKinniry, 5 Ct.
6-18-31	Arthur Flegenheimer	NYC	1897 PL & Fel.Asslt.	Salke, MOD	7-2-31, Acquitted, Jdg. Corrigan, Genl Sess Ct.
7-1-31	Arthur Schultz	NYC	Gun	Quinn, 5Sq	7-7-31, Discharged, Jdg. Weil, 1st Ct.
X11-28-34	Arthur Flegenheimer	Utica,NY	Vio Income Tax Law		8-1-35, Acquitted, Jdg. Bryant, US Ct. Malone, NY
9-25-35	Arthur Flegenheimer	Perth Amboy,NJ	Suspicion	Murray	TOT Fed. Auth.
9-26-35	Arthur Flegenheimer	Perth Amboy, NJ	Conspiracy		Case was pending when killed.
10-24-35	Was shot by unidentified assailants in tavern at 12 East Park St., Newark, N.J. at 10:30 P.M. 10-23-35 (Died 10-24-35) with Otto Berman, E3998, Leo Franks, alias Abe Franks, alias Abr. Landau, B43447, and Bernard Rosenkrantz, E9840. All removed to City Hospital where they died.				

Chapter XV

The Offender—Case Studies

The four case studies in this chapter offer a review of the content of many of the foregoing chapters. In addition, they develop the problem of drug abuse in relation to criminal behavior—not from the viewpoint of providing clues to the causes of drug abuse or other facts about it, but rather to develop it as a not uncommon problem of many offenders. Case study no. 1 concerns a juvenile from a substantial family setting; case study no. 2 is about a poor and disadvantaged youth who murders a man after several years of adult criminal behavior; and case studies no. 3 and no. 4 tell of a single offender on his first entry into state prison, and his reentry after violating parole.

These case studies are presented in dialogue form to preserve the verisimilitude of coauthors reviewing official records and making notes and comment. All the names of the offenders have been changed to avoid any future embarrassment, and some place names were changed to avoid identification of the offender. Otherwise, the case materials are untouched.

Case Study No. 1—Sharon Weldon

Weston: This is the story of the life situation and—now—the criminal history of a young lady: Sharon Weldon, a girl just 17 years old.

Wells: I think the best point to start is the present situation of this girl, the event that led to her arrest. Here are the facts from the police report (the date of the arrest was November 2):

Sharon Weldon was taken into custody along with her crime partner, young, 19-year-old Carl Beadle. The crime was the strongarm robbery of a drunk old man on a downtown street. Sharon served as lookout for Carl, and drove the car he intended to use for a getaway. Here are the policeman's words:

> After knocking down the victim, the suspect ran around the northeast corner of Main and 20th Streets, toward High Street. Three men (named below as witnesses) standing on this corner heard the victim scream when he was struck by the suspect and watched the suspect run toward them. They blocked the suspect's flight, threw him to the ground and held him until the RO (that's reporting officer) arrived in response to the radio call of 9:36 P.M.

Weston: Sometimes the very simplicity, or lack of planning, of a crime is a tipoff to police investigators that this is the work of someone on the drug scene, a person who is not on drugs and planning a crime has a sophisticated modus operandi. A person on the drug scene, trying to get money to buy drugs, or slightly stoned on drugs and wanting money for one reason or another has no more than one-tenth of a decent modus operandi. (That is taking modus operandi to mean skill in committing a crime and getting away from the scene without being arrested.)

Wells: This girl is classed as a crime partner, There is a page about it on the police report. I'll try to sum up: They have apprehended Carl and are thanking the three civilians who held him. After all, they are good citizens. This Carl might have had a knife or gun and injured them and they are getting their names. Then, the two policemen noticed a car down the street—on 20th, between Main and High—but down toward High Street, blinking its headlights on and off. The three good citizens said it wasn't their car, or their friends; the six of them walk down to the car (two other officers were helping the victim). It's a little blue Volkswagen and Sharon is sitting behind the wheel and blinking the lights. She looks up at the police, smiles, and speaks to Carl: "Where have you been?"

Weston: The police found drug and narcotic paraphernalia in the car, and the car was registered in Sharon's mother's name. That's what put her into this case as a crime partner. Another thing, Carl had a bad habit of keeping the wallets of his victims. When the police searched the trunk compartment of Sharon's Volkswagen, they found three more wallets, all with credit cards and identification, and all linked up with past strongarm on-the-street robberies of old men.

Wells: The police report is a fine example of trying to help youngsters. Listen to this at the end:

> Suspects possibly under the influence of some drug. There was no smell

of alcohol on either suspect and they were very slow to answer questions of the reporting officer. Suspects also indicated some drug use by lack of response to light test: unresponsive pupils of eyes.

Weston: That's good reporting, sometimes the youngsters think police are "zinging" them when something like this goes into a police report, but these facts help everyone trying to help any of these youngsters after an arrest.

Wells: Legally, in some crimes requiring a specific intent, it could be used as a defense; as a claim of diminished responsibility; of being unable to form the necessary intent.

Weston: The offense is assault and robbery, legally it is called grand theft, stealing from the person, and it is a major crime. She is a principal. The second charge is a lesser one: possession of needles, hypodermic syringes and the like.

Wells: The intake or initial probation officer's report highlights the fact that Sharon was 17 years old. They attach her statement as given to the probation officer. Let me read it:

> Minor admits to the allegations contained in the petition. She stated that on the night of the crime she went to the home of Carl Beadle, a 19–year–old juvenile, and upon arrival she suggested, "Let's go downtown." When they arrived downtown, she states "We needed some junk and had no money." Minor explains that the two of them parked and talked at the spot where police arrested her; she cannot remember who first mentioned stealing, that it just came up and neither she nor Carl were totally for the suggestion, but that Carl finally got out of the car and the incident occurred as indicated in the police report.

That pretty well amounts to a plea of guilty.

Weston: Sharon is a drug abuser. It's pretty long story, but here is the substance of it: Sharon admitted she first used heroin a year ago, and she quickly became a regular user. She said she "shot" one or two times a week; that is, when she had money. She first became exposed to drug abuse and began experimenting when she was 15 years of age—that is two years ago—using "Freds" and "grass" (dropping pills and smoking marihuana).

Wells: About Sharon's previous record. A year ago, and this date fits in with Sharon's own story of when she first began to shoot heroin, she was arrested with three other juveniles in a drive–in movie. There was a *disorderly juveniles* call to the sheriff's office, and when the deputies tried to calm down the two boys and two girls in the car, they noted the distinctive smell of marihuana. Briefly, Sharon and her friends were charged with being disorderly in public and possession of marihuana and dangerous drugs. Police found Seconal pills and marihuana in the car and one pill in the pocket of Sharon's slacks. The disposition at this time—for Sharon—by the juvenile court judge was to make her a ward of the court and put her on a program of six months court probation. She was released in the care and custody of her parents.

Weston: You look through this record and this young lady had everything going for her. Her father was a retired Air Force colonel now working for the state, a budget analyst; her mother was active in the PTA and Girl Scouts. But one of the first progress reports about Sharon by her new probation officer commented: "Minor has many conflicts with her parents over minor's *not accepting responsibility.*" The probation officer noted that her parents believed Sharon has not acted in any way to help herself, even though she verbalizes her need for help. He reports the parents state Sharon has been treated since she was 15 years old by a private physician specializing in emotional disorders, but they don't believe she cooperated with him, and she has not been helped by this treatment—that's for sure.

Wells: You mean Sharon's probation officer does not believe she is going to discontinue her use of drugs. In other words, after Sharon's first contact with the wheels of criminal or, better yet, juvenile justice, Sharon in her present situation hasn't been helped by all that was done, or attempted, since her first arrest a year ago.

Weston: Here's the data on Sharon's school attendance. Her record is very good. However, two things noted here may be of importance: (1) Sharon is just maintaining a C–average, and (2) she is enrolled in one of the local continuation schools. This indicates to me that Sharon has had trouble at school. It means she was transferred from her regular school to a continuation school and even there she has difficulty. The absence of truancy may only be an indication of a desire to get away from home, rather than any motivation to attend school and learn.

Wells: There is a clinical report attached to the juvenile court petition, and the words "personality disorder" are repeated time and time again, sometimes in connection with "infantile personality" or "sociopathic features." I won't put definitions on these words, they are hard to pin down, but it appears that Sharon had a year of in–hospital medical care and was released with the diagnosis of improved. Again, the terminology, the meaning of the words in these clinical reports are very difficult to pin down. It doesn't really inform us about either the girl or her problems.

Weston: The juvenile as a person and as a problem is covered in the "Analysis and Plan" section of the probation officer's recommendation to the juvenile court. I'll read it:

Minor's previous functioning suggest an impetuous juvenile who can possibly be described as a failure. She tends to act on sudden impulse without thinking. There is evidence of self-destruction tendencies (she reportedly attempted suicide at the age of 15 years), and now has resorted to the use of drugs—hard narcotics. There are suggestions that minor sees herself as a cold and unloving person.

Commitment to an institutional situation is the only alternative for this minor. At this time, minor is a threat to herself and the health and safety of others.

Wells: In this plan for Sharon, there is a complete rejection of the concept that treatment by a private agency would help her. An earlier report stated, "There is a possibility that private medical care would be successful." However, a probation officer interviewed Sharon's doctor, and he strongly suggested the need of "locked ward" treatment for this young lady. That means a state hospital.

Weston: As part of the program to rehabilitate Sharon, the probation officer making the analysis and plan recommended a program to the juvenile court. This recommendation is for release into the care and custody of minor's parents *provided* the minor is voluntarily committed to a state institution with facilities for appropriate care of the minor; that further action be suspended for six months while the minor is continued on probation supervision; and that final disposition of the charges be made at the end of this period.

Wells: That about sums up the case. Sharon liked the idea of the locked ward concept. She now believes this is what she needs. Both parents are fine people, and they agreed to the voluntary commitment. Sharon was held in juvenile hall until the parents and the probation office could arrange the commitment. Her final disposition comes up in about May or June.

Weston: I'd like to review this case study, so that the facts are in some order:

1. The crime charged against 17–year–old Sharon Weldon was grand theft (person) and possession of narcotics equipment.
2. The minor's present situation is that she is a crime partner in a major felony. She was reported to be under the influence of drugs at the time of the crime, and she admits to an extensive use of a variety of drugs for at least 12 months.
3. Sharon's previous record only reveals one arrest prior to her present one, but she could have been arrested once or twice a week according to her statements—if the police had caught up with her.
4. Her drug-scene way of life complicated her adjustment under probation supervision after the court made her a ward in disposing of the first arrest situation.
5. Her school record shows she was a C–average student in a continuation school.
6. The doctor's report on Sharon did sum up a personality disorder—

for whatever meaning you get out of these words.

7.   The probation officer's petition to the juvenile court stated a good analysis and a good program for the young lady, and a locked ward type of institutional setting as the only alternative.

Wells: Sharon was termed a threat to herself, but the facts of this case study indicate that a young girl and her parents have a problem. They have, and admit to, a responsibility for their child. Then, her crime partner has a problem. We don't know in these juvenile cases just who leads and who follows. In any event, the juvenile court's disposition is responsive to the facts of the case insofar as this girl is concerned. Let's hope that Carl Beadle receives an equally just treatment.

Weston: It is difficult to finish a case study such as this without some wise word as to the event or events in Sharons's childhood that caused her behavior, as we have just reported it. But it is not in these records —unless there are some clues to her behavior in the data about her family, the school record, or her own self–image.

Wells: That's true, we lack data. However, in the disposition of this case there is an inherent provision to work up these factors as part of the diagnosis of Sharon and her problem when she is first admitted to the state hospital. That is the hope and the aim of this disposition. Then, there's the provision for a review in six months. At that review, there will not only be more data on this girl, but the girl herself will be back in court along with her parents, and the juvenile court judge can take it from there.

Case Study No. 2—The Gene Wilson Story

Weston: This case study concerns a young man named Eugene Wilson. Gene is 27 years old. He was born in Texas. He was about four years old when his mother died. Gene says she was "cut to death" in a pocketknife brawl.

Gene Wilson's father left Texas after the death of his wife. He moved himself and Gene to the central valley of California, settling in Fresno, a fair–sized town between Sacramento and Los Angeles. Soon, Gene's father had a common–law wife, and Gene a stepmother. Unfortunately, Gene's father was sent to prison. He had been in the business of selling women, narcotics, and stolen property.

Gene has two stepsisters or half sisters (it isn't clear whether they are children of a previous marriage or the outcome of the common–law marriage), but one thing is certain: the family never had any money. Gene says they were on welfare most of the time, and to get "regular eating" he had to go next door, with his grandparents, most of the time.

Wells: Gene Wilson's criminal history and its beginnings tie in with his schooling. Gene's first arrest was for assaulting his school teacher. Gene was 17—going on 18—years of age and struggling along in school at about the eighth grade level. (Gene is what is termed a dull normal.) His next arrest was also for assault. It was processed in the juvenile court. He was just about 18. Gene's third arrest was more serious. He and several crime partners were arrested for armed robbery. Gene was convicted and the presentence investigation revealed he had committed a series of robberies with an assortment of five crime partners, and in all of these holdups a sawed–off rifle was used as the weapon and each crime had some unnecessary violence in it. He was sentenced to 5–15 years in state prison.

Weston: Gene was paroled to his grandparents about 3 years later and he worked as a car washer. In a few months he was again arrested for armed robbery with a knife. He was sentenced to the local jail because the charge had been reduced to petty theft and he was released at the end of a 90–day sentence to return to state parole.

Wells: He filed a guilty plea. No doubt there were negotiations for a short term and a reduced plea. It could not have been much of a robbery. The parole authorities apparently did not evaluate it as a major problem or they would have returned him to state prison.

Weston: Gene was next arrested for armed robbery with a rifle (while on parole). It was only about six months after his release from county jail. He pled guilty and received a sentence of five years to life with a five–year minimum, and a two–year minimum on parole release.

Wells: Gene Wilson went through the classification work-up on reception at state prison. I'll be brief. The diagnostic reports said Gene was aggressive, a dull normal, and a problem. Here's the story of Gene's conduct in prison:

1. He spent a good portion of his time in the adjustment center "for his own protection," requesting this isolation from the general population. The record states: "Wilson cannot avoid getting into trouble with other inmates."

2. He was transferred once to "rescue him from his gambling debts."

3. He was noted for a homosexual involvement with another inmate.

4. He attended group counseling on a voluntary basis: both the alcoholic and narcotic users' groups. He was noted as having little self–motivation, and is said to have just participated enough to satisfy the staff.

5. He spent ten days in the adjustment center for "stealing and dealing" (theft and selling stolen property).

6. He became a cook, and was transferred to a forestry work camp, where his good physical condition, and something not identified, made him an outstanding worker.

7. His camp transfer was rescinded because of thefts and a developing history of homosexual coercion, but the prison disciplinary committee found the evidence insufficient, and Gene was returned to camp. He did well for a short time, and walked away, escaped. . . .

Weston: This is not a sad, but a tragic story. Gene escaped from a conservation camp high in the hills above Yosemite Park. He worked his way down into the valley in the nighttime, no flashlight, no-moon hike. Here he met a child and her parents. They were camping in a remote area. He ate with them. He wanted wheels and he fought with the man and killed him for his car. Gene wanted to continue his flight, his escape. He was arrested the next day, and charged with first degree murder. He pled guilty to second degree murder. Here is Gene Wilson's statement to the probation officer who conducted the presentence investigation on his plea of guilty:

> A man was beaten to death in a fight by a mistake on my behalf. I was not aware of the man's death at that time. I am 27 years old and I have been in prison going on ten years now. And I need help, I have an uncontrollable temper and during one tantrum, I beat a man to death. I'm in heavy trouble already, I know this, and I know this could mean I might not ever walk the street again.

Wells: It was an ugly crime. Beating a man to death always is an ugly murder technique. They assigned defense counsel to Gene, and the decision was to negotiate.

Weston: Speaking for the community, I wonder. A father and husband is dead, beaten to death before the eyes of his wife and child. Yet, the killer was an inmate in a forestry work camp, a place without walls or fences, an honor camp. In fact, this is a preparole release setting. What went wrong?

Case Study No. 3—Thomas Marlow

Weston: This case study is concerned with Thomas Marlow, also known as (aka) Tommy Milo. When Thomas Marlow was received at the state corrections guidance and reception center he was 25 years of age. He had no recorded crime partner. He was a first termer at state levels, but he had previously served time in a county jail, two terms of

90 days, both for possession of narcotics. In between, in 1956, he had been fined for assault and battery and failing to pay five traffic citations. More recently, he served a 60–day jail term for another narcotics violation. At the time of this arrest he was still doing a year's probation on his last narcotic arrest. These arrests were all processed as misdemeanor cases. Tommy Marlow had no prior felony convictions at the time he was received in the state prison system.

Wells: Tommy was sentenced on two felonies. Six months to 10 years and five years to life—all to be served concurrently. His minimum term of imprisonment was five years, but he would be eligible for parole in 20 months. There was a weapon (a pistol) involved in Tommy's crimes, and this might negate any early parole because of the violence potential. Tommy Marlow committed a series of crimes. He was convicted of two of them. These are the facts of the crimes:

1. At 5:15 P.M., defendant entered the Crown Drug store with a gun and demanded money and narcotics from a clerk. The victim crouched behind the store's counters and successfully fled the store through a side door. Defendant pursued him a short distance, then fled on foot.

2. Four days later, at 11 P.M., defendant entered the Regal Pharmacy with a gun, demanded money and narcotics from the two clerks present in the store. Clerk No. 1 gave him money ($84) from the cash register, and narcotics (some morphine) from a safe. Clerk No. 2, unseen by defendant called police. The police arrived and talked defendant into dropping his gun and surrendering to them.

Weston: We pick up the data in this case study of Tommy Marlow after the professional staff of the state corrections agency has processed him during his reception into the state prison system. There's a great deal of data on Thomas Marlow:

1. The intelligence level of this inmate (he is no longer a defendant) is classed as average intelligence, with a penciled plus–sign; indicating the upper portion of the average intelligence grouping.

2. His educational level is at the twelfth–grade level.

3. Marlow had a natural father, unknown to him. His mother is a 47–year–old housewife; his stepfather a 48–year–old restaurant owner. His mother married (for the first time) about five years after Tom's birth in 1933.

4. Tom Marlow's brother and sister are, in reality, half brother and sister: a brother 17 years old, and a sister, 15 years old.

5. The residence of the Marlow family was originally New York City. They moved when Tommy was seven years old, to Las Vegas, and then lived there until Tommy was nine years old. From this time on, the family lived in the one city in California.

6. Tom has a prior juvenile record: he was picked up when he was 16,

as a delinquent boy—a runaway from home. He was released to his parents. He had not been reported missing by the parents, who explained this lapse of parental concern by saying that Tommy was a chronic runaway, but in the past had always come back home in a few days, or had gone to the home of a relative or friend—who would call the parents. Juvenile authorities kept Tommy for six days, reviewing his behavior, before the decision was made to release him in the care and custody of his parents.

7.   The history of Tommy's marriage offers some insight into the problems of this inmate. In 1953, at the age of 20, Tommy married his first wife, Geraldine. She was 18 years old at the time. Tommy was working in Ventura, and they drove to Las Vegas, to get married. Tommy had just finished a very unhappy period of military service. There was a whirlwind courtship, and they were married within 90 days of the time they met each other. This was a childless marriage. Geraldine was a Ventura girl, from a good family. Unfortunately, she picked up a flu bug that hospitalized her. In the hospital she died. The doctors told Tommy that the complication that had fatal results was a streptococcal infection that raced through her body.

8.   Thomas Marlow was a salesman, with a total employment of about three years in this occupation, from the time he was 18 years old. Tommy had 14 jobs in his seven years of employment. He was a warehouseman at an air force base for a short period. He also worked as a dry cleaner and as a laborer for a concrete mixing crew. Otherwise, it was some form of selling position. He was route salesman for a linen concern and a bread company; he sold home improvements for a short time; and he worked on several occasions as a used car salesman.

9.   Tommy was a Catholic. This was also the religion of his family.

10.   Tommy's financial condition was balanced: (1) he had no assets, and (2) he had no dependents.

11.   Tommy described himself as a moderate drinker, and it is true that the use of alcohol had no relation to his criminal behavior (his offense pattern). However, Tommy admitted to using marihuana from 1953 to 1956; and heroin from 1956 to 1958. He is addicted, and his rate of use at the time of arrest was four grams a day.

The social evaluation in these work–ups of inmates repeat some of the foregoing data, but this will help to firm up the facts in your mind: This is the report of a professional member of the prison staff:

Unlike the usually observed narcotics user who is passive in orientation, subject (as suggested by his offenses) is an aggressive individual. Hostility toward authority figures seems to be a displacement of feelings regarding his parents, from whom he has experienced real or fancied rejection.

There is a highly neurotic component to subject's behavior, apparently he has had a behavioral disorder for many years, characterized by: (1) running away at age 18, and (2) poor adjustment to the U.S. Army.

His acting–out behavior is related to his problems with authority figures:

((1) stepfather; (2) U.S. Army superiors) and feelings he has not been loved by parents.

Subject describes the series of crimes that resulted in his imprisonment as a "nightmare," and he has very little understanding of the reasons for his involvement in the offenses, apart from his need for narcotics or the money to buy them.

Subject is moderately depressed, partly as a result of his experiences, but depression is probably more directly related to underlying and behavioral problems.

However, subject indicates sufficient anxiety at his behavior to respond to specialized forms of treatment.

In a backup report, another professional member of the prison staff filed this social evaluation of Marlow:

Subject did not like to discuss antecedents, he found it painful. He has a good deal of suppression of certain events: (a) that stepfather was in home almost from time of subject's birth, and (b) siblings' competition for parental affection and attention.

Subject began expressing behavior problems during latency. This acting –out was apparently the result of then unresolved problems which continued to remain unresolved.

Subject's behavior problems were most unstable during adult adjustment, notably:
a. Employment (short terms, varied jobs).
b. Military history (subject was a disciplinary problem, returned once by police for being AWOL or over–leave).
c. Early marriage (search for attention).

Subject began using narcotics at age 20, principally marihuana; and introduced his wife to narcotic use prior to marriage. Most of subject's heroin use followed the untimely and unfortunate death of his wife.

Subject directs his anxiety—anxieties—to trememdous energy for work, but this outlet is not satisfactory or stabilizing. He gets bored with work after a short period of employment.

Present offenses were committed to obtain money or drugs during a period of addiction. Apart from narcotic addiction, there is a neurotic component to his behavior which finds expression in serious acting–out behavior.

Wells: This is a personality evaluation by a psychologist on the staff at the prison's reception center. This evaluation of the personality of an inmate begins by administering a battery of tests. It is usually termed a group battery and the specific tests in this group are a professional decision of staff personnel as to usefulness, validity and reliability.

Tommy was found to be average in his intellectual classification as the result of his responses to this group battery of tests. His functioning was reported as commensurate with an intellectual capacity in the upper portion of the average range classification.

The concluding segment of this report speaks for itself:

> This is an individual who, according to current psychological test results, displays symptoms related to the presence of neurotic feelings. The fact of strong dependency needs is completely below the level of conscious awareness, although subject expressed anxiety. At this time, subject seems incapable of expressing hostile or aggressive feelings toward the environment and these are directed inwardly, resulting in an intensification of his depressive mood.

> Subject's stepfather did little to establish meaningful relations with subject; and mother openly rejected subject. Subject's greatest difficulty at this time is that he cannot admit he wants to reject his mother and cannot admit he has any feeling but love for her.

> Originally, subject's feelings of being rejected took the form of running away from home (he was a chronic runaway). On at least one of these occasions, there was a prior dispute with his mother. The incident appears to be an acting–out against his mother.

> Prognosis is poor as long as subject remains in present condition. Subject needs psychiatric treatment for the deep–seated conflicts surrounding both his mother and his father surrogate (stepfather).

> Subject's future successful adjustment in society depends upon therapeutic gains which he may derive from specialized treatment during confinement.

Weston: Tommy was given the Kuder preference test. He was found to have an above–average interest in scientific and clerical pursuits; there was a clustering of interests around personal service and sales work (ties in with sales experience of subject). It was recommended that vocational training be deferred because of subject's disturbed feelings; defer until (1) more academic schooling, and (2) specialized group therapy treatment. Subject might qualify for training in science, provided he becomes: (1) less anxious, and (2) less demanding for work that demands gross physical activity. The other reports in Marlow's work–up do not indicate he will be a custody problem, but indicates that there may be some acting–out against authority figures.

Tommy wasn't a custody problem while serving this term of imprisonment, but he did not receive the program of recommended treatment. In fact, he was paroled despite not receiving this treatment.

Wells: Tommy was released, but after a few months, Tommy's parole officer ordered his return to prison pending final determination of the facts surrounding his failure to comply with regulations and failure to cooperate with parole supervision. He "violated" Tommy on these facts:

1. Parolee left residence without prior permission (believed moved to L.A. area).

2. Parolee failed to submit monthly reports (as required).

3. Parolee failed to attend regular Nalline test sessions.

Weston: Parole authorities, and the police could not locate Tommy— at least, not for three months. Then, Thomas Marlow also known as Tommy Milo, was arrested in the Los Angeles area. He had moved to L.A. with his girl friend, an ex–drug addict and present prostitute.

Case Study No. 4.—Tommy Marlow, Recidivist

Weston: Tommy was indicted, tried and convicted on four counts of armed robbery; two counts of assault with intent to commit robbery: and two prior felonies alleged in the indictment. Tommy pled guilty. These offenses explain the complex sentence.

Wells: The facts of Tommy's offenses are:

Defendant entered the Medical Arts Pharmacy and went to the drug clerk where he mumbled something about a prescription. The clerk asked for the prescription; the defendant reached into his pocket and pulled a pistol. He then went down–counter to the proprietor at the cash register, where he demanded money and narcotics. The proprietor gave defendant $150 in cash, and a bag of narcotics (such as Dilaudid, cocaine and Dolophine). At this time, defendant ordered the proprietor and clerk to lie on the floor and made his escape.

Five days later the defendant entered the Threeball Camera Exchange and pretended to shop until other customers left. When alone with the two clerks, defendant produced a pistol, demanded money and instructed one clerk, James Rae, to empty the cash register, He then marched both victims into the rear room, where he had them empty their pockets onto a chair. A female customer entered the store, defendant seized her and ordered her to the back room, where he told her to empty her purse. A clerk, Ralph Jones, grappled with defendant, hollered for the other clerk to grab his gun. A shot was fired, Jones was wounded, but he seized gun from defendant, and he fired a shot at the defendant, when defendant held a bottle and threatened Jones with it in an attempt to escape. Police were notified, arrived at the crime scene and the defendant was arrested. Jones, the wounded victim, was transported to the hospital. At the hospital, Jones was found to have a wound in the upper abdomen; and a .22 caliber bullet was removed.

The defendant's release on bail facilitated a new crime. On September 21, 1963, eleven days later, the defendant entered the Variety Drug Store. He went to the drug counter. When approached by the proprietor, the defendant produced a gun, said he was a drug addict and wanted narcotics and money, and instructed him to open the safe and give him whatever money there. A female customer entered, and defendant demanded and got the keys to her car. Defendant took $750 in cash from the drug store proprietor and he escaped in the 1962 Valiant of victim No. 2, after telling the proprietor and this woman to wait before calling police. Later on the same day, the defendant entered Howe's Drug store, produced a gun, ordered the female clerk to the back room, demanded and got money and narcotics: $30 from cash register, $3 from the clerk's purse, and approximately $250 worth of Dilaudid and morphine.

The probation officer who conducted the presentence investigation for the Los Angeles court filed a memorandum in addition to his recommendation for imprisonment (mandatory in the case of a defendant with two prior felonies and standing convicted on his own plea of guilty to four more felonies). This memorandum reads: "This defendant should spend a substantial amount of time in state prison."

Weston: This item does not appear on prison records: Tommy Marlow and his common–law wife, the ex–addict and working prostitute, were suspected of the attempted robbery of a supermarket in the same general area of East Los Angeles where Tommy robbed the two drug stores and the camera shop. In the investigation of this case, the police went to Tommy's apartment. They found a considerable amount of narcotics and "hardware" for injecting drugs. He was arrested, but the prosecutions attorney made the decision not to charge Tommy in this case because the police search was illegal. When police entered Tommy's apartment, they had no identification of Tommy as the man in the supermarket robbery attempt. They had just developed him as a suspect because of the modus operandi and his criminal activity in the area. The time of the supermarket attempt was on the same day as Tommy's third and fourth robberies.

Wells: A wise decision not to prosecute. There was more than enough evidence in the robbery cases to prosecute, and the guilty plea was entered, no doubt, because Tommy and his counsel were quite aware of this.

Weston: The version given by Tommy of his crimes, his explanation: "I committed all the offenses to obtain narcotics to support my drug habit. I would not have committed these offenses had it not been for my addiction."

Wells: That is a self–serving declaration. There is always a risk in accepting these statements, to know whether it is the truth or some attempt to rationalize serious misbehavior.

Weston: Tommy's classification work–up on his return to state prison was very similar to his first one. The data base records system in the prison only requires a few entries to bring it up to date as an inventory of Tommy Marlow.

Wells: This is interesting, his social evaluation was by the same psychologist that did Tom's social evaluation at the time of his first commitment. Here are his professional views on this second evaluation.

> Subject is a heroin–addicted recidivist returning after a crime spree similar to his prior commitment. He appears to have a sincere desire to utilize this new term to his best advantage.

> Subject did well on parole for the six months when first released, from July to about December, but admits to coping fear.*

> Subject did try to do something about it, he went to an out–patient clinic after discussions with his parole supervisor, but he did not like the OP therapist and stopped attending.

> Subject states he believes the trigger to his offenses was the denial by state authorities of his application for a dry–cleaner's license because of his prior history of a felony conviction and drug abuse. He states his parents would have bought him a dry–cleaning store and he could have made a decent living if he had been licensed to operate it.

> Subject rejected the hoped–for adequacy of his parole supervisor in fulfilling subject's dependency needs and he sought female companionship. He states this created friction with his parole officer, and he began to use drugs again. There was more friction with his parole officer when this supervisor suspected deception in passing Nalline tests. Finally, drug use got so heavy, he knew he could not pass tests, and he fled to L.A. with his girl friend.

Weston: Tommy did have skills in the dry–cleaning field, but he should have realized any licensing board is unlikely to be as understanding about a criminal record as the prison and parole personnel.

Wells: The psychological evaluation of Tommy was enriched by interviews with a psychiatrist on this second classification work–up. Tommy is described in this doctor's report as a bright normal person, and an individual he viewed as follows:

> Subject cannot express his aggressiveness in socially acceptable fashion and his inwardly directed hostility has now reached the point where he is markedly self–destructive. His situation is not at the point where suicide in prison is likely, as prison serves to satisfy this inmate's feelings of guilt, but if released without treatment, he is almost certain to kill himself or arrange for someone else to do it!

> Subject has considerable dependency needs, he is basically a passive and insecure person who needs moral support and assistance. He makes friends easily but at superficial levels of intimacy; underneath he is lonely and isolated and does not feel he is up to the standards of others. To compensate, subject has lied to his parents, parole officer, and girl friend,

*Unable to cope with his problems on parole.

and when this deception creates enough pressure he had to run away from the situation.

The previous evaluation of this subject* indicated a favorable parole adjustment, and—again—this examiner feels he will make a favorable parole in spite of his past serious offense. Subject's chance of success on parole is good if he receives intensive group therapy. He is motivated for treatment, and has the capacity and possible potential to make use of it. He is an ideal therapy candidate at this time.

To sum up: This subject is a recidivistic drug addict who displays a self–destruction pattern that becomes marked once he succumbs to the pressure he allows to build up and reverts to drug use.

Weston: I can condense Tom Marlow's years in prison by itemizing some claims Tommy made in his application to the parole board for release on parole. These items were listed as indicating rehabilitation while in prison:

First Year: A note from the Catholic chaplain saying Tommy was sincerely preparing for a normal life.

Second Year: A high school diploma and a certificate of completion of one year's carpentry school. A memorandum of a medical examination attesting to his good health and fitness for work in a forestry camp.

Third Year: A transcript from a junior college showing the completion of three units of credit for a course in American literature, with a grade of B. A letter from a research assistant saying that Tommy was one of the most hard–working members of a project studying the blood chemistry of convicted offenders. A certificate of completion of an introductory course in data processing. A transcript from a junior college showing the completion of three units of credit for a course in reading development with a grade of B.

Wells: On the other hand, the parole board had the prison disciplinary record, and this revealed that Tommy had been placed in the adjustment center for failing to cooperate in the investigation of an in–prison narcotics peddling ring. The record shows that an alert correctional officer noticed a strange smell coming from a small room in the carpentry shop. He had another officer seal off the room and returned with a third officer. The three of them found the door locked. It was opened after some delay, and Tommy and three other inmates were found in the room. At the prison disciplinary board hearing, all three officers said the room smelled "like marihuana had just been smoked" and a search of the room revealed a large quantity of contraband, but no grass.

*On first classification and reception at the state prison.

Weston: After reviewing the case, the recommendation of the parole board was to continue the case without setting a date for parole release.

Wells: It is a case with many problems. I don't see anything in these records that indicate any in–depth psychiatric care or even group counseling participation. That's strange.

Weston: Odd.

Wells: He kept busy in prison, and on a self–treatment program with the institution providing the opportunity for study, vocational training, and the other activities he engaged in, but it wasn't enough to keep him out of trouble in prison, and it was not treatment aimed at his problems.

Weston: It wasn't treatment; he was not helped in any significant way by these three years of care–and–custody.

Wells: That is the reason the parole review was negative.

. . .

When case studies of offenders are used in a college classroom, there is always a demand foɪ more facts about the offender. Unfortunately, additional data is not available. The data base system in most courts and corrections agencies operate with no more, and often less, data than presented in the foregoing cases. On such data, decisions must be made about the needs of an offender, the problem areas, and solutions for the offender's problem or problems which are amenable to treatment.

Case studies such as these indicate clearly that only some of the basic problems can be isolated and adequately treated. Broad corrections and rehabilitation programs which are accomplished on a sweeping impersonal level can only achieve limited success. Solutions for the problems of many offenders are peculiarly individual and vary, just as each person and his reaction to his environment and heredity is different from every other person. Economically, it is feasible to find no more than one or a few problem˙ It is much more costly to recognize that each individual offender has his own set of problems. Extensive diagnostic work is involved at first and then treatment is required for all the complex factors of childhood and adult life that have contributed to the criminal behavior. To rehabilitate an offender requires a reshaping of his life style. The result of storage while in prison is failute on parole. The price of parole failure is recidivism for the offender, and property loss, injury, or death for his victims during a career of crime.

Chapter XVI

Criminal Justice as a System

Criminal justice is a system comprised of four major functional parts: sanction law, police, courts, and corrections. Or, to rephrase, it is a system of lawmakers, law enforcement agents, the judiciary, and the personnel of corrections and rehabilitation agencies.

America's lawmakers enact new laws and amend old ones to provide at state, federal, and oftentimes municipal levels, the criminal codes of our country which punish violations by the application of penalties.

Police and other agents of law enforcement serve as the foragers of criminal justice, discovering and apprehending violators; and in their role as peace officers the police have a function in which they adjust various differences and disputes without arrest.

The prosecuting attorney, the defense counsel, and the presiding judge make up a court for the prosecution of offenders. The prosecutor and the defense lawyer are both officers of the court, despite being opposing counsel as part of our adversary method of seeking truth in court proceedings.

At the conclusion of the criminal proceedings against an accused the probation–prison–parole complex (organized to rehabilitate offenders) takes over. This complex uses the sentencing power of the trial judge, the field supervision of probation and parole officers, and the professional competence of correctional counselors, caseworkers, psychologists, sociologists, and psychiatrists in a bifurcated program aimed at alternatives to imprisonment, and release on parole rather than lengthy incarceration. This complex of people, facilities, theory, and practice strive for new goals in rehabilitation: clean lives by persons previously convicted of crime and a diminishment in the number of persons who return to criminal acts after arrest, prosecution, conviction, sentence, and rehabilitation.

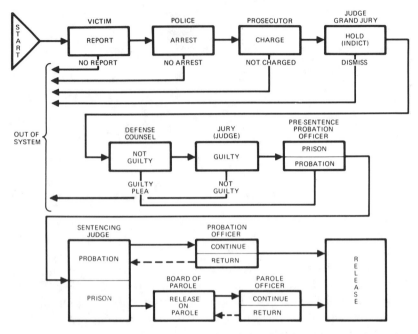

A model of criminal justice as a "system" based on the *offender* and the network of decision points which determine the offender's fate in the system.

At this time there is a balance in dealing with crime and delinquency: (1) control through sanction law enforcement with its individualized treatment of offenders oriented to their individual rehabilitation, and (2) control through removal of the causes of criminal behavior. Therefore, social control is a method of reducing crime and delinquency by maintenance of an effective criminal justice system. Through the integration of various social science and social justice programs in clinics and the community, crime can be prevented by removing causative factors related to poverty (deficiences in education, vocational preparation, and job and career opportunities), and emotional problems related to constitutional defects or acquired in early childhood.

In social control there is a coexistence of two major thrusts, the one by agents and agencies of criminal justice, and the other by family, church, school, and government. The common goal of social control in any free society is to make life in a community of people manageable and sufficiently permissive so that each individual has a maximum amount of liberty and freedom to grow and develop—and in America, to pursue life, liberty, and happiness. The founding fathers were not unmindful of the necessary controls and limits to liberty which are necessary to allow many people to live together with a minimum of conflict. Each man could not be a law unto himself; deciding what is right and wrong; enforcing his own moral or social concepts on others; and acting as policeman, prosecutor, judge, jury, and executioner, all rolled into one. If society were so constituted it would have destroyed itself long ago.

On the other hand, each person must have some individuality, some area of decision as to how he lives his own life, and some privacy from the protective eye of government. The first eight amendments to the Constitution recognized that a person is an individual and that the individual must be protected from oppression by the government. Those amendments were not meant for the protection of a majority, but rather for the protection of any minority from the oppression of the majority. There are many diverse ways in which a person may live his life without infringing unnecessarily or substantially on the lives of others. The American system allows for—and even encourages—such divergence, and cautions government against unnecessary or unreasonable interference. The mere fact that there may be some benefit which accrues to a person who has committed a crime is unimportant when weighed against the specter of unlimited and uncontrolled government interference in the personal and private lives of its citizens. There are many examples of such unlimited government power over the citizen in both ancient and recent history to warn us of the dangers of power. Benjamin Franklin put it nicely: "Those who are willing to give up an essential liberty for the sake of a little security are deserving of neither liberty nor security."

While the zeal and expertise of many individuals in criminal justice and social science have contributed to a systems strategy for combatting crime and delinquency, there is need for new management resources. These agencies of criminal justice have been splintered by geography and function, and social science research programs and demonstration projects have been equally fragmented. Such management resources may be nondirective to protect the concept of local government, but through funding and fiduciaries sufficient control can be exercised to insure a new uniformity in planning, decision making, and field direction of the day–to–day work of social control. Under program budgeting procedures the attainment of objectives at reasonable costs can be emphasized.

Absolutely necessary for the control of crime and delinquency is an approach keyed to the following objectives:

1. A data base information system containing not only the factual data on offenders, but also the relationship of this data to the efficacy of arrest–to–release programs to which these offenders have been exposed.

2. Systematic studies of criminals and crime–prone groups, the social dependency of problem families, and the criminal-creating impact of the labels of juvenile delinquent and ex–convict.

3. A law of crimes that does not overreach, but rather confines itself to legislation concerning crimes that injure persons or cause financial loss; and a system of sanctions in the law which are not vengeance directed (punitive in nature). A system of penalties which will allow for dealing with an individual rather than mandating an inflexible punishment for a particular crime.

4. A cost analysis of the costs of crime and delinquency in relation to the impact of crime on the offender and victim: the loss of productivity while offenders are in prison or pursuing a lifetime crime career; the welfare costs of supporting the families of offenders; and the victim's loss of property, injury, or death.

5. The development of action programs keyed to social control projects organized for crime prevention and *management* of offenders; development and training of manpower to carry out such action programs; and projects which will reveal innovative methods of utilizing communications media to notify the public and secure their support and cooperation.

6. A continuing overall systems research survey–and–report project which will speak out in public to the police, the prosecutors, the lawyers for the defense, the judiciary, the personnel of correctional agencies, and the scientists of the social sciences and other disciplines and technologies. They must be informed about the effectiveness or ineffectiveness of the criminal justice system and its goal of controlling crime and delinquency with justice rather than injustice.

There is a costs–to–benefits theme in the above planning by objectives. There is also a base of knowledge for the action programs, for revised laws, and for overall supervision and report by research technicians which is tied in with the ratio of costs to benefits. Action programs not based on factual knowledge are like shooting without aiming (a waste of ammunition). There is also a base point for developing and training adequate manpower, and this too reveals a costs–to–benefits consciousness. Untrained or poorly selected personnel is wasteful. Lastly, if the *real* costs of crime, rather than the costs of supporting the criminal justice agencies, are known, there is a better basis for funding programs with objectives of managing offenders, and turning them away from their criminal behavior patterns.

Action programs would be situated in four major functional areas:

(1) prevention of crime and delinquency, (2) discovery of crime and the apprehension and prosecution of offenders, (3) fair trial and due process in criminal proceedings, and (4) case management of offenders. Measurements for evaluation can be established which will indicate whether the operations of these programs are meeting with success. Based on population, the rate of crime has always indicated the general failure of socialization and special programs to prevent crime. Offense and arrest data, correlated with statistics on conviction and final disposition of arrestees, has served to roughly measure the functioning of the apprehension process (from discovery to prosecution). Judicial review and circumstances disclosed by a series of cases or individual landmark cases are indicative of the prevailing practices threatening the concept of fair trial and due process. The criminal offender population, with its recidivism and escalation in the seriousness of crimes, is a fair indication as to the actual success or failure in the rehabilitation processes.

The law schools of America are reacting constructively to the challenge of crime, enforcement, prosecution, and postconviction problems. Only a few years ago the only courses offered were one semester of criminal law, constitutional law, and evidence (the last two only partially related to the subject of criminal law). An example of present day law school concern for law enforcement and criminal justice may be found in the listing of courses related to criminal justice in the catalogue of one law school:*

1. Criminal Law (two quarters)

2. Criminal Procedure (one quarter)

3. Constitutional Law (one quarter)

4. Evidence (two or more quarters)

5. Advanced California Trial Practice (one quarter)

6. Juvenile Law (one quarter)

7. Psychiatry and the Law (one quarter)

College level police science education, dating back to 1916 at the University of California at Berkeley, has discarded many of the courses that duplicated the basic course given to police recruits at police academies during entrance level or vestibule training. Course offerings at community colleges, or the first two years of a four–year college or university program, offer courses with content which ranges from evidence and investigation to criminal justice and its administration. Requirements for a degree in the community colleges, or to attain third-year scholastic levels in a four–year college or university, require approximately two–thirds of the courses taken to be in the area of general

*University of Pacific, McGeorge Law School, 1971–72.

education: science, art, humanities, mathematics, writing and speaking, psychology, political science, philosophy, and sociology. Police science programs at third and fourth year levels now range from criminalistics and police administration to proseminars in current problems in criminal justice.

Closely aligned with the police science programs of education at academic institutions is the development of a similar public service program in the area of corrections. This is a breakaway from the traditional social work programs in the past, and it will provide greater educational opportunities in this field for many more individuals. Among the recommended courses in corrections education are:

1. Crime and delinquency

2. Correctional services in the community

3. Introduction to corrections

4. The court system

5. Probation, pardons, and parole

6. Group and individual counseling

7. Institutional procedures

8. Principles of correctional administration

9. The prison society

10. Administration of criminal justice

11. Crime and the criminal

12. Contemporary practices in corrections.[1]

There is a continuum in the criminal justice process: from a greater to a lesser involvement—with the victim and with the offender. At one end is law enforcement, with its agents exposed to the violence of crime, the agony of injured victims, and the hazards of fighting crime. Just beyond this sphere are the prosecutor and defense counsel who are more remotely aware of the many brutal aspects of crime and its impact on victims and offenders. The judiciary occupies a central or neutral position. They are aloof from both victim and offender and are mainly concerned with the facts in dispute. Sentencing neutralizes the judiciary: they must evaluate the seriousness of the crime (victim) against the offender's need for rehabilitation. Correctional personnel are remote from the victims of crime and in direct and frequent contact with offenders. Except for considering the potential victims of future crimes when evaluating parole readiness or continuance on probation, their role is one of almost total involvement with the offender.

1. Vernon B. Fox, *Guidelines for Corrections Programs in Community and Junior Colleges* (Washington, D.C.: American Association of Junior Colleges, 1971), pp. 29–30.

The central tendency of educational programs in law, police science, and corrections to form around the theme of criminal justice is indicative of new horizons in the administration of criminal justice as a system. In addition, these educational programs are being re-grouped into departments of Criminal Justice or Administration of Justice at many community colleges and four–year colleges and universities.

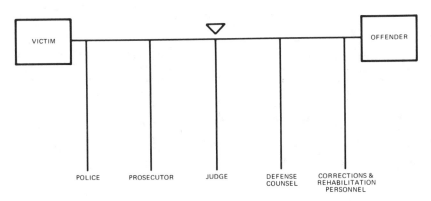

The continuum between victim and offender and the relative positions of the agents of criminal justice.

The control of crime and delinquency will certainly be enhanced when the agents and agencies of criminal justice shorten the continuum between police and corrections, and work together to reduce crime and rehabilitate offenders.

List of Cases

Index